NEOLIBERALISM AND THE MEDIA

This book examines the multiple ways that popular media mainstream and reinforce neoliberal ideology, exposing how they promote neoliberalism's underlying ideas, values and beliefs so as to naturalize inequality, undercut democracy and contribute to the collapse of social notions of community and the common good.

Covering a wide range of media and genres, and adopting a variety of qualitative textual methodologies and theoretical frameworks, the chapters examine diverse topics, from news coverage of the 2016 U.S. presidential election to the NBC show *Superstore* (an atypical instance in which a TV show, for one brief season, challenged the central tenets of neoliberalism) to "kitchen porn." The book also takes an intersectional approach, as contributors explore how gender, race, class and other aspects of social identity are inextricably tied to each other within media representation. At once innovative and distinctive in its illustration of how the media is complicit in perpetuating neoliberal ideology, *Neoliberalism and the Media* offers students and scholars alike an incisive portrait of the intersection between media and ideology today.

Marian Meyers is a professor in the Department of Communication and an affiliate of the Institute of Women's, Gender and Sexuality Studies at Georgia State University. Her research interests are in the areas of feminist media studies and neoliberalism and the media. Her publications have focused on intersectionality within the representation of women, including the role of neoliberalism within that representation, as well as women in higher education. This is her sixth book.

NEOLIBERALISM AND THE MEDIA

Edited by Marian Meyers

NEW YORK AND LONDON

First published 2019
by Routledge
52 Vanderbilt Avenue, New York, NY 10017

and by Routledge
2 Park Square, Milton Park, Abingdon, Oxon, OX14 4RN

Routledge is an imprint of the Taylor & Francis Group, an informa business

© 2019 Taylor & Francis

The right of Marian Meyers to be identified as the author of the editorial material, and of the authors for their individual chapters, has been asserted in accordance with sections 77 and 78 of the Copyright, Designs and Patents Act 1988.

All rights reserved. No part of this book may be reprinted or reproduced or utilised in any form or by any electronic, mechanical, or other means, now known or hereafter invented, including photocopying and recording, or in any information storage or retrieval system, without permission in writing from the publishers.

Trademark notice: Product or corporate names may be trademarks or registered trademarks, and are used only for identification and explanation without intent to infringe.

Library of Congress Cataloging-in-Publication Data
A catalog record for this title has been requested

ISBN: 978-1-138-09442-0 (hbk)
ISBN: 978-1-138-09443-7 (pbk)
ISBN: 978-1-315-10604-5 (ebk)

Typeset in Bembo
by Swales & Willis Ltd

Printed in the United Kingdom
by Henry Ling Limited

For Talia and Emma

CONTENTS

Acknowledgments   *x*
Preface   *xii*
Notes on Contributors   *xiv*

PART I
Where We Are and How We Got Here   **1**

1 Neoliberalism and the Media: History and Context   3
   Marian Meyers

PART II
Corporations and Markets   **19**

2 Reality TV "Gets Real": Hypercommercialism and
   Post-Truth in CNN's Coverage of the 2016 Election
   Campaign   21
   Liane Tanguay

3 The Girl Effect: Philanthrocapitalism and the Branded
   Marketplace of Philanthropic Governance   39
   Dana Schowalter

4 Neoliberalism and Women's Right to Communicate: The Politics of Ownership and Voice in Media 60
Carolyn M. Byerly

PART III
Responsibility and Choice 75

5 Numinous Fortune and Holy Money: Dave Ramsey's Cruel Optimism 77
John Ike Sewell

6 From Homo Economicus to Homo Sacer: Neoliberalism and the Thanatopolitics of The Meth Project 91
Michael F. Walker

7 As American as Capitalist Exploitation: Neoliberalism in The Men Who Built America 108
Christopher M. Duerringer

PART IV
Consumers and Advertising 129

8 Affirmative Advertising and the Mediated Feeling Rules of Neoliberalism 131
Rosalind Gill and Akane Kanai

9 Kitchen Porn: Of Consumerist Fantasies and Desires 147
C. Wesley Buerkle

PART V
Identity and Representation 163

10 "I Deserved to Get Knocked Up": Sex, Class and Latinidad in Jane the Virgin 165
John S. Quinn-Puerta

11 An Intersectional Analysis of Controlling Images and Neoliberal Meritocracy on Scandal and Empire 176
Cheryl Thompson

12 Doing Whiteness "Right": Playing by the Rules of
   Neoliberalism for Television's Working Class   192
   Holly Willson Holladay

13 Negotiating Identity and Working Class Struggles in
   NBC's *Superstore*   209
   Lauren Bratslavsky

Index   229

ACKNOWLEDGMENTS

Neoliberalism and the Media would not have been possible but for the scholars, journalists, other writers and activists whose hard work, dedication and writings have brought to light the hold that neoliberal ideology has on our consciousness, as well as the ways that neoliberal policies and laws have undermined our democracy and government institutions while simultaneously reshaping our culture and society.

I include in the above the contributors to this book, to whom I am deeply indebted. Their original chapters, written specifically for *Neoliberalism and the Media*, provide the kinds of valuable insights and knowledge that is necessary to more fully grasp the media's role in perpetuating neoliberalism in thought and practice. Their work, dedication – and patience – have shaped this volume in ways that I could not have imagined when I embarked upon this project, and for that I am very thankful.

I also am indebted to my graduate research assistants, Josephine (Josie) Leide and William Canter, who have been instrumental in the practical matters involved in the production of a manuscript of this nature. To the extent that this book was formatted properly and that all references were where they should be prior to submission to the publisher, they are largely responsible. Josie, in addition, is owed a huge debt for helping to keep me organized throughout this project – not an easy task given that I can be, at times, preternaturally disorganized.

I want to thank, as well, my publisher at Routledge, Erica Wetter, who believed in this book from the outset and has been most gracious and generous in her support.

Finally, I owe a debt I simply cannot repay to my most demanding of editors, Lauren Rich, whose unwavering encouragement and close reading of every word in this book, in addition to her comments and suggestions concerning my own writing, has not simply resulted in fewer typos but also has immeasurably improved *Neoliberalism and the Media*. To her, I offer my deepest gratitude and love.

PREFACE

I often have told my students that my research interests are motivated by what most makes me mad. Toward this end, my previous research has focused primarily on violence against women and the representation of women within the media, as well as the status and treatment of women in higher education. Over the past decade, however, I have become increasingly troubled by the multiple ways many politicians in the United States, Europe, and in countries around the world – with the help of the media – have inflamed social divisions around race, immigration, gender, and sexuality, as well as undermined confidence in our governmental institutions and democracy itself. I have also become increasingly concerned about the rapid escalation in wealth inequality and the commensurate drop in social mobility in the United States and worldwide. Those inequities have gained traction in recent years as uber-wealthy donors and their corporate collaborators work to entrench oligarchy in place of democracy and to continue the transfer of global and national wealth from the working and middle classes to themselves.

As a society, we appear to be moving into a new gilded age in which real power and the levers of government are in the hands of the wealthiest among us – indeed, some scholars argue we are already there. And it has become increasingly clear to many that this transition has been aided and abetted by the media. Here, I am not just talking about social media, which have become suspect these days as both the diffuser of Russia-generated disinformation, in addition to homegrown, right-wing conspiracy theories and other forms of "fake news." Instead, I am referring to the so-called mainstream media – the "legitimate" news programs, movies, TV sitcoms and dramas, self-help books, advertising, etc. – which, in their seeming neutrality and innocence, are both ubiquitous and effective as purveyors of neoliberal ideology in the mediated world outside the realm of the internet.

I came up with the idea of an edited book about neoliberalism and the media because I kept bumping up against neoliberalism – in its material forms within government policies and laws, as well as in my own work about the representation of women in the media. For example, in examining the narrative about First Lady Michelle Obama created by the White House and spread by the mainstream media, I found a neoliberal discourse that advanced the notion that the systemic disadvantages of racism and poverty can be overcome by dedication, persistence and hard work. After all, the narrative goes, if she can do it, so can you (see Meyers & Goman, 2017). In this, as well as other research, I kept having to bring neoliberalism into my analyses to explain what was going on.

So I embarked on the journey of creating *Neoliberalism and the Media* – the work of putting together a book, whether authored or edited, is always a journey – as an attempt to better understand, and to illustrate, how the media have come to be complicit in embracing and promoting neoliberal ideology, and how they have normalized and offered as common sense the ideas that individualism and free markets, with their emphasis on "freedom," "choice" and "liberty," should supplant democracy, the social, and related beliefs in community, compassion, the common good and solidarity.

The first step in countering this slide into oligarchy is to arm ourselves with knowledge about the tactics and strategies of the multi-billionaire, corporate donor class that got us here. The next step is to mobilize to defeat it. Audre Lorde has famously said that "the master's tools will never dismantle the master's house. They may allow us to temporarily beat him at his own game, but they will never enable us to bring about genuine change." The tools of our would-be masters are stealth, deception, divide-and-conquer appeals based on the social divisions of race, sex, gender, ethnicity and class, and the wholesale purchase of politicians, government institutions and media industries. Our tools, then, must be solidarity, compassion, community, a vision of the collective good, and – most importantly – the vote. There is no time to be lost.

Reference

Meyers, M., & Goman, C. (2017). Michelle Obama: Exploring the narrative. *Howard Journal of Communications*, *28*(1), 20–35. doi:10.1080/10646175.2016.1235520

CONTRIBUTORS

Lauren Bratslavsky is an assistant professor at Illinois State University's School of Communication, where she teaches in the mass media division. Her research interests focus on how television became cultural and historical material by entering into archives, as well as more contemporary television studies about the hegemonic processes in sitcoms and other satirical media.

C. Wesley Buerkle is an associate professor in the Department of Communication & Performance at East Tennessee State University. His research primarily focuses on issues of gender and sexuality in the media. Of particular interest to him are the ways that neoliberalism situates individuals as fully in control of their lives and identities.

Carolyn M. Byerly is a professor and chair in the Department of Communication, Culture & Media Studies at Howard University. She takes a political economy approach to the study of gender and race issues in media policy, media employment, and other aspects of media industries. Her most recent work examines women and journalism unions, as well as the political economy of gentrification in urban neighborhoods.

Christopher M. Duerringer is an associate professor in the Department of Communication Studies at California State University, Long Beach. His research interests include the constitution and maintenance of publics and counterpublics; rhetorical strategies employed by powerful publics to silence dissent; and the relationships among the economy, ideology, and rhetoric.

Contributors **xv**

Rosalind Gill is a London-based scholar who is author or editor of many books and articles, including *Gender and the Media* (Polity, 2007), *New Femininities: Postfeminism, Neoliberalism and Subjectivity* (with Christina Scharff, Palgrave, 2011), *Gender and Creative Labour* (with Bridget Conor and Stephanie Taylor, Blackwell, 2015) and *Mediated Intimacy: Sex Advice in Media Culture* (with Meg-John Barker and Laura Harvey, Polity, 2018).

Holly Willson Holladay is an assistant professor in the Department of Media, Journalism & Film at Missouri State University. Her research interests involve representations of identity, including gender, race, and class, in popular media, and how media audiences and fans negotiate their own identities in relationship to the media they consume. Her previously published work has explored audience reactions to Lady Gaga, the TV shows *Breaking Bad, Mad Men*, and *The Office*, and rural, working-class representations on television.

Akane Kanai is a lecturer in the School of Media, Film and Journalism at Monash University, Australia. Her research explores feminism, affect, and identity in neoliberal media culture. Her book, *Gender and Relatability in Digital Culture*, has recently been published with Palgrave Macmillan.

Marian Meyers is a professor in the Department of Communication and an affiliate of the Institute of Women's, Gender and Sexuality Studies at Georgia State University. Her research interests are in the areas of feminist media studies and neoliberalism and the media. Her publications have focused on intersectionality within the representation of women, including the role of neoliberalism within that representation, as well as women in higher education. This is her sixth book.

John S. Quinn-Puerta has a master's degree from the Department of Communication at Georgia State University. His research interests include race and ethnicity in film and television, with a focus on representations of Latinx and immigrant stories seen through the lens of media criticism.

Dana Schowalter is an assistant professor in the Communication Studies Department at Western Oregon University. Her research interests include feminist media studies, global consumer culture, and gendered-based bullying and harassment. Her current project focuses on the social media backlash against women-led films.

John Ike Sewell is an assistant professor of convergence journalism in the Department of Mass Communications at The University of West Georgia. His research interests include queer studies, constitutive rhetoric, neoliberalism and post-structuralism. His publications have concerned issues of collective identification for queer social movements.

Liane Tanguay earned a Ph.D. in English at the University of Manchester and is the author of *Hijacking History: American Culture and the War on Terror* (McGill-Queen's University Press, 2012) and several articles and book chapters on neoliberalism and contemporary popular culture. She is currently an assistant professor of English at the University of Houston-Victoria, where she teaches courses in composition, literary theory, cultural studies, and critical studies in race, class and gender.

Cheryl Thompson is an assistant professor in the School of Creative Industries, Faculty of Communication and Design, at Ryerson University. She was a Banting Postdoctoral Fellow (2016-2018) in the Centre for Drama, Theatre and Performance Studies at the University of Toronto. Her research interests are critical media studies, visual culture, and promotional culture. She has published articles on black beauty politics, postfeminism, and blackface minstrelsy.

Michael F. Walker is an instructor in Communication Studies in the New College of Interdisciplinary Arts and Sciences at Arizona State University's West Campus. His research focuses on the discursive formation of social issues, with an emphasis on the governance of addiction and recovery.

PART I
Where We Are and How We Got Here

1
NEOLIBERALISM AND THE MEDIA
History and Context

Marian Meyers

The past several decades have seen seismic changes in the global and national political, economic and cultural landscape. Those shifts have rapidly accelerated in recent years, reflecting not only the schism between the major political parties in the United States, but also influencing the political economy of the European Union and nation-states around the globe. While there are numerous explanations for these changes, including an increase in anti-immigrant hostility and racism, much can be attributed to the ascendance of neoliberalism, a form of capitalism whose goals and related policies have been commonly embraced by the radical right and conservatives internationally and within the United States, where it has become the leitmotif of the modern Republican Party.

This shift over the past 40 years "from governmental philosophies of social welfare to neoliberalism" (Collins & Bilge, 2016, p. 16) has led to an increase in global economic inequality and a concomitant decrease in social mobility (Picketty, 2014) as "inequality and commodification mutually reinforce each other" (Giroux, 2011, p. 11). Critics of neoliberalism note that it is inherently anti-democratic in that it legitimizes government by a wealthy elite rather than a representative citizenry (Giroux, 2011; MacLean, 2017; Mayer, 2016; McChesney, 2013; Taplin, 2017). Under a neoliberal regime, governments no longer have a practical or ethical responsibility to their citizens and have abdicated any obligation to level the playing field for women, people of color, gender- and sexually-non-conforming people and others who have been disadvantaged by systemic discrimination. Instead of instituting policies to promote social and economic equality, neoliberalism calls for individual choice and personal responsibility as antidotes to the barriers of bias and prejudice.

Advocates of neoliberal policies have long recognized the need to convince the public of the rightness of their cause – and they understood the role that the media would have to play to accomplish this. In this regard, they have been spectacularly successful, spending untold billions to influence public opinion. Indeed, much of the effectiveness of neoliberal ideology – its global reach and acceptance as a common-sense way of understanding the world – can be attributed to the media. For example, the Institute for Contemporary Studies, funded by the right-wing Scaife Family Charitable Trusts, targeted the mass media to spread neoliberal ideas by developing economics curricula for schools and training businessmen and journalists to provide a "libertarian analysis of social problems" (MacLean, 2017, p. 121). But ICS has been far from alone in its outreach to the public. It has been joined by a web of think tanks, nonprofit centers, universities and other organizations in spreading the libertarian gospel. The result is that neoliberalism has permeated both traditional and new media channels, extending its influence far beyond news stories to encompass entertainment, advertising, social media and other mediated genres.

This book explores how the media have espoused and normalized neoliberal beliefs, ideas and values – that is, neoliberal ideology – to a public that would otherwise reject any attempts to undermine democracy and institute the economic, political and social policies and laws of a neoliberal regime. Here, we are not talking about right-wing media outlets such as Fox News, whose alliance with the Republican Party and promotion of conservative politics has been well documented (Brock & Rabin-Havt, 2012; Sherman, 2014) or the Sinclair Broadcast Group which, as the largest operator and owner of television stations in the U.S., has been able to push a conservative agenda through local news broadcasts in nearly 100 markets (de la Merced & Fandos, 2017; Farhi, 2017; Folkenflik, 2018; Wemple, 2018). Nor are we referring to conservative AM talk radio, with hosts like Rush Limbaugh, Glenn Beck, and Sean Hannity, among others, or Breitbart News and InfoWars, two truly "fake news" outlets – among many – that traffic in conspiracy theories and radical-right propaganda. Rather, the focus here is on the seemingly neutral or objective media – the mainstream news, ad campaigns, books, movies and TV shows that are ubiquitous and appear innocuous but which, nevertheless, promote neoliberal ideology.

The late cultural theorist Stuart Hall (1988) pointed to the melding of "neoliberal doctrine within conservative philosophy" (p. 46) in Britain during the 1980s to explain the rise of an "authoritarian populism" (p. 7) spread by the nation's media industry. The media's primary work, he insisted, is to support and preserve this dominant ideology, which itself reflects the ideas and values of the economic, social and political elite. Today, within the U.S. and globally, that ideology is neoliberal capitalism.

Indeed, Harvey (2005) points out that its advocates have held considerable sway over a broad array of U.S. and international institutions and organizations, including education, the media, the financial and banking industries, and governmental regulatory agencies. In effect, it has touched all aspects of our lives, both conscious and unconscious. "Neoliberalism has, in short, become hegemonic as a mode of discourse," Harvey (2005) explains. "It has pervasive effects on ways of thought to the point where it has become incorporated into the common-sense way many of us interpret, live in, and understand the world" (p. 3).

The work of this chapter, then, is to lay the foundation for the rest of *Neoliberalism and the Media*, to situate it within the recent history and core tenets of neoliberalism, and to connect its ideas and values to popular media. In addition, because neoliberalism is far from neutral in the face of gender, race, class, sexuality, ethnicity, and other signifiers of systemic inequality, the chapters that follow also take into account how aspects of social location and identity intersect within the neoliberal discourse and practice of the media. Feminist scholars Collins and Bilge (2016) point out that, "The neoliberal world order relies on a global system of capitalism that is inflected through unequal relations of race, gender, sexuality, age, disability and citizenship" (p. 138). By utilizing an intersectional perspective, it is possible to not only understand neoliberalism's impact on disenfranchised people, but also to link "theory with practice that can aid in the empowerment of communities and individuals" (Collins & Bilge, 2016, p. 36).

Defining Neoliberalism and Its Effects

Harvey (2005) defines neoliberalism, in the first instance, as a "theory of political economic practices that proposes that human well-being can best be advanced by liberating individual entrepreneurial freedoms and skills within an institutional framework characterized by strong private property rights, free markets and free trade" – the role of the state being limited to creating and preserving this framework (p. 2). In the second instance, he adds, neoliberalism "has entailed much destruction" in almost all aspects of our social, political and economic life – specifically in the areas of state sovereignty, labor, social relations, welfare, technology, "ways of life and thought, reproductive activities, attachments to the land and habits of the heart" (p. 3).

This definition of neoliberalism, while commonly understood as advocating for free markets and limited government, is misleading because it does not reflect the current realities of the relationship between the theory and the state. Neoliberalism is supposed to severely restrict intervention by governments on the grounds that they cannot possibly second-guess the market and "because powerful interest groups will inevitably distort and bias state interventions (particularly in democracies) for their own benefit" (Harvey, 2005, p. 2). However, nation-states and their regulatory agencies do, in fact, enact policies and laws to advance the accumulation of wealth and political power by corporate entities and multi-billionaire donors.

In addition, the meaning of "neoliberal" itself is widely misunderstood. First, it is often used interchangeably with libertarian and conservative. While this may be confusing, its use as a substitute for those terms is for good reason given that those who identify as either conservative or libertarian tend to support the same neoliberal policies and laws.[1] Second, "neoliberal" is sometimes confused with political liberals, left-wing politics, progressives and even the Democratic Party in the United States. In this case, there is a vast difference between "liberal" within a political context and "neoliberal" within the political *economic* sense indicated by Harvey. While political liberals assert the need for government to provide for the common good by regulating markets and providing public services, neoliberals counter that free markets and private property rights must be primary to insure individual freedom, liberty and choice. Neoliberal capitalism extols the virtues of personal responsibility as opposed to the collective good, an unfettered marketplace rather than one regulated by government, and the privatization of public institutions and services as opposed to government programs, agencies, and interventions. Phelan (2014) views the competition between these oppositional worldviews as at the heart of neoliberalism, which he sees as deriving from antagonisms during "a specific historical juncture" characterized by the "political and ideological contestation over the very meaning of modernity, progress, reason and human freedom" (p. 143).

What neoliberalism looks like in practice is the denial of global warming and the elimination of environmental protections and climate treaties; the decimation of unions and workers rights; the privatization of public schools, detention centers, prisons, roads, and services; the enactment of voter suppression laws and other legislation aimed at the curtailment of civil and voting rights protections; the gutting of taxes for corporations and the wealthy; and the drop in wages and benefits for workers. In essence, neoliberals primarily see human beings as consumers, and freedom as the ability to make choices within the marketplace. As Duke University historian Nancy MacLean (2017) explains, the goal of neoliberalism is to protect "capitalism from government" (pp. 74–87). In doing so, it undermines social values such as compassion, "the public good, community, and the obligations of citizenship" (Giroux, 2011, p. 9).

How We Got Here

Numerous scholars have linked the undermining of democracy and the social, cultural and governmental institutions that uphold it to the gradual enactment of neoliberal policies, laws and court decisions that, over that past half century, have privileged private property and wealth over the Keynesian social contract that views government as a necessary corrective to the excesses of capitalism.

Among the primary researchers who have focused on the role of an ultra-wealthy donor class in the crusade for a radical right agenda are Duke University historian Nancy MacLean (2017) and investigative journalist Jane Mayer (2016, 2017). Both note that in a confidential memorandum written by Lewis Powell in 1971, shortly before he was nominated to the U.S. Supreme Court by President Richard Nixon, the future justice laid out a plan to allay potential skepticism and persuade the public to embrace neoliberal policies and thought. According to Mayer (2016), Powell viewed with alarm the increase in wealth equality and government regulation in the 1960s, as well as campus unrest that saw students protest *against* the Vietnam war and *for* social and economic equality for women and minorities; he considered those actions an attack on the free enterprise system that would lead to economic ruin for the moneyed classes. Powell proposed a multi-faceted approach that called on corporations and the U.S. Chamber of Commerce to fund organizations and groups that would: enlist scholars to publish and lecture in support of free enterprise; establish a speaker's bureau; evaluate and influence the content of textbooks; influence college and high school curriculum and faculty; monitor the media so as to challenge unfavorable coverage; buy ads in support of neoliberal causes; increase political power through funding conservative politicians; and gain the support of the judiciary, which, Powell noted, "may be the most important instrument for social, economic and political change" (Powell Memo, 1971).

Powell's challenge was taken up by a handful of multi-billionaires and like-minded corporate collaborators over the past half century. Chief among those in this elite group are the brothers Charles and David Koch. In particular, Charles Koch[2] – the world's 12th wealthiest person, with an estimated worth of $50.7 billion, and the chairman and CEO of Koch Industries – was singularly influential in deciding, in response to lawsuits filed against his company due to flagrant violations of the law, to transform the nation's politics and laws through changing the outcome of its elections. He and others of the conservative donor class were subsequently aided by the U.S. Supreme Court in its 2010 ruling in *Citizens United*, which further consolidated the notion that corporations have the same free speech rights as individuals, thereby opening the floodgates of untraceable – but tax-deductible – "dark money" that could be given to non-profit "social welfare" organizations to influence elections, cut corporate taxes, and advance their interests more generally (Mayer, 2016).[3] A wide-ranging network of foundations, think tanks, academic centers, advocacy groups, and corporations were among the recipients of the Kochs' and other donors' largesse, including the Heritage Foundation and the Federalist Society, which vetted the list of potential U.S. Supreme Court nominees provided to President Donald Trump,[4] and the American Legislative Exchange Council (ALEC), which for years has provided Republican state legislators with boilerplate, model legislation with the aim of advancing gun rights, deregulating industry, limiting abortion, voting and LGBT rights, privatizing public education, curtailing labor unions, and accomplishing a host of other conservative goals. These model bills are then provided with scholarly legitimacy by the Koch-funded State Policy Network (MacLean, 2017).

The far-reaching tentacles of this "Kochtopus," as it is sometimes called, also includes organizations with such innocuous sounding names as the Reason Foundation, a national voice for privatization, the Liberty Fund, which recruits and trains graduate students and others to build an "intellectual cadre" for the cause (MacLean, 2017, p. 145), the Institute for Humane Studies, a training center for academicians, and the Center for Independent Education, which advocates for private schooling and vouchers rather than public education. In addition, the Charles Koch Foundation, American Enterprise Institute and the Cato Institute are part of this network, whose ultimate goals are to change the laws and direction of U.S. society, and to dismantle the state and its institutions so that corporations and the wealthy are free to do as they please.

Realizing that the majority of U.S. citizens were unlikely to support these goals, Koch and other champions of free market capitalism engaged in a program of deception to incrementally alter laws and work to amend the Constitution, thereby making these changes impossible to rescind (MacLean, 2017; Mayer, 2016). One prong of this stealth attack involves "astroturfing" – secretly funding organizations so that they appear to represent a grassroots movement but, in actuality, are a mouthpiece for their billionaire sponsors. Mayer (2016) points to the Tea Party movement as just one of the astroturf groups funded by the Koch brothers. The most successful of these groups, the Tea Party, effectively stoked racial animosity and social anxiety to win support for Republican Party opposition to any legislation or goals backed by President Barack Obama, including those addressing health care and global warming, and worked to elect President Trump and other conservative politicians.

Another part of their plan involved spreading discontent with government and its institutions – including public schools and government agencies. This ends-justifies-the-means strategy, communicated in "training manuals for subversion by stealth" (MacLean, 2017, p. 209), was used to promote the privatization of schools and prisons, as well as to undermine faith in Social Security and other government programs and institutions. Moving slowly and using piecemeal steps so as not to raise public concern or awareness until it was too late, they presented to the public the opposite of what was really intended – which was to jettison public services that the majority of U.S. citizens supported, such as Medicare and Social Security. For example, the first step in eliminating Social Security was to "soften public support for the system by making it seem unreliable" (MacLean, 2017, p. 179). The next step was to apply the classic strategy of divide and conquer by pitting current recipients against soon-to-be recipients and younger workers. Those seeking to undercut Social Security and other entitlement programs were encouraged to proclaim the need for "reform" so as to save them from going bankrupt, "even though the real goal was to destroy them" (MacLean, 2017, p. 194). Similarly, ending public education relied on convincing the public that the problem with schools was that teachers unions have too much power. According to MacLean (2017):

> Under the influence of one wealthy individual in particular (Charles Koch), the movement was turning to an equally troubling form of coercion, achieving its ends essentially through trickery, through deceiving trusting people about its real intentions in order to take them to a place where, on their own, given complete information, they probably would not go.
>
> *(p. 208)*

Of course, the Kochs are not alone in funneling vast fortunes to conservative politicians and causes, as well as distorting the truth to get what they want. Others in this donor class are father and daughter team Robert and Rebekah Mercer (Mayer, 2017), Richard Mellon Scaife, John M. Olin, and the Bradley brothers (Mayer, 2016), casino magnate Sheldon Adelson, and wife and husband Liz and Dick Uihlein, all of whom have contributed millions to push a neoliberal agenda – often through the dissemination of fake news. For example, the Mercers were the primary benefactors of Stephen Bannon, a former Trump chief strategist and executive chair of the radical-right *Breitbart News*, an outlet for what has been called "'hate news' – a toxic mix of lies, white-supremacist content and bullying that can inspire attacks on Muslims, gay people, women, African-Americans and others" (Kennedy, 2017). Similarly, the Uihleins' "brand of political engineering" involves "candidates and tactics sometimes audaciously distorting the truth," often reinforced through "a network of broadsheets and websites that resemble news outlets but that make one-sided attacks against their opponents" (Saul & Hakim, 2018). And Olin – whose company dumped 66,000 tons of chemical waste into Niagara Falls, creating high rates of mercury poisoning there and near its factory in Saltville, Virginia, which became one of the first federal superfund sites[5] – secretly funded cells or "beachheads" of conservative intellectuals on college campuses who published non-peer reviewed studies with fabricated data (Mayer, 2016).

To create the kind of permanent political, economic and social change that they desired, however, it was necessary not only to get the public and conservative politicians on board, but to change jurisprudence through a "campaign for the courts" (MacLean, 2017, p. 126) that both trained judges to protect corporate profits and private wealth and also pumped unheard of money into state judicial races.[6] If they could amend the Constitution, "public officials would be legally constrained from offering new social programs to the public or engaging in regulation on their behalf even when vast constituencies were demanding them" (MacLean, 2017, p. 184).

This would, of course, overturn majority rule and the very idea of the United States as a representative democracy. But the goal, according to MacLean (2017), was to change the rules rather than the rulers, to enshrine unregulated corporate capitalism into the Constitution, thereby ushering in oligarchy in place of democracy. "To value liberty for the wealthy minority above all else and enshrine it in the nations' governing rules, as … the Koch network is achieving," MacLean (2017) asserts, "is to consent to an oligarchy in all but the outer husk of representative form" (p. 233).

Indeed, research has affirmed that, other than the amending of the Constitution, we are pretty much already there. A recent study that measured democracy in 178 countries found that a third of the world's population is living in a declining democracy – and that the measurable drop in democracy in the United States is both "precipitous and unprecedented," plunging 24 places in the ranking between 2015 and 2017 (Lührmann & Wilson, 2018). In addition, the United States fell from seventh place to 31st for the worst downward trend among the countries studied, and declined to 48th place from among the top countries worldwide in terms of government compliance with the U.S. Supreme Court. The researchers credited Donald Trump and Congressional Republicans for this swift decline:

> Experts lowered their estimates of democracy in the United States because they began to be skeptical that the U.S. Congress will rein in executive overreach. Similarly, experts lost faith that the opposition party can contribute to overseeing, investigating or otherwise checking the majority party. The U.S. executive branch was assessed as showing less respect for the Constitution and compliance with the judiciary, two indicators that the judicial branch can restrain the executive.
> *(Lührmann & Wilson, 2018)*

Similarly, a groundbreaking analysis of political influence on public policy by Gilens and Page (2014) found that "economic elites and organized groups representing business interests have substantial independent impacts on U.S. government policy, while mass-based interest groups and average citizens have little or no independent influence," thereby supporting theories of economic-elite domination (p. 565). In other words, oligarchy and plutocracy, or plutarchy, may have already supplanted the democratic process.

The Media in Context

Of course, the shift toward neoliberalism did not come about solely through the efforts of Republican politicians, conservative judges, a cadre of trained believers, or even a stealth campaign orchestrated by a donor class of multibillionaires willing to spend lavishly on an extensive and complex web of mutually reinforcing think tanks, centers, advocacy groups, and universities. Nor can it be attributed to voter anger at stagnant or declining wages and standards of living – which, in themselves, are largely the result of neoliberal tax and trade policies, laws, and court decisions that have greatly increased corporate profits while leaving "Americans living on a paycheck … with a shorter end of the rope" (Cohen, 2018). All of these certainly have contributed to the cultural maelstrom that has enabled neoliberalism to spread. But it is the mainstream media – from the news to reality TV, advertising campaigns, television sitcoms, and dramas – that has been most effective in selling an agenda and ideology that supplants as societal goals the notions of "democracy," "equality," "the common good," and "community" with the neoliberal ideals of "freedom," "individualism," and "choice."

Guardino and Snyder (2012) argue that "One of the least appreciated – and, arguably, most consequential – political-economic shifts during the neoliberal era concerns the relationship between the state and the media industry" (p. 532). Their findings in a study of the "right-wing" Fox and "moderate" CNN news coverage of the Tea Party confirm the pervasiveness and hold of neoliberal thought in mainstream news: both portrayed the Tea Party in a highly favorable light and framed it as a legitimate social movement, with CNN's coverage even more favorable than Fox's. In addition, they note that the "populism" of the "New Right" idealizes the "self-reliant, rugged individual" and the market's assurance of the "personal freedom" to choose, while articulating "a vision of government as an inefficient, cumbersome, overly bureaucratized entity prone to meddling in the private affairs of hardworking citizens to the benefit of the 'undeserving' poor (minority) populations" (p. 530). Their conclusion:

> Not only does news media under the neoliberal policy regime operate as a hegemonic site for propagating information and ideas that advance New Right political goals, but the media serves as an ideological figure in itself, as the very conservatives who increasingly drive the actual media agenda strategically construct popular understandings of what "the Media" is – namely, a key arm of the "liberal elite."
>
> *(p. 542)*

But the news is just one of a number of media channels championing neoliberal discourse. Reality television, too, has played its part, defining neoliberal citizenship for viewers by emphasizing personal responsibility and self-empowerment in shows like *Dr. Phil* and *Judge Judy*, the benevolence of private enterprise in make-over charity shows like *Extreme Makeover: Home Edition*, the constant need for self-improvement and reinvention in various personal make-over shows, and the requirement that neoliberal citizens be solely responsible and thus prepared at all times for any emergency or disaster – financial, natural, physical or other (Ouellette & Hay, 2008).

In addition, media scholars have emphasized not just content, but also the political economy of the media in supporting and maintaining neoliberal capitalism. Taplin (2017) points to the internet as increasing global inequality while the men behind the "tech capitalism" of digital behemoths such as Facebook, Amazon, and Google achieve cultural, political, and economic power "unseen since the Gilded age" (p. 25). Many of the libertarian tech billionaires, such as venture capitalist and PayPal founder Peter Thiel, support authoritarian government and view capitalism and democracy as incompatible (Taplin, 2017). According to McChesney (2013), the internet "has become one of the greatest generators of monopoly in economic history" (p. 130). He adds that the internet can be thought of as "a planet where Google, Facebook, Apple, Amazon, Microsoft and the ISP (Internet service provider) cartel members each occupy a continent that represents their monopoly base" (p. 137). None of these monopolies would be possible, however, without government policies that expedite and facilitate their creation and economic power (p. 142). As Giroux (2011) states:

> The dominant media largely function as a moral anesthesia and political firewall that legitimate a ruthless and fraudulent free market system while failing to make visible the workings of a casino capitalism that rejects as weakness any measure of compassion, care, trust and vulnerability.
>
> *(p. 12)*

About the Book

Neoliberalism and the Media aims to make visible the workings of neoliberalism within the media by shedding light on the ways the media are complicit in mainstreaming neoliberal ideology and establishing a neoliberal hegemony and regime that places capital and control in the hands of the few and the uber-wealthy at the expense of nearly everyone else. Despite the machinations of right-wing foundations, think tanks, centers, and other organizations, the grip neoliberalism has on our economics, politics, and culture would not be possible without the co-optation and cooperation of the traditional media. Certainly, social media – Facebook, Twitter, YouTube, Instagram, etc. – have played their part, often with the assistance of the Russian government. But they are no match for the pervasiveness of advertising, television sitcoms and dramas, movies, local and national news, books, and the other forms of traditional media that continue to form the core of our mediated worlds.

The following chapters explore how the media have been complicit in espousing and normalizing the neoliberal values and ideas that have saturated our lives, undermined our democracy, reshaped our culture and shifted the nation's wealth and power from workers to corporations and the elite. They focus on the main themes underlying neoliberalism, but also include an example of how the media can, in fact, challenge the tenets of neoliberalism. In addition, a number specifically focus on the representation of social identity and the intersectionality of different aspects of gender, race, ethnicity and class in neoliberal discourse.

In the next section, Part II of *Neoliberalism and the Media*, the chapters explore the corporatization of the media, how political economic issues such as media ownership, financialization, hypercommercialization and campaigns that highlight corporate philanthropy serve the interests of conglomerates and capital at the expense of democracy, equality and our understanding of the roots of – and solutions to – social and economic equity. Liane Tanguay examines in Chapter 2 the ways that a marketized mediascape of hypercommercialization, financialization and the pursuit of ratings at CNN subordinated meaningful journalism to a horse-race approach to elections that helped Donald Trump win the presidency. In Chapter 3, Dana Schowalter explains how philanthrocapitalism and marketplace branding in the Girl Effect campaign were designed to create a positive corporate image while misrepresenting complex social issues hindering the advancement of girls and women in developing countries. And in Chapter 4, Carolyn M. Byerly discusses the connection between conglomerate ownership and control and the lack of representation, voice and status of women within the media. She concludes with suggestions for leveling the playing field for women.

Part III illustrates one of the primary messages of neoliberal ideology as expressed in the media – that of individual responsibility and choice. Indeed, the lessons provided by the media in this section emphasize the importance of pulling yourself up by your own bootstraps rather than expecting or relying on any government assistance. The ruthlessly competitive scenario presented here is devoid of compassion or empathy; it also does not recognize that the playing field is far from level. Those who are unable to succeed are considered weak and/or to have made bad choices. Hence, they have no one to blame but themselves for their lack of success or limited material circumstances. In Chapter 5, John Sewell shows how Dave Ramsey, a financial self-help guru with a wide-ranging media empire, markets himself by invoking a paternalistic, faith-based strategy of austerity and self-discipline as a way to amass wealth. In Chapter 6, Michael F. Walker looks at a national campaign to prevent methamphetamine addiction, The Meth Project, and how it represents addiction as a fall not only from grace, but from the respectable, white, middle-class. Those who make the poor choice to use meth, he argues, are marked as dangerous, diseased criminals and deviants who are not deserving of life. In Chapter 7, Christopher M. Duerringer concludes that a History Channel series, *The Men Who Built America*, not only denotes capitalism as our national religion, but it also positions these "robber baron" captains of industry as role models whose heroic choices, self-reliance, singular determination and absolute ruthlessness were necessary to "build America."

Part IV addresses another key theme within neoliberalism – advertising, consumerism and the creation of desire. "Choice" is equated with marketplace freedom within neoliberal discourse, but consumers must nonetheless be manipulated by advertisers to buy their products. In Chapter 8, Rosalind Gill and Akane Kanai view neoliberalism as not simply about economic and political power, but about an everyday sensibility that shapes our views of self and others. They examine a L'Oréal ad campaign to demonstrate the workings of the psychology of neoliberalism. In Chapter 9, C. Wesley Buerkle further explores the psychology of consumerism and marketplace demand through the creation of pornographic desire in the "kitchen porn" of the online cooking, shopping and recipe site Food52.

Part V focuses more specifically than the previous chapters on the representation of social identity within media entertainment – that is, on the ways in which the intersectionality of race, ethnicity, gender and class are represented within the neoliberalized discourses of reality TV, sitcoms and television drama. Intersectionality highlights how various facets of social location are inextricably linked.[7] A focus on intersectionality rather than a sole focus on political economy, Duggan (2003) suggests, is necessary for progressives to wrest power from neoliberal authoritarianism and to stem their "culture war" attacks on racial or sexual minorities, the poor and women: "Neoliberal politics must be understood *in relation* to coexisting, conflicting, shifting relations of power along multiple lines of difference and hierarchy" (p. 70). Thus, in Chapter 10, John S. Quinn-Puerta explores the ways that Latinx culture, social class and gender identity are interconnected in their portrayal on the television sitcom *Jane the Virgin* as he explores the choices of the main character and her family, as well as the cultural stereotypes invoked in the narrative. In Chapter 11, Cheryl Thompson explores the dramas *Scandal* and *Empire*, both of which celebrate "self-made" Black entrepreneurship in narratives that reify a neoliberal meritocratic form of citizenship in a discourse marked by race and class. Holly Holladay, in Chapter 12, examines the reality TV shows *Here Comes Honey Boo Boo* and *Duck Dynasty* to show how neoliberal ideology has impacted expectations of the body, work and normative femininity and masculinity in Southern white, working-class representation.

Finally, in Chapter 13, Lauren Bratslavsky provides an example of how the media *can* challenge neoliberal ideology with her analysis of the sitcom *Superstore*. Bratslavsky focuses on the first season of the NBC series, which critiqued oppressive corporate policies such as the lack of adequate pay, health benefits and poor working conditions. Unfortunately, the narrative in the second season of the show moved away from issues of worker solidarity and anti-worker corporate policies – for reasons that are unknown but could well be related to pushback from corporate sponsors of the show. Nevertheless, the first season stands apart as an example of how the media *can* defy neoliberal logic and, instead, promote social values of democracy, solidarity, compassion, equality and community.

Conclusion

While the first season of *Superstore* remains outside the norm for television sitcoms and dramas, as well as news and advertising, it is important to remember that some movies and radio shows, as well as certain television programs – notably MSNBC's night-time news lineup and many of the late-night talk shows and political comedy and commentary aired on broadcast and premium cable channels – consistently do challenge neoliberal discourse and ideology. The hosts on *The Late Show with Stephen Colbert, Jimmy Kimmel Live!, Full Frontal with Samantha Bee, Last Week Tonight with John Oliver* and other programs often have been vocal opponents of neoliberal policies and politicians, including Donald Trump. Articles in the nation's prestige press, the *New York Times* and the *Washington Post*, as well as local newspapers (many of which use the *Times'* and *Post's* news services) have highlighted escalating income and wealth inequality, the debilitating effects of skyrocketing housing, pharmaceutical and health care costs, and the effects of neoliberal tax reform that has ballooned the federal deficit while shrinking taxes for corporations and the ultra-wealthy. In addition, progressive publications such as *Mother Jones, The Progressive* and *The Nation* magazines have long provided a media presence that has staunchly opposed neoliberalism.

While these media outlets, programs and articles may challenge neoliberal ideology, in and of themselves, they have not proven sufficient to turn the tide. Hall (1988, 1977, 1982), Althusser (1971) and others within the areas of critical and cultural studies emphasize that the media are effective in supporting and maintaining the interests of the ruling classes because they are able to create an ideological consensus that appears natural and common-sensical. Indeed, ideology is most effective when people are not aware that their beliefs, values and ideas *are*, in fact, ideological – that is, when they consider their worldview to be related to "truth" rather than to ideology. Hall (1977, 1982) further notes that the dominant ideology is neither monolithic nor secure; it must be continually shored up against the encroachment of alternative or oppositional ideologies to maintain its position of dominance. Hence, neoliberalism must be continually fought for and renewed against the advances of a progressive ideology that values democracy, equality, community and the common good – as well as clean air and water, access to health care, reproductive and LGBTQ rights, freedom from fear, and the right to live with dignity.

The first step in challenging neoliberalism, therefore, is to see through the self-serving and duplicitous attempts to legitimize and naturalize it in the media, and to recognize neoliberalism for what it is – an ideological formation (notwithstanding its political and economic structures) that is inherently anti-democratic, devoid of compassion and care, and that seeks to accumulate ever more wealth and power in the hands of a corporate and moneyed elite. This book seeks to contribute to that first step by making visible the ways that neoliberal thought has surreptitiously permeated our media and come to shape our politics, economics, and our lives. Underlying this work is the belief that the media, rather than acting as purveyors of neoliberal ideology, can be repurposed.

Clearly, additional steps are needed to accomplish this, for the media to reflect the values, beliefs and ideas that provide the foundation for social, political and economic equality, as well as democracy and all it entails. Feminist activist and writer Audre Lorde famously cautioned that "the master's tools will never dismantle the master's house." (Lorde, 2007). The would-be masters of what some consider our current state of plutarchy have built their "house of cards" using the tools of deception, greed, lies and social division. The tools necessary to dismantle it, then, must be compassion, inclusion, benevolence, fairness, generosity, community and – above all – truth.

Notes

1 Adding to our understanding of the fluid nature of these terms, MacLean (2017) points out that the libertarians of the Mont Pelerin Society considered referring to themselves as neoliberal but adopted the term conservative to attract more allies (pp. 50–51).
2 Charles Koch was influenced by "public choice" economics as advanced by Nobel Prize-winning economist James McGill Buchanan, who posited that public officials were ultimately self-serving.
3 More recently, the *New York Times* reports, the Trump administration has ended "a longstanding requirement that certain nonprofit organizations disclose the names of large donors to the Internal Revenue Service, a move that will allow some political groups to shield their sources of funding from government scrutiny" (Cohen, Vogel, & Tankersley, 2018). The article goes on to state that this change has been sought for years by conservatives and Congressional Republicans and will affect "labor unions, social clubs and political groups as varied as arms of the AARP, the United States Chamber of Commerce, the National Rifle Association and Americans for Prosperity, which is funded partly by the billionaire brothers Charles and David Koch."
4 One of those appointments was to fill the vacancy left by the retirement of Justice Anthony Kennedy, himself a participant in programs funded by the Kochs. Kennedy also had previously been recruited to serve as the vice president of the Institute for Contemporary Studies.
5 Mayer (2016) points out that Charles Koch, like Olin, was motivated in his anti-government crusade by government regulations and lawsuits against Koch Industries.
6 MacLean (2017) notes that by 1990, "40 percent of the U.S. federal judiciary had been treated to a Koch-backed curriculum" whose aim was to apply free market

economics to legal cases (p. 195). Donald Trump has been extremely successful in appointing those federal judges.
7 Intersectionality as a theoretical construct was developed by Black feminist scholars such as Angela Davis, Patricia Hill Collins, and Kimberlé Crenshaw as a way to understand how multiple forms of oppression are inextricably connected within the complexity of individual social location and identity.

References

Althusser, L. (1971). Ideology and ideological state apparatuses. In *Lenin and philosophy and other essays* (pp. 127–186). New York, NY: Monthly Review Press.
Brock, D., & Rabin-Havt, A. (2012). *The Fox effect: How Roger Ailes turned a network into a propaganda machine.* New York, NY: Anchor Books.
Cohen, P. (2018, July 13). Paychecks lag as profits sour, and prices erode wage gains. *The New York Times (Online).* Retrieved from www.nytimes.com/2018/07/13/business/economy/wages-workers-profits.html
Cohen, P., Vogel, K. P., & Tankersley, J. (2018, July 17). I.R.S. will no longer force Kochs and other groups to disclose donors. *The New York Times.* Retrieved from www.nytimes.com/2018/07/17/us/politics/irs-will-no-longer-force-kochs-and-other-groups-to-disclose-donors.html?partner=rss&emc=rss
Collins, P. H., & Bilge, S. (2016). *Intersectionality.* Malden, MA: Polity Press.
de la Merced, M., & Fandos, N. (2017, March 3). Fox's unfamiliar but powerful television rival: Sinclair. *The New York Times.* Retrieved from https://search-proquest-com.ezproxy.gsu.edu/nytimes/docview/1894674653/fulltext/C50FB99A34934153PQ/1?accountid=11226
Duggan, L. (2003). *The twilight of equality? Neoliberalism, cultural politics, and the attack on democracy.* Boston, MA: Beacon Press.
Farhi, P. (2017, May 8). Here's what happened the last time Sinclair bought a big-city station. *The Washington Post (Online).* Retrieved from www.washingtonpost.com/lifestyle/style/heres-what-happened-the-last-time-sinclair-bought-a-big-city-station/2017/05/08/92433126-33f7-11e7-b4ee-434b6d506b37_story.html?utm_term=.d679c38137f1
Folkenflik, D. (2018, April 3). Warm relations with Trump appear to benefit Sinclair Broadcasting. *NPR.* Retrieved from www.npr.org/2018/04/03/599077733/warm-relations-with-trump-appears-to-benefit-sinclair-broadcasting
Gilens, M., & Page, B. I. (2014). Testing theories of American politics: Elites, interest groups, and average citizens. *Perspectives on Politics, 12*(3), 564–581.
Giroux, H. A. (2011). The crisis of public values in the age of the new media. *Critical Studies in Media Communication, 28*(1), 8–29. doi:10.1080/15295036.2011.544618
Guardino, M., & Snyder, D. (2012). The tea party and the crisis of neoliberalism: Mainstreaming new right populism in the corporate news media. *New Political Science, 34*(4), 527–548. doi:10.1080/07393148.2012.729741
Hall, S. (1977). Culture, the media and the "ideological" effect. In J. Curran, M. Gurevitch, & J. Woolacott (Eds.), *Mass communication and society* (pp. 315–348). Beverly Hills, CA: Sage.
Hall, S. (1982). The rediscovery of "ideology": Return of the repressed in media studies. In M. Gurevitch, T. Bennett, J. Curran, & J. Woolacott (Eds.), *Culture, society and the media* (pp. 56–90). London, UK: Methuen.
Hall, S. (1988). *The hard road to renewal: Thatcherism and the crisis of the left.* London: Verso.

Harvey, D. (2005). *A brief history of neoliberalism*. New York, NY: Oxford University.
Kennedy, P. (2017, January 7). How to destroy the business model of breitbart and fake news. *The New York Times*. Retrieved from www.nytimes.com/2017/01/07/opinion/sunday/how-to-destroy-the-business-model-of-breitbart-and-fake-news.html
Lorde, A. (2007). The master's tools will never dismantle the master's house. In *Sister outsider: Essays and speeches* (pp. 110–114). Berkeley, CA: Crossing Press.
Lührmann, A., & Wilson, M. (2018, July 3). One-third of the world's population lives in a declining democracy. that includes the united states. *The Washington Post*. Retrieved from http://ezproxy.gsu.edu/login?url=https://search-proquest-com.ezproxy.gsu.edu/docview/2064061028?accountid=11226
MacLean, N. (2017). *Democracy in chains: The deep history of the radical right's stealth plan for America*. New York, NY: Viking.
Mayer, J. (2016). *Dark money: The hidden history of the billionaires behind the rise of the radical right*. New York, NY: Doubleday.
Mayer, J. (2017, March 27). The reclusive hedge-fund tycoon behind the Trump presidency: How Robert Mercer exploited America's populist insurgency. *The New Yorker*. Retrieved from www.newyorker.com/magazine/2017/03/27/the-reclusive-hedge-fund-tycoon-behind-the-trump-presidency
McChesney, R. W. (2013). *Digital disconnect: How capitalism is turning the Internet against democracy*. New York, NY: The New Press.
Ouellette, L., & Hay, J. (2008). *Better living through reality TV: Television and post-welfare citizenship*. Malden, MA: Blackwell.
Phelan, S. (2014). *Neoliberalism, media and the political*. New York, NY: Palgrave Macmillan.
Picketty, T. (2014). *Capital in the 21st century*. Cambridge, MA: Harvard University Press.
Powell Memo (also known as the Powell Manifesto) (1971). Reclaim democracy. Retrieved from http://reclaimdemocracy.org/powell_memo_lewis/
Saul, S., & Hakim, D. (2018, June 7). The most powerful conservative couple you've never heard of. *The New York Times (Online)*. Retrieved from www.nytimes.com/2018/06/07/us/politics/liz-dick-uihlein-republican-donors.html
Sherman, G. (2014). *The loudest voice in the room: How the brilliant, bombastic Roger Ailes built Fox News – and divided a country*. New York, NY: Random House.
Taplin, J. T. (2017). *Move fast and break things: How Facebook, Google, and Amazon cornered culture and undermined democracy*. New York, NY: Little, Brown & Co.
Wemple, E. (2018, April 5). Sinclair's remarkable gaslighting operation. *The Washington Post*. Retrieved from http://ezproxy.gsu.edu/login?url=https://search-proquest-com.ezproxy.gsu.edu/docview/2022035385?accountid=11226

PART II
Corporations and Markets

2

REALITY TV "GETS REAL"

Hypercommercialism and Post-Truth in CNN's Coverage of the 2016 Election Campaign

Liane Tanguay

Aaron Sorkin's *The Newsroom* (HBO, 2012–2014), modeled on his Bush-era hit *The West Wing*, features an old-school Republican news anchor named Will McAvoy (played by Jeff Daniels) who brazenly bucks the norms of commercialized journalism, rejecting spectacle and scandal in favor of hard-hitting, fact-based coverage centered on meaningful events. McAvoy insists he is on a "mission to civilize" (Sorkin and Poul, 2012), decrying the Glenn Becks and Ann Coulters[1] of the U.S. mediascape and blaming their unethical practices for the increase in political polarization. The series was blatantly and relentlessly liberal – hewing closely to the Democratic vision of its producer – and was cancelled after only three seasons, having never achieved the popularity of its White House-based predecessor. However, a video clip of its main character's opening tirade on American "greatness" made a viral comeback on social media around the time of Donald Trump's election to an office that many still wish was occupied by *The West Wing*'s Jed Bartlett. In the clip, when asked at a panel discussion what makes America the "greatest country in the world," McAvoy replies:

> There is absolutely no evidence to support the statement that we're the greatest country in the world. We're seventh in literacy, 27th in math, 22nd in science, 49th in life expectancy, 178th in infant mortality, third in median household income, number four in labor force, and number four in exports. We lead the world in only three categories: number of incarcerated citizens per capita, number of adults who believe angels are real, and defense spending, where we spend more than the next 26 countries combined, 25 of whom are allies.
>
> *(Sorkin and Mottola, 2012)*

Following this barrage of verifiable statistics so seldom covered in mainstream news, he appeals to the glorious past it is his mission to bring back:

> We sure used to be [the greatest country]. We stood up for what was right. We fought for moral reasons, we passed and struck down laws for moral reasons. We waged wars on poverty, not poor people. We sacrificed, we cared about our neighbors, we put our money where our mouths were, and we never beat our chest. We built great big things, made ungodly technological advances, explored the universe, cured diseases, and cultivated the world's greatest artists and the world's greatest economy. We reached for the stars, and we acted like men. We aspired to intelligence; we didn't belittle it; it didn't make us feel inferior. We didn't identify ourselves by who we voted for in the last election, and we didn't scare so easy. *And we were able to be all these things and do all these things because we were informed. By great men, men who were revered.* The first step in solving any problem is recognizing there is one – America is not the greatest country in the world anymore.
>
> (Sorkin and Poul, 2012; emphasis mine)

Making Journalism Great Again

For McAvoy (and presumably Sorkin), America's former "greatness" depended on great or "civilized" journalism as the condition for a Habermasian public sphere in which democracy could thrive. But the show's unsubtle critique of the infotainment society – the extent to which commercial motives have undermined journalistic integrity and betrayed the public interest – rests on the assumption that we can turn the clock back to a kinder, gentler form of capitalism as well as the civility lost with it. So, along with the fact that McAvoy's "great" America was decidedly less so for people of color, women, and other marginalized populations, the show forgets as well that its idols, "great" journalists like Edward Murrow and Walter Cronkite, were themselves the products of a media culture incapable of delivering serious content. Entertainment, as Neil Postman (2005) argues in *Amusing Ourselves to Death*, has become in the televisual age "the metaphor for all discourse" (p. 108), disposing viewers to consume its products in a decontextualized and dehistoricized manner that reduces them to interchangeability. In other words, to wax nostalgic for a time when television journalism was truly "great" is about as delusional as either the Trumpian *or* the "Sorkinian" version of a golden age gone by.

Nonetheless, the fact that the clip went viral some four years after it was initially aired suggests that many who were dismayed with the election were of broadly the same opinion as Sorkin – that America was by no means "great" and that the media had failed in their civic duty.

Coverage of the 2016 election took the form of a market-driven media spectacle that generated false equivalencies between two vastly unequal candidates and rewarded Trump's outrageous antics with billions' worth in free airtime (Mahler, 2017).[2] In itself this is not surprising, given the revenues Trump brought to news outlets across the board: as CBS's CEO, Les Moonves, remarked, Trump was "bad for America but ... damn good for [us]" (Goodman, 2016). Furthermore, for the media to operate in this way is obviously nothing new. Critics both scholarly and popular (Chomsky and Herman, 1988; McChesney, 2004; Postman, 2005) have long lamented the subordination of journalistic integrity to the profit motive – the crass commercialism, the dearth of analysis, the embrace of scandal and spectacle, the impoverishment of discourse, the "horse race" imperative, and the endless punditry and pugilism – that has grown worse with every election cycle. But to view the most recent elections as marking a merely *quantitative* intensification of the contradiction between the profit motive and the public interest does not account for why, in 2016, the media were unable to meaningfully confront an apparent white supremacist sexual predator bent on dismantling an "establishment" that encompasses the media themselves. Predictable platitudes about the commercialization of journalism cannot account for the fact that, in an ostensibly race- and gender-blind neoliberal "meritocracy," which has now seen a black president serve two terms and a white woman secure the nomination to succeed him, a candidate widely seen as openly racist and misogynistic with a vocal following of self-proclaimed white nationalists assumed the presidency in 2016.

This is a position that, even a decade earlier, Trump's apparent racism, misogyny and overall crassness would have placed out of his reach. An "increase" in commercialization of news media therefore does not explain it; a qualitative shift must also be at stake to account for the white, patriarchal power structures at work in the political economy of mass media. It is this shift that this chapter seeks to illuminate. Without underestimating the material harm that has already been and will continue to be inflicted on women, the LGBTQ community and communities of color by Trump's occupation of the White House, or the very real dangers posed by the white supremacists and "alt-righters" who in Trump see their concerns legitimized and worthy of taking to the streets, I argue in this chapter that a "neoliberalized mediascape" was not only a necessary condition of Trump's success but that it effectively emptied the most objectionable (i.e., racist and misogynist) aspects of his platform of their content. Although the racism and misogyny should have been a "deal breaker" for all but the most extreme of his supporters, I believe the grounds for such a "deal" were never really there, that they were eroded by a mediascape in which his racist and sexist proclamations, as well as other unsavory revelations about his character, were never simply *objects* of media coverage but instead were *always-already subjected to the media logic* in which they were swept up. That is, they were hollowed out and reconfigured by a reality-TV, post-truth, neoliberalized mediascape in a way that made them less "real," and thus more palatable, for Trump's more moderate supporters. Though there is no question of simply blaming the media for the outcome of the election,[3] the symbiosis between Trump's iconic and toxic white masculinity, on the one hand, and the neoliberalized mediascape, on the other, needs to be explored beyond the now commonplace assertion that the campaign was *"like* reality TV."[4] Rather, in 2016, reality TV "got real" – and it was precisely over the course of this "reality TV" election that even the "liberal," color- and gender-blind media found themselves at a loss to manage the "truth."

Though the analysis that follows describes a condition shared by both mainstream and less mainstream (but still wildly popular) news organizations like Fox, I will focus primarily on CNN, as the network has both prided itself on its journalistic integrity and struggled to redefine itself against its cable news rivals within a constantly changing digital environment – and has capitalized perhaps more successfully than its rivals on the 2016 race (Mahler, 2017). Furthermore, the way in which CNN, a prime example of "identity-neutral" news, effectively shed its staid, predictably centrist image over the course of the campaign, saving itself from relative obsolescence, makes it the most useful network for understanding the neoliberalized mediascape as a whole.

Theorizing the Neoliberalized Mediascape

News reporting is unavoidably conditioned by the forms and logics of different media, and these, in turn, develop within and through the capitalist networks that sustain them. Neoliberalism, in its close correspondence to financialization,[5] inflects both form and content in specific ways; no medium has a single, immutable logic of its own that resists the economic forces in which it is caught up. Walter Benjamin (2007) recognized this in 1936, conceding that the emancipatory potential of the cinema would never be realized so long as it remained under capitalist control (p. 231). As such, "neoliberalism" and "media" are not here considered separate entities whose effects, one upon the other, can be empirically observed. I posit instead a "neoliberalized mediascape" that accommodates the mutual inextricability of the logics of media and neoliberalism respectively.

Television, which emerged only after Benjamin's death, is a relic of the age of mass production. Initially a dedicated broadcasting medium, it now hosts and coexists with "narrowcasting" and digital content platforms as well as the internet and social media, and it is undeniably transformed by these. But it is also transformed in tandem with the economic infrastructure with which its logic has always been articulated. The key infrastructural shift is the shift to financialization; the logic that emerges does so in the interstices of financialization and communication, and it is a logic we identify with the blanket term "neoliberalism." This is a "neoliberalism" that is always already mediated, and media are "neoliberalized" under the domination of finance, which changes the terms and conditions under which the "reality" of television – that is, not just television as a "reality" but the world that television itself puts forth – is produced, commodified and consumed. In other words, a qualitative change has taken place as financialization bears upon the political economy of mass media while digitization changes the relations between producers and consumers across all platforms.

A further consideration is undeniably that of commercialism, or the logic of advertising. Postman (2005) identified the television commercial, in 1985, as the "fundamental metaphor for political discourse in America," one that made "emotional appeal, not tests of truth, the basis of consumer decisions" and that emptied political ideas of "authentic political substance" (pp. 142–152). More recently, John Bellamy Foster and Robert W. McChesney (2003) have expounded on the link between commercialism and communication, noting that advertising is "part of the bone marrow of contemporary capitalism." Hannah Holleman, and Inger L. Stone, along with Foster and McChesney (2009), have similarly described the "sales effort" as forming "part of the system's DNA from the firm level all the way up to the economy as a whole." At stake is "the marriage of editorial/entertainment and commercialism to such an extent that they are becoming indistinguishable" (Foster and McChesney, 2003).[6] But there is something more deep-structural about advertising under contemporary capitalism that can help to shed light on the present-day mediascape. Although it builds on trends established earlier in the relationship between monopoly capitalism and the media, its logic has only fully permeated television programming under the financial and technological pressures of more recent decades. It arises from a contradiction in advertising under monopoly-finance capitalism whereby, as Holleman, et al. (2009) explain, "the more products are alike, the more the prices are similar, the more the firms must advertise to convince people they are different." What ensues is a sort of runaway commercialism driven by differentiation:

> The more firms advertise to distinguish themselves … the more commercial "clutter" there is in the media and culture. As a result firms are forced to increase their advertising that much more to get through the clutter … Commercialism in this sense is not unlike a hurricane picking up speed as it crosses the warm salt waters of late summer. Monopoly capital begets advertising begets hyper-commercialism.
>
> *(Holleman et al., 2009)*

Hypercommercialism is not a new concept. McChesney, a co-author of the quote above, included a chapter on it in *The Problem of the Media: U.S.*

Communication Politics in the 21st Century (2004), claiming that through advertising, "corporate power is woven so deeply into the culture that it becomes invisible, unquestionable" (p. 167). Robin Andersen (2008), likewise, discusses hypercommercialism in terms of product placement, "branded entertainment" and increasing media consolidation (pp. 171–181). But under present conditions the issue is not only the extent to which advertising has penetrated other areas of programming: it is the way in which its logic has subsumed those areas themselves under specific technological and financial pressures.

On one hand, the proliferation of platforms and increasing availability of free content has seriously threatened the profitability of television news. On the other, the financialization of media corporations, combined with conditions of generalized austerity, has forced news itself into a more commercially amenable format. If the tension between public interest journalism and commercialism has always been unavoidable, financialization, as Nuria Almiron (2010) explains, has "[exacerbated] the contradictions within journalism" (p.11), subjecting it to short-term profitability requirements that differ from those associated with commodity capitalism. For Almiron, financialization changes how media corporations govern themselves, and this is even more the case as austerity imposes a mandate now all too familiar across all sectors – the requirement to do more with less. Rather than focus on sales returns, finance demands that gains be assured up front in the form of cuts to expenditures, staffing, and so forth, with the company "immersed in a scenario of major instability and larger fragility" (Almiron, 2010, p. 80). The result is a "chronic resource deficit that generates impossible-to-meet agendas, impossible-to-confirm information, and the inability to go beyond press-release journalism" (Almiron, 2010, p. 170). On television, in particular, journalism is substituted with a "sort of superficial, pointless, and irrelevant flow of show business" (Almiron, 2010, p. 177) that standardizes the formatting of news production across the board.

But standardization, as the concept of hypercommercialism makes clear, intensifies the need for differentiation, as the most pressing imperative becomes that of distinguishing one "brand" – in this case, one news network identity – over another. As such, "hypercommercialism" is more than just an intensification of commercialism of the sort that critics like Postman are concerned with. The prefix "hyper" suggests a doubling of sorts, a sort of il-logic that sees *differentiation itself* superseding the "content," or referent, of a brand. Applied to saleable commodities, this is not particularly remarkable; applied to news reporting, it is considerably more so, and portends the very shift to "post-truth" that many intuited both during the campaign and following the political upset that ended it. Further, as this chapter will explain, these processes do not unfold seamlessly in some abstract realm, uncomplicated by racialized and gendered structures that privilege some identities over others while exacerbating existing tensions between them. Much like ostensibly neutral machine learning algorithms replicate the racial and gender biases embedded in the societies that create them,[7] so too do the apparently disinterested forces of financialization and hypercommercialism elevate the white masculinity that remains at the helm of neoliberal capitalism despite its inclusive, meritocratic claims.

Reality Television and the Political Economy of Outrage

Ultimately, my claim is that the neoliberalized mediascape is defined by financialization and hypercommercialism, by a relentless imperative of differentiation that has infused all strands of programming and reformatted them within the circuits of the neoliberal media in uniquely disabling – as well as persistently gendered and racialized – ways. How this played out on CNN in 2016 can be considered in relation to two of the most common observations about the election – first, that it unfolded "like a reality TV show," and second, that it pointed to "post-truth" (Davies, 2016; Jordan, 2016; Sharockman, 2016) as some new existential condition in the West. These claims were made in both the popular and scholarly registers, and elaborated upon to varying degrees. But considered separately, they are of decidedly limited value. For instance, to call Trump a "reality TV president" has less to do with his 13-season stint on *The Apprentice*, or the fact that, with an initial 17 candidates, the Republican primaries played out like a particularly dispiriting season of *American Idol*, than it does with the format of the coverage itself. To this extent, what reality television *is*, and how it operates in the context of neoliberalism, has not been sufficiently explored in the many accounts of how Trump "gamed" the system and drove the media coverage.

This is not to say that it has not been explored at all. Noted television scholar Laurie Ouellette, in a short piece on the Trump campaign as reality television (2016), does note "[r]eality TV's relationship to the free market political rationalities that Trump so powerfully signifies and embodies," and credits *The Apprentice* with "[establishing] the rogue businessman as a new kind of expert and leader extraordinaire"; she connects the show's neoliberal politics to Trump's "embodiment of ... a 'no nonsense' approach to leadership," and insists, quite rightly, on understanding the "social, economic and political contexts in which reality television as a genre is embedded" (pp. 2–3). Indeed, it is crucial to consider the context of a financialized, upwardly redistributive economy that disempowers ordinary citizens along axes of race, class, and gender alike, pressuring them to cultivate entrepreneurial subjectivities in increasingly inhospitable conditions and to subsequently internalize their inevitable failures. But this is also the same context in which, had the Democratic National Committee put Bernie Sanders forward as its candidate, we might now be facing an entirely less abysmal set of circumstances. Thus, an analysis too focused on content – as if the medium were merely a vessel – ignores the place of reality television within the neoliberalized mediascape, including journalism, itself. It also fails to account for its part in the resurgence of an increasingly vocal, white supremacist masculinism.

Likewise, the canonization of "post-truth" as Word of the Year by Oxford Dictionaries (2016) does not tell us much, in itself, about the coverage. *New York Times* columnist Paul Krugman (2011), for one, had already claimed the term "post-truth campaign" for the Obama-Romney presidential race in 2011. Well before that, in 2004, Ralph Keyes penned a book called *The Post-Truth Era* to explore what he called the "routinization of dishonesty" in public life. More memorably, in 2005, Stephen Colbert coined the term "truthiness" to describe the experience of "believing something that *feels* true, even if it isn't supported by fact."[8] But the use of "post-truth" to describe how Trump ran a successful campaign on the most easily verifiable of lies is too limited; in fact, "truth" was nothing if not fully central to the campaign, with 2016 "the year of the fact-checker" (Stelter, 2016) in independent and mainstream media alike. And again, it is silent on questions of race and gender.

Considered together, however, and in the context of the neoliberalized mediascape, the "post-truth" and "reality television" claims explain a lot more. What most closely connects them – and explains why the 2016 campaign was so widely hailed as both a "reality television" *and* a "post-truth" campaign – is the logic of hypercommercialism and differentiation described above. The combination of neoliberalization, financialization and hypercommercialism has helped make reality television – a genre that entertains an especially fraught relationship to "truth" – the model for all communication. And the appearance of Trump on the political scene combined with these factors, catastrophically, to drive the direction of the coverage into an epistemological "state of exception" in which his unique brand of authoritarianism, racism, and misogyny was able to flourish.

Reality television, to begin with, is an amalgam not only of other entertainment genres but of what Niklas Luhmann (2000) identified as three separate "strands" of programming that establish the rules for selection, formatting and presentation of content: news, entertainment, and advertising. Briefly, Luhmann sketched out the criteria for each programming "strand": news seeks surprises, conflicts, norm violations – especially "of the moral code, and ... of 'political correctness'," celebrities, and so forth (pp. 28–34) – while entertainment provides a "doubling of reality," as in a game or a "world in which a fictional reality of its own applies" (pp. 51–52). But advertising has a special function: it directly confronts the "suspicion of manipulation" (p. 40) that results from our awareness that the mass media's "reality" is always highly selective (p. 42) and subject to control by vested interests. The key is that advertising conceals nothing. In it, "[e]verything we had always suspected anyway suddenly appears as truth"; it "works insincerely, and assumes that that is taken for granted" (p. 44). Its "open hand" (p. 44) relieves its claims of any obligation towards the truth. One is not expected to *believe*, for instance, that Red Bull "gives you wings." And although reality television qualifies as both entertainment and as news – its second-order reality is not exactly "fictional" insofar as the participants are "real" people, and it must meet the criteria established by news programming (surprise, conflict, norm violations) in order to draw ratings – its dominant logic is advertising, which absorbs the logics of both news and entertainment into its undiscriminating maw.

Reality television came into its own under the same technological and commercial pressures described above. As Chad Raphael (1997) explains, "changing patterns of distribution" in the 1980s threatened the networks' "oligopolistic control" over programming, and reality television "fit the bill" by enabling producers to bypass labor and save on costs associated with "higher-priced stars and union talent" (pp. 102–109). But as the genre flourished and proliferated across networks, the drive to differentiate took over, superseding the actual content of any given product with the sheer fact of its distinction from the others. And now, in a shift which accounts in large part for the increasing (re-)normalization of overt racism and misogyny, distinction has become entirely a function of the ability to shock. The relatively innocuous scenario of a dozen strangers sharing a house (*The Real World, Big Brother*) has given way to the moralizing voyeurism of shows like *Jersey Shore* or *16 and Pregnant*, to the intensified Darwinian competitiveness and backstabbing of *Survivor* and its urban counterpart, *The Apprentice*, and to shamelessly exploitive experiments like *The Briefcase*. The capacity to shock and appall is part of the branding strategy. Indeed, June Deery (2004), who classifies the genre under the neologism "advertainment," sees its "brand identity" as offering a "special access to 'reality'" (p. 7), promising viewers, in its unscriptedness, "the thrill of seeing something intimate and taboo" (p. 9).

It was from intensified conditions of scarcity and increasing competition that *The Apprentice*, under Jeff Zucker's supervision, saved NBC (Mahler, 2017). And it is easy to see how television news, facing the same set of pressures, has since reformatted itself along the lines of reality television, with ever-expanding panels of celebrity anchors and paid provocateurs making themselves, and their outrage, the "story" rather than the events they are discussing. News, too, has submitted to the principle of differentiation as the need to distinguish one network's squabbling panel over another's has made the substance of the coverage irrelevant. Thus, the cost-saving measures of the financialized newsroom – the preference for cheaper, in-house, interpretive reporting over the costlier and more time-consuming investigative kind, as well as, on CNN, the retention of Trump campaign surrogates and unpaid "guests" like *Apprentice* star-turned-White House aide Omarosa Manigault[9] – were also *differentiating* measures that saw CNN's panels become news events unto themselves, and its daytime and prime-time viewership climb 50% and 70% respectively in what became the most profitable year (2016) in its history

(Mahler, 2017). Former campaign manager Corey Lewandowski and Trump surrogates Jeffrey Lord and Kayleigh McEnany proved a windfall for CNN, amplifying the largely gendered and racialized shock value already provided by the candidate himself in such a way that the nature of the coverage came to subsume the actual content of those "shocks." As Trump abandoned his dog whistle for a bullhorn, the reality television spectacle generated around him effectively neutralized what should have been downright alarming, serving it up in the form of entertainment rather than subjecting it to any serious critical scrutiny.

The sheer entertainment value of CNN's coverage lent itself nicely to social media, where clips uploaded by ordinary users feature titles like "Anderson Cooper OWNS Jeffrey Lord, 'Trump Could Take a Dump on his DESK and you would defend him'" (Act Now, 2017); "Van Jones BLOWS UP on Kayleigh McEnany 'You Need to Back Off!'" (G4Viral Videos, 2016); "CNN Contributor has a MELTDOWN!! AFTER!! Kayleigh McEnany TOLD HER THE ELECTION WAS FAIR !!!" (Fox Conn, 2016); "Kayleigh McEnany Rips CNN Panel Apart over Trump" (DC Statesman, 2016); and so on *ad infinitum*. What should have been serious discussions of race, class and gender translated into spectacular fights between news personalities. Hence, what Sarah Sobieraj and Jeffrey M. Berry (2011) have called the "outrage industry," explaining that whereas "during the era of the big-three network dominance ... the goal was to offend the fewest, to program with the least objectionable content," now audience fragmentation and "entertainment imperatives" have created a "media environment ... uniquely supportive of outrage-based political discourse" (pp. 20–22). To this I would add that hypercommercialism and the drive to differentiate have made the strategy of "offending the fewest" tantamount to "blending in," a fate that had all but befallen CNN before Donald Trump appeared on the scene. The retention of Trump surrogates – designed precisely to infuriate rather than contribute to a meaningful discussion – by a network that once prided itself on avoiding extremes and on privileging "the facts" shows to what extent the imperative of differentiation through shock value has penetrated newsroom culture. And Trump's appeal to white, nativist masculinity served this imperative perfectly.

The Normalization of Hate

The presence of CNN's Trump surrogates serves not only to increase the "outrage factor" and draw more ratings and social-media shares, it also effectively normalizes racist, sexist, homophobic, and nativist discourses that not so long ago would have been considered unacceptable. Characters brought on to defend the indefensible end up bringing it into the bounds of "rational" discourse while appealing to the same voyeuristic instincts and appetite for scandal that fuel the popularity of reality TV. Statements that even a decade ago would have been cause for alarm are thus radically decontextualized. Though Postman (2005) points out that decontextualization is intrinsic to the televisual epistemology, hypercommercialism and the reformatting of news along the lines of reality television have so thoroughly done away with any standards of reasonableness and decency that the media themselves were unprepared for the long-term consequences of a racist, misogynistic campaign like Trump's. A tacit assumption throughout the campaign, for instance, was that Trump's bottomless ignorance and flamboyant racism would ultimately keep him out of office. But with decontextualization, the value of Trump's statements *as content* – that is, their veracity or lack thereof – is subordinated to their value as a tool of differentiation. Thus, the impact of such statements, no matter how offensive, is measured primarily by their domination of what Jayson Harsin (2015) calls the "attention economy." It is, in other words, their value as an instrument of pure differentiation that overrode the righteous outrage of the center and the left during the 2016 campaign.

Unsurprisingly, the same logic obtains at the level of CNN's coverage itself, even of the most blatantly regressive proclivities of the Republican candidate. Trump's alarming March 2016 refusal to disavow the support of former Ku Klux Klan Grand Wizard David Duke saw its most prolonged treatment, on CNN, in a face-off between CNN commentator Van Jones and Trump surrogate Jeffrey Lord (CNN, 2016a) that *CNN itself* reported had "distilled" the "racial tension underlying the 2016 race … into a single cable news moment" (CNN, 2016b). To be sure, the segment hadn't done anything of the sort. The "debate" was utterly absurd, thanks to Lord's intellectual acrobatics and misleading appeals to the racially fraught, early history of the Democratic Party. It ultimately yielded nothing by way of an effective response to Trump's indifference vis-a-vis the KKK. On the whole, Trump's capacity to generate outrage ultimately overwhelmed the "outrage industry" itself, rendering even "good" journalists incapable of steering the conversation.

The same applies to Trump's equally outrageous misogyny. CNN seemed quite nearly convinced that the leaked *Access Hollywood* tape in which Trump famously bragged of "grabbing [women] by the pussy" would ultimately cost him the White House (CNN, 2016c). The footage of the *Access Hollywood* bus advancing at a crawl, overlaid with the infamous audio feed, was replayed *ad nauseam* while journalists and commentators feverishly speculated about its impact on his chances at the presidency as well as on the upcoming second debate with Clinton. The most memorable coverage, however, took the form of a five-member panel on Don Lemon's *CNN Tonight* in which political commentator Ana Navarro and campaign surrogate Scottie Nell Hughes broke into a screaming match over Trump's choice of words (CNN, 2016d). Trump, for his part, dismissed the remarks as "locker-room talk" and used the occasion of his first public apology to go after former

President Bill Clinton for his own treatment of women. But, ultimately, neither the revelation nor his apology mattered – it was their domination of the "attention economy" that counted, and by October 2016 it was far too late for a return to responsible, deliberative journalism. Trump won the election a month later.

Authenticity, Post-Truth and Fascism through the Looking-Glass

The bus tape was all the more exciting as "reality television" in that it offered a (supposedly) privileged, voyeuristic glimpse into who Trump "really" is off-camera (and this voyeurism trumped, so to speak, the revelation that he is "really" a sexual predator). After all, this is the promise of "advertainment," as Deery (2004) notes in her comments on reality television – that of a special "access" to "reality" (p. 9) that other genres do not afford. This is all the more appealing given that, where no independent criteria exist against which to measure truth-claims – where, as Mark Andrejevic (2010) says, "the criteria for adjudication are themselves called into question" (p. 20) – the suspicion Luhmann (2000) associated with the "reality" of the mass media resolves itself in the paradoxical conviction that some kernel beyond the appearances is within the subject's reach. Thus we come to "post-truth," to choosing *affectively* on what seems like "gut instinct" but really corresponds to the medium's command of the attention economy (Harsin, 2015, p. 331). Naturally, this ersatz empowerment produces a certain amount of anxiety as well, insofar as one can never be sure whether one is making the "right" choice; hence the desire, Andrejevic (2010) argues, to access "hidden, underlying truths" (p. 17) common to reality television and news coverage alike. And again, though this would seem to apply on an abstract or "identity-neutral" plane, it nonetheless brings androcentric norms and expectations into play.

In particular, Andrejevic (2010) attributes to this desire for "access" the increasing retention of "body language experts" in political news coverage. Although this strategy had been used in earlier elections, it was especially gendered in 2016, with the burden placed on Clinton to prove her "authenticity." Thus Trump, in the first debate, was deemed by the expert to be "more emotional, his hand gestures projecting strength and confidence, his demeanor indicating he's trying to play offense," while Clinton's great achievement – never mind her superior knowledge of the issues and fluency in addressing them – was to "[get] under [his] skin in the first 12 minutes" (CNN, 2016e). However, according to the expert, Clinton's "emotions" failed to "match the message she [was] delivering"; she was also described as remote and "dismissive," but her principal problem was disingenuousness, such that "while she's making excellent points verbally, she's not making them non-verbally; you're feeling them here [in the head] and not here [in the heart]" (CNN, 2016e). In the third debate, Clinton is deemed at times "more human," while Trump is "consistent with his overall anger"; Clinton is more "composed" but also less "relatable" and less "sincere," as well as more likely to show signs of having "rehearsed" her answers to questions about her emails. At the key moment that came to dominate the post-debate panels on CNN and MSNBC – Trump's refusal to commit to accepting the election results – the expert (Anthony Locascio) assures us that Trump is "absolutely sincere … absolutely genuine" (CNN, 2016f). Honesty and truth are subordinated to "sincerity," a priority echoed millions of times over by Trump voters justifying their support: he "tells it like it is." This brand of sincerity is, to be sure, inescapably masculine – no woman could "tell it" like Trump does. But the scrutiny placed on physical "tells," on aspects of performance that cannot but be gendered, reinforces suspicions about the female candidate's untrustworthiness while privileging Trump's own domineering presence.

That "telling it like it is" entailed a steady stream of lies was not, apparently, a problem for many viewers. Perhaps the truest statement to come out of the Trump campaign was Corey Lewandowski's oddly astute critique of the media:

> You guys took everything that Donald Trump said so literally. The American people didn't. They understood that sometimes, when you have a conversation with people, whether it's around the dinner table or at a bar, you're going to say things, and sometimes you don't have all the facts to back it up.
>
> *(Hawkins, 2017)*

Yet, in such moments, you are perceived as "authentic" and "sincere," and perception, in the neoliberalized mediascape, is everything. When the differentiating, hyper-commercialist drive of reality television reduces all political discourse to outrage-value, when no authoritative truth is perceived to speak through the proliferating shocks and offenses perpetrated through the logic of differentiation, what obtains is what Harsin (2015) calls a "regime of post-truth." A final blow is struck to the presupposition, necessary to deliberative democracy, of a "truth" that stands outside ideology and partisanship as a common terrain on which public policy can be meaningfully, and inclusively, debated. The arc of communication, in the neoliberalized mediascape, tends towards nihilism and willful ignorance, providing a welcoming environment for the racism and misogyny that came to infuse every aspect of Trump's campaign and, eventually, his presidency.

Michel Foucault (1990, 1995) understood "truth" to be contingent in any case, and always intrinsically linked to power. And if a certain coordination between industrial capitalism, the institution of mass media and what Benjamin (2007) called the "formation of masses" (p. 241) enabled a "truth regime" that still pointed to some shared understanding of "truth" in the scientific or Enlightenment sense of the word – a relic, Postman might say (2005), of the print culture that at that time was only just beginning to fade into oblivion – then it follows that the relationship between neoliberalism, the shape of communication today and contemporary power portend the change to the "regime of post-truth" that Harsin (2015) describes.

This was the point of this chapter all along – to explore certain aspects of the 2016 campaign as a mediatized event where hypercommercialism drives the production, distribution and consumption of information, and to explain its unique positioning in relation to "truth" as well as the ascendancy of a hate-fueled, racist and misogynistic politics that not so long ago would have been shut down in the earlier stages of an electoral campaign. It is now a question of, as Harsin (2015) puts it, "truth markets" centered around the attention economy (p. 330), where the commitment is not to the public interest but to the degree of interest shown by the public – that is, to ratings. Trump's lies helped him win the election, but not in the way that lies usually win elections; it was the fact of the lies themselves, their brazenness and frequency, that allowed him to dominate the field.

This would all be merely academic, so to speak, if Trump had been a more conventional candidate. But his authoritarian streak and divisive, damaging rhetoric – which proved more than the "liberal" media could handle – made the 2016 campaign a perfect storm. In *Amusing Ourselves to Death*, Postman (2005) juxtaposes Orwell's dystopian vision in *1984* with Aldous Huxley's in *Brave New World*, arguing that the latter is the one that has triumphed. Orwell's "warnings," he writes:

> have customarily been directed against those consciously formulated ideologies that appeal to the worst tendencies in human nature. But what is happening in America is not the design of an articulated ideology. No Mein Kampf or Communist Manifesto announced its coming.
>
> *(2005, p. 173)*

Perhaps no announcement preceded it and the present-day ideology of the Right does lack the coherence of any manifesto. Yet, where differentiation as such empties racist proclamations and misogynistic behaviors of their substantive content, perhaps the result is the same – such that, indeed, the authoritarianism of a figure like Trump – for whom *Mein Kampf* is reputed to be bedtime reading – is able to thrive once again. The cult of Trump was not a conscious creation of the television and cable networks that granted him a free outlet for his racist, xenophobic and misogynistic views; most of the networks (and even at times the odd Fox commentator) were openly critical of Trump, and after he secured the nomination many of them set about digging up various scandals and misdeeds from his past, albeit to no effect. There was no need, as Walter Benjamin (2007) warned with the advent of cinema, to mobilize the "masses," to show them their "reflections" (p. 251) in organized spectacles and military parades of the sort that Trump is now busily arranging for the coming year.[10] But if reflection (in the newsreels of Benjamin's day) implies a sort of mirroring function, whereby the "masses" are induced to recognize themselves in large-scale spectacles, then reality television brings us "through the looking glass," as it were, shifting the grounds for knowledge from cognition to affect and making the "gut," or individual instinct, the impossible arbiter of truth. Stepping into this context at a time of record inequality and generalized precarity – a condition also in part facilitated by the same decline in public communication lamented in Sorkin's short-lived drama – Donald Trump, of reality television fame, brought with him a bit more "reality" than the media were able to handle. Even traditionally centrist and "liberal" networks were unable to meaningfully confront his attacks on the American social fabric given the epistemological crisis precipitated by hypercommercialism and differentiation, a crisis conducive to the fantasies of authenticity, patriarchal domination and racial purity that helped propel him into power. Perhaps in this light his occupancy of the Oval Office is not the affront to "normality" that his liberal opposition takes it to be, but a revelation of the truth behind it: the still racialized and gendered contempt for human life on which capitalist accumulation has always depended, not least in its ostensibly color-blind and gender-blind, neoliberal phase.

Notes

1 Glenn Beck and Ann Coulter are prominent right-wing political commentators. Beck hosted a show on the conservative Fox News network while Coulter has appeared regularly on television and radio talk shows. Both are extremely conservative and they have contributed substantially to the political polarization of the past 20 years.
2 According to Mahler (2017), "[t]he media-measurement firm mediaQuant calculated that Trump received the equivalent of $5.8 billion in free media – known as 'earned media,' as opposed to paid advertising – over the course of the election."
3 No single factor "caused" Trump's victory. Russian interference, voter suppression, voter apathy, economic insecurity amid a recovery that has benefited primarily the 1%, a "whitelash" following Obama's two terms, Hillary Clinton's limited appeal on the left as well as the right, and sexism directed against her count among the numerous other factors that combined to put Trump in the White House.
4 See, among others, Michael Rosenblum (October 30, 2016); Jay Newton-Small (September 26, 2017); Michael Atkinson (November 7, 2016); Tom Engelhardt (August 10, 2016); Laurie Ouellette (June 2016); David Showalter (June 8, 2017); Hank Stuever (July 16, 2016).
5 "Financialization" refers to the ascendancy of the financial sector over the "real" or productive economy, giving financial institutions and elites (including shareholders) greater influence over both policy and production by prioritizing short-term profits. Its impacts on the communication sector are further explained below, with reference to Nuria Almiron's (2010) *Journalism in Crisis: Corporate Media and Financialization* (Hampton Press, 2010).

6 The essence of this critique can arguably be traced all the way back to the Frankfurt School.
7 Numerous studies are revealing how computer programs designed to be more "objective" than humans are instead further entrenching racial and gender bias in areas like risk assessment, lending, employment, etc. See, for instance Hannah Devlin (September 13, 2017); Dina Bass and Ellen Huet (December 4, 2017).
8 *The Colbert Report* (2005). Season 1, Episode 1. Comedy Central. October 17, 2005.
9 Manigault was fired from the White House in December 2017, apparently for misusing the White House's car service.
10 Trump has secured funding for a military parade to be held in Washington, D.C., on Veterans Day 2018.

References

Act Now. (2017, May 9). *Anderson Cooper OWNS Jeffrey Lord, "Trump Could Take a Dump on His DESK and You Would Defend Him."* [Video File]. Retrieved from www.youtube.com/watch?v=S_DJ8CvjIFc

Almiron, N. (2010). *Journalism in Crisis: Corporate Media and Financialization.* New York, NY: Hampton Press.

Andersen, R. (2008). Hypercommercialism. In Robin Andersen and Jonathan Gray (Eds.), *Battleground: The Media Volume 1 (A–N)* (pp. 171–181). Westport, CO: Greenwood Press.

Andrejevic, M. (2010). Reading the Surface: Body Language and Surveillance. *Culture Unbound: Journal of Current Cultural Research* 2(1), 15–36. Hosted by Linkoping University Electronic Press. Retrieved from www.cultureunbound.ep.liu.se

Atkinson, M. (2016, November 7). Trump TV: How Election 2016 Officially Turned Politics into Reality Television. *Rolling Stone.* Retrieved from www.rollingstone.com/tv/news/how-election-2016-officially-turned-politics-into-reality-tv-w448487

Bass, D. and Huet, E. (2017, December 4). Researchers Combat Gender and Racial Bias in Artificial Intelligence. *Bloomberg.com.* Retrieved from www.bloomberg.com/news/articles/2017-12-04/researchers-combat-gender-and-racial-bias-in-artificial-intelligence

Benjamin, W. (2007). The Work of Art in the Age of Mechanical Reproduction. In Hannah Arendt (Ed.) and Harry Zohn (Trans.), *Illuminations: Essays and Reflections* (pp. 217–251). New York, NY: Schocken Books. (Originally published 1936)

Chomsky, N. and Herman, E. (1988). *Manufacturing Consent: The Political Economy of the Mass Media.* New York, NY: Pantheon Books.

CNN. (2016a, March 2). *Van Jones Rips Donald Trump and the KKK.* [Video File]. Retrieved from www.cnn.com/videos/politics/2016/03/02/cnn-analysts-heated-exchange-trump-race-divide-sot.cnn

CNN. (2016b, March 2). *Van Jones, Jeffrey Lord Launch into Fiery Debate.* [Video File]. Retrieved from www.cnn.com/2016/03/01/politics/jeffrey-lord-van-jones-cnn-debate/index.html

CNN. (2016c, October 8). *Can Donald Trump Recover from This?* [Video File]. Retrieved from www.cnn.com/2016/10/07/politics/donald-trump-campaign-crisis/index.html

CNN. (2016d, October 8). *Leaked Trump Video Sparks Heated Exchange.* [Video File]. Retrieved from www.cnn.com/videos/tv/2016/10/08/ctn-navarro-hughes-trump-offenseexchange.cnn

CNN. (2016e, September 27). *Expert: Clinton Got Under Trump's Skin in 12 Minutes.* [Video File]. Retrieved from www.cnn.com/videos/politics/2016/09/27/donald-trump-hillary-clinton-presidential-debate-body-language-marquez-dnt.cnn

CNN. (2016f, October 20). *Anderson Cooper 360 Degrees*. [Transcript]. Retrieved from http://transcripts.cnn.com/TRANSCRIPTS/1610/20/acd.01.html

The Colbert Report. (2005, October 17). Season 1, Episode 1. Comedy Central.

Davies, W. (2016, August 24). The Age of Post-Truth Politics. *The New York Times*. Retrieved from www.nytimes.com/2016/08/24/opinion/campaign-stops/the-ageof-post-truth-politics.html

DC Statesman. (2016, October 19). *Kayleigh McEnany Rips CNN Panel Apart over Trump*. [Video File]. Retrieved from www.youtube.com/watch?v=xUbxqbrrPlc.

Deery, J. (2004). Reality TV as Advertisement. *Popular Communication: The International Journal of Media and Culture 2*(1), 1–20.

Devlin, H. (2017, September 13). AI Programs Exhibit Racial and Gender Biases, Research Reveals. *The Guardian*. Retrieved from www.theguardian.com/technology/2017/apr/13/ai-programs-exhibit-racist-and-sexist-biases-research-reveals

Engelhardt, T. (2016, August 10). Better than Reality Television: The 2016 Election Is Proving to Be the Greatest Show on Earth. *Salon*. Retrieved from www.salon.com/2016/08/10/better-than-reality-televisio_partner/

Foster, J. B. and McChesney, R. W. (2003, March). The Commercial Tidal Wave. *Monthly Review: An Independent Socialist Magazine 54* (10). Retrieved from https://monthlyreview.org/2003/03/01/the-commercial-tidal-wave/

Foucault, M. (1990). *History of Sexuality, Vol. 1: An Introduction*. New York, NY: Vintage Books.

Foucault, M. (1995). *Discipline and Punish: The Birth of the Prison*. New York, NY: Vintage Books.

Fox Conn. (2016, December 26). *CNN Contributor HAS A MELTDOWN !! AFTER !! Kayleigh McEnany TOLD HER THE ELECTION WAS FAIR !!!* [Video file]. Retrieved from www.youtube.com/watch?v=L21OsLt_f98

G4Viral Videos. (2016, November 9). *Van Jones BLOWS UP on Kayleigh McEnany 'You Need to Back Off!'*. [Video File]. Retrieved from www.youtube.com/watch?v=5d4_DR6wtEU

Harsin, J. (2015). Regimes of Posttruth, Postpolitics, and Attention Economies. *Communication, Culture & Critique 8*(2), 327–333.

Hawkins, D. (2017, September 6). Getting to Harvard, the Corey Lewandowski Way. *The Washington Post*. Retrieved from www.washingtonpost.com/news/morningmix/wp/2017/09/06/corey-lewandowski-who-once-balked-at-obamas-harvardcredentials-is-headed-there-himself/?utm_term=.19f88f68e211

Holleman, H., Stone, I. L., Foster, J. B. and McChesney, R. W. (2009). The Sales Effort and Monopoly Capital. *Monthly Review: An Independent Socialist Magazine 60*(11). Retrieved from https://monthlyreview.org/2009/04/01/thesales-effort-and-monopoly-capital/

Goodman, Amy. (interviewer) (2016, November 9). "It Might Not Be Good for America, But It's Good for Us": How the Media Got Rich on Trump's Rise. *Democracy Now*. Retrieved from www.democracynow.org/2016/11/9/it_might_not_be_good_for

Jordan, M. (2016, October 27). In a Post-Truth Election, Clicks Trump Facts. *The New Republic*. Retrieved from https://newrepublic.com/article/138201/post-truth-electionclicks-trump-facts

Keyes, R. (2004). *The Post-Truth Era: Dishonesty and Deception in Contemporary Life*. New York, NY: St. Martin's Press.

Krugman, P. (2011, December 22). The Post-Truth Campaign. *The New York Times*. Retrieved from www.nytimes.com/2011/12/23/opinion/krugman-the-post-truthcampaign.html?mcubz=3

Luhmann, N. (2000). *The Reality of the Mass Media*. Translated by Kathleen Cross. Cambridge: Polity Press.

Mahler, J. (2017, April 4). CNN Had a Problem. Donald Trump Solved It. *The New York Times Magazine*. Retrieved from www.nytimes.com/2017/04/04/magazine/cnnhad-a-problem-donald-trump-solved-it.html?mcubz=3

McChesney, R. W. (2004). *The Problem of the Media: U.S. Communication Politics in the 21st Century*. New York, NY: Monthly Review Press.

Newton-Small, J. (2016, March 23). How Reality T.V. Took Over U.S. Politics. *Time*. Retrieved from http://time.com/4268109/donald-trump-reality-television-apprenticedancing-stars/

Ouellette, L. (2016). The Trump Show. *Television & New Media*, 1–4. Retrieved from http://journals.sagepub.com/doi/abs/10.1177/1527476416652695?journalCode=tvna

Oxford Dictionaries. (2016). *Oxford Dictionaries Word of the Year 2016*. Retrieved from www.oxforddictionaries.com/press/news/2016/11/17/WOTY-16

Postman, N. (2005). *Amusing Ourselves to Death: Public Discourse in the Age of Show Business*. New York, NY: Penguin Books. (Original work published 1985)

Raphael, C. (1997 May). Political Economy of Reali-TV. *Jump-Cut: A Review of Contemporary Media 41*, 102–109. Retrieved from www.ejumpcut.org/archive/onlineessays/JC41folder/EconomyRealiTV.html

Rosenblum, M. (2016, October 30). How the 2016 Presidential Election Became a Reality Show. *The Huffington Post*. Retrieved from www.huffingtonpost.com/michael-rosenblum/how-the-2016-presidential_b_12715398.html

Sharockman, A. (2016, August 16). The Post-Truth Election? Comparing 2016 to past Elections on the Truth-O-Meter. *Politifact.com*. Retrieved from www.politifact.com/truth-o-meter/article/2016/aug/16/post-truth-electioncomparing-2016-past-elections-/

Showalter, D. (2017, June 8). Donald Trump and the Political Aesthetics of Reality Television. *Berkeley Journal of Sociology*. Retrieved from http://berkeleyjournal.org/2017/06/donald-trump-and-the-political-aesthetics-of-realitytelevision/

Sobieraj, S. and Berry, J. M. (2011, February 8). From Incivility to Outrage: Political Discourse in Blogs, Talk Radio and Cable News. *Political Communication 28* (1), 19–41.

Sorkin, A. (Writer) and Mottola, G. (Director). (2012, June 24). We Just Decided To [Television series episode]. In Aaron Sorkin (Producer), *The Newsroom*. HBO Entertainment.

Sorkin, A. (Writer) and Poul, A. (Director). (2012, July 15). I'll Try to Fix You [Television series episode]. In Aaron Sorkin (Producer). *The Newsroom*. HBO Entertainment.

Stelter, B. (2016, November 7). How Donald Trump Made Fact-Checking Great Again. *cnn.com*. Retrieved from http://money.cnn.com/2016/11/07/media/donald-trump-fact-checking/index.html

Stuever, H. (2016, July 16). How Reality TV Gave Us Reality Candidate Trump. *The Washington Post*. Retrieved from www.washingtonpost.com/entertainment/tv/how-reality-tv-gave-us-reality-candidatedonald-trump/2016/07/16/0ebc5963-4454-11e68856f26de2537a9d_story.html?utm_term=.2f2f39ff9382

3

THE GIRL EFFECT

Philanthrocapitalism and the Branded Marketplace of Philanthropic Governance

Dana Schowalter

The Nike Foundation launched its Girl Effect campaign in 2009 with a YouTube video highlighting that 62 million girls still lack access to formal schooling and claiming that small interventions in educational opportunities for girls would have the power to improve the gross domestic product (GDP) of entire nations. Unlike philanthropic programming that links a corporation with a single intervention or location, the Girl Effect aimed to serve as an umbrella brand; individuals and organizations could download and use the official logo to market an array of girl-empowerment activities. The Nike Foundation's stated goal was to use its $100 million campaign investment to control the conversation about the need for increasing educational opportunities for girls worldwide by offering free publicity for any subsidiary of their umbrella philanthropy (Kylander, 2011). By the time the Nike Foundation spun the Girl Effect into its own organization in 2015, the program had: partnered with major international governance, economic, and philanthropic organizations, such as the United Nations Global Compact, Clinton Global Initiative, the G20 Summit, the World Bank, and the World Economic Forum; received millions of hits on YouTube and thousands of followers on Facebook; and been the subject of an episode of *Oprah* (Carella, 2011; ICAI Report, 2012).

The campaign, which was largely aimed at attracting the attention of consumers in the Global North,[1] served as an informational hub for social media followers who were encouraged to share viral content, including do-it-yourself crafting guides for making homemade Girl Effect stickers, examples of activism girls could replicate in their own communities, and campaign videos suggesting that funding schools for girls would enable financial and political independence even without any additional interventions.

In this chapter, I conduct a discourse analysis of the Girl Effect initiative, focusing on the official online and social media sites (girleffect.org, facebook.com/girleffect, and youtube.com/user/girleffect); web-based mobilization materials, including two Girl Effect reports summarizing internal research on educational access ("Your Move" and "Smarter Economics"); two toolkits informing people about ways to get involved ("Toolkit" and "Plan an Event Guide"); and the *Girls Count* research series funded by the Nike Foundation to assess the importance of global investments in educational infrastructure for girls. Together, I look at what these materials say about the best avenues for involvement, activism, and citizenship for individuals and corporations. I highlight these sources because they are the predominant means through which the campaign communicates with individuals and corporations who wish to get involved with the project, and also because these sources tend to cross-reference each other.

In analyzing official online and social media pages, campaign videos, mobilization materials, and affiliated research studies, I argue that the Girl Effect campaign deflects attention from the complexities of gendered global poverty and instead directs attention toward individualized acts of caregiving and privatized philanthropic governance. Indeed, the Nike Foundation has funded five research studies—with organizations such as the Population Council and the Center for Global Development—that offer systemic and critical analyses of the problems and potential solutions to intergenerational poverty among women and girls. However, official Girl Effect campaign materials direct consumer attention away from these robust analyses and toward individualization and self-empowerment. In other words, girls in the Global North are encouraged to feel good about using online cause networks to "save" girls in the Global South.

To assess the connection between the focus on hyperindividualism and the deflection away from complex understandings of gendered global poverty, I integrate the theoretical frameworks of neoliberalism, cause marketing, citizenship, and critiques of education as economic development, and aim to offer explanations for how and why the Girl Effect campaign constitutes a market for branded philanthropy. I argue that this notion of philanthropic economic development creates a marketplace of branded philanthropy where active citizenship is defined as sharing online content or selling brand-inspired cookies. The ideal corporate citizen in this model participates in philanthropic activities that expand the Girl Effect brand in neoliberal terms, and the ideal woman citizen in both the Global North and the Global South gives back to the community using these branded resources.

Gendered Global Governance

The rise in public–private partnerships between multinational corporations that have previously been accused of violating human rights and environmental standards and the international governance organizations tasked with policing their behavior is no accident. In fact, the U.N. has encouraged such partnerships through the Global Compact, a program that encourages corporations to comply with human rights, labor, environmental, and anti-corruption standards regardless of whether the countries in which they operate demand such high benchmarks. However, critics of these partnerships have been quick to point out not only the irony of allowing corporations like Nike, Goldman Sachs, and Royal Dutch Shell to "solve" the exacerbating inequalities they helped to create, but also the fact that U.N. policies are not legally enforceable, so companies can "sign onto the Global Compact and then violate every one of the nine principles with impunity" (Bigge, 2004, p. 12). Thus, transnational corporations have reason to want to sign onto the contract: they can reap the rewards of marketing their social responsibility to potential consumers and clients regardless of whether they actually abide by any such standards (Bradford, 2012).

The push for this form of for-profit philanthropy has its roots in neoliberal theory. Neoliberalism is a contested term with several competing definitions, but I use it here in line with the work of David Harvey (2005) and Robert McChesney (2008) who conceptualize the neoliberal turn as the push to privatize goods and services such as transportation infrastructure and education that were previously under the purview of the state. Although this philosophy had been around for decades, President Reagan ushered it into the mainstream when he argued that "the private sector still offers creative, less expensive, and more efficient alternatives to solving our social problems" (Reagan, 1981, para. 9), and business leaders should put those skills to use by helping nonprofit organizations administer social programs previously funded by government.

Before companies realized they could earn a profit for this work, a large contingent of the business community rejected the idea that corporations would spend a portion of their profit doing community service and social welfare work. Milton Friedman and other economists felt engaging in this type of large-scale philanthropy would dip into dividends, while other economists rejected company-wide corporate giving initiatives, claiming that the only "social responsibility of business is to increase its profits" (Friedman, as quoted in Richey & Ponte, 2011, p. 125). Many shareholders demanded that companies limit philanthropic and social welfare engagement if it would impact the dividends they received from their investments (Bradford, 2012). However, Reagan (1981) sold his philosophy to private enterprises by suggesting that engaging in philanthropic work might eventually lead to "a buck for business" (para. 11). Reagan's policies—including tax breaks for philanthropic giving and opportunities to invest in privatizing global economies—helped to ensure that corporate social responsibility was seen not only as a way to increase positive public perceptions of expanded corporate activities, but also as a means to increase corporate profits (Richey & Ponte, 2011).

Perhaps nowhere is the conflation of marketization and philanthropy more apparent than in the rise of cause marketing, which aims to combine purchasing power with philanthropic donation. In cause marketing, corporations align their brand or product with a prosocial cause and promise to donate a percentage of each unit purchased to a non-profit organization (Richey & Ponte, 2011). Because neoliberalism asks us to address these problems on an individual basis through the market (such as by "voting" with our dollars), consumers conflate consumption with activism, suggesting that the best means to solve systemic social problems is purchasing products from corporations who donate a portion of their profits to such causes (even when the acts of consumption exacerbate the very inequalities they proclaim to fight against). Thus, consumers can feel good about engaging in conspicuous consumption because their purchases are literally and figuratively sold to them as the most efficient way to address social, political, and economic inequality. However, the idea that consumers should seek out responsible or ethical purchases highlights the underpinnings of the neoliberal system, which advocates for corporate impunity through deregulation and then asks the market to address the very inequalities it has helped to create. In *Radical Consumption*, Jo Littler (2009) writes that the "responsible" label:

> reveals both some of the key problems of our culture (global warming, global poverty, stark inequalities of wealth) and indicates the scale of our collective failure to deal with these problems on any significant or systemic level other than through small palliative measures orchestrated through the lifestyle choices of the sufficiently privileged.
>
> *(p. 14)*

Instead of pushing for collective action, cause marketing asks consumers to further privatize these solutions by making the individual solely responsible for policing corporations through their purchasing power.

Correcting the problems of large government bureaucracies "involves not only making private agencies more responsible for public assistance ... but also transforming individuals into more responsible, accountable, and enterprising managers of themselves" (Ouellette & Hay, 2008, p. 24). Using a financial mentality to define citizenship moves people away from thinking about finance as the accumulation of wealth and toward thinking about finance as a means of regulating and monitoring our bodies and minds (Martin, 2002; Schowalter, 2012). Those who properly monitor themselves are therefore "good" citizens, and those who do not are considered burdens on the system. We can see both the promise and the perils of this financialization in the recent push for microlending programs aimed predominantly at women in the Global South, including the Building Resources Across Communities (BRAC) program. BRAC, initially formed in Bangladesh in 1972, is currently the world's largest non-governmental development organization and an official partner of the Girl Effect. Approximately 20 percent of all Bangladesh women use microlending, and BRAC disbursed $1.1 billion in loans to women in Bangladesh in 2009 alone ("Bangladesh," 2011). Though they claim that 99 percent of women repay the loans in full, recent investigations show the actual number is much smaller and that many repay their loans by taking out additional loans to make payments ("Bangladesh," 2011). Repayment is difficult in part because of high interest rates. BRAC charges between 18 and 60 percent interest on each loan, which it claims is necessary to cover the administrative costs associated with distributing small sums ("BRAC," 2014). So while microlending programs are often held up as an exemplary way for women to take control of their own financial independence and are often equated with granting women access to basic human rights such as bodily autonomy, safety and health services (Esty, 2014), there is little evidence to support the idea that they lift women in general and/or entire communities out of poverty (Aizenman, 2016).

Whereas microlending offers women small-scale loans for individual businesses, the Girl Effect offers businesses and community organizations opportunities for funding and branding for initiatives aimed at empowering girls via educational access. What sets the Girl Effect apart from previous educational philanthropic programs is that the Girl Effect fuses cause marketing with privatization in such a way that it also serves as a global development project aimed at creating long-term opportunity and wealth. Carol Cone, the managing director of brand and corporate citizenship for the global communication strategy firm Edelman, argues that philanthropy is increasingly used as a tool for gaining lucrative business contracts in the Global South:

> Companies need a license to operate. There are many, many competitors … In China, for example, the government wants to know, "What are you doing for my people? What are you doing for my communities?" even before they're allowed to do business. When you give back through a cause, you earn the license to operate.
>
> *(as cited in Pool, 2011)*

By engaging in philanthropic initiatives that expand business pools and globalize their consumer base, corporations have found a way to engage in philanthropy that appeals to consumers in the Global North while simultaneously maximizing profits for shareholders who adhere to Friedman's corporate mandate. This new model of philanthropy blurs the line between business and charity by making all acts of charity subject to the same profit motive of other standard business activities. This blurring also occurs in governance communities, most notably in the World Bank, whose official policy holds itself accountable to a for-profit business model when engaging in efforts to solve social problems ("Historical Chronology," 2006).

This is not to say that for-profit philanthropy is necessarily bad, nor do I intend to state that these interventions lack merit as important interventions in the lives of individuals. The Girl Effect has been beneficial to many women and girls who are given access to money and resources they might not otherwise receive, and increasing educational opportunities goes a long way toward increasing women's sense of self efficacy, access to rights, and involvement in community and political organizations (Levine et al., 2008; Greene et al., 2009). Efforts to decrease gendered discrepancies in educational access, including opportunities created through the Girl Effect, are important in drawing attention to the millions of girls who are kept out of schools worldwide.

However, in addition to acknowledging the possibilities this program provides, the critique leveled in this chapter suggests it is also important to consider how possibilities may be constrained by the particular vision of empowerment made possible through the program's channels. For example, the emphasis on encouraging individualized activism among women and girls in the Global North deflects attention away from empowering the actual women and girls this project aims to serve. While the genuine desire among women and girls in the Global North to be involved in the push for positive change is co-opted and directed toward particularly shallow interventions like baking cookies and sharing images on Facebook, the voices of women and girls in the Global South are almost completely absent. In the current era of corporate-driven global development, empowerment is increasingly tied to short-term Band-Aid solutions—such as microloans to start a sewing business or to purchase chickens whose eggs might feed the family—and not to more systemic changes that would challenge the structures that create and perpetuate gendered intergenerational poverty in the first place. As such, this chapter highlights the ways that the language of empowerment has become increasingly depoliticized and individualized.

It is important to note that the Girl Effect directs its individualized empowerment campaign almost exclusively at women and girls. While the campaign does not ban men and boys from involvement, most of the examples of activism shared on social media and included in press materials feature the work of women and girls in the Global North working on behalf of women and girls in the Global South. Additionally, the suggestions for how to get involved offered through press materials and shareable toolkits offer a particularly feminized vision of activism, including stereotypically feminine tasks like bake sales and craft projects. Placing women and girls in the Global North at the center of these materials suggests it is their responsibility to do the work of fixing issues of educational access plaguing women and girls in the Global South. Excluding men and boys from these discussions also serves to exclude them from any responsibility in perpetuating or fixing issues of inequality, thereby letting them off the hook when it comes to these gendered forms of neoliberal work.

These interactions take center stage in the Girl Effect campaign, as consumers are encouraged to invest in their own identities as consumers and as global citizens through a professed support for the campaign on social media sites and through financial support for products that raise money for girls' education. However, these interactions also discourage consumer citizens from engaging in activism that questions the basic tenets of globalization and neoliberalism, both of which have led to vast social and economic inequalities as they have taken root in countries across the globe. These inequalities include the hypocrisy of Nike engaging in corporate social responsibility to address global poverty while eschewing responsibility for what many view as a long history of egregious labor and environmental practices (Bigge, 2004). As Mukherjee and Banet-Weiser (2012) state, the tendency for corporations to direct criticism away from global neoliberal policies is especially important to unpack as global businesses and campaigns "exact their heaviest price from marginalized constituencies—women, nonwhites, and the poor" (p. 9). The Girl Effect campaign is a prime example of deflecting attention away from systemic discourses and toward individual neoliberal solutions.

Girl-Centered Philanthropy

The Girl Effect campaign materials draw from a series of five studies funded by the Nike Foundation, the World Bank, and the United Nations and conducted by the Population Council, the International Center for Research on Women, and the Center for Global Development. Titled *Girls Count*, these research reports repeatedly tout the importance of creating multi-faceted health and education programs for women and girls in the Global South in order to reverse the systemic gendered discrimination that consistently disadvantages women.[2] The authors iterate the importance of focusing on girls by stating, "This report takes as a starting point that the wellbeing of girls matters, above all, because they are individuals with inalienable human rights" (Levine et al., 2008, p. 11). The authors go on to showcase areas where violence, discrimination, and an unequal distribution of resources prevent women around the world from exercising their basic human rights (Levine et al., 2008, p. 11). The researchers acknowledge that investments in girls may lead to positive economic changes within communities, but they clearly state that the most important reason to invest in girls' education is because girls are human beings with inalienable rights.

When *Girls Count* does address economics, researchers focus on how girls are motivated by economics, including the motivation to be economically independent in order to avoid forced child marriages and to have enough money for basic rights such as food, healthcare, and education (Greene et al., 2009). Most other references to economics in the reports address the ways that girls' human rights are impacted by the unequal distribution of power, jobs, and resources (Levine et al., 2008, p. 11). These reports do not discuss how corporations might benefit economically by investing in girls' education, nor do they quantify the benefits countries would receive if they increased educational opportunities for women and girls. This is an important exception in a neoliberal era that consistently demands that social services run on a for-profit business model and asks that governance organizations extend rights and privileges to people only when it is cost effective or profitable. The authors' resistance to financializing the benefits of extending full human rights to girls in the Global South disrupts the neoliberal model of economic globalization, saying that even in areas where it is not economically beneficial to expand rights and privileges to girls, governance organizations must do this work anyway.[3]

Still, a major roadblock in expanding girls' rights is that many are not aware of what rights are afforded them, and even if they are, many know that deeply entrenched societal values and norms restrict their access to those rights. A study summarized in one of the Nike Foundation reports states that only "53 percent of girls ages 9–17 knew they had a right to education; only one-third believed they had a right to express their ideas or opinions" (Greene et al., 2009, p. 38). A teen girl living in a slum in Brazil told researchers, "Rights exist on paper, but in reality they aren't put into practice" (Greene et al., 2009, p. 38).

To address the incongruity between girls' formal rights, their knowledge of those rights, and the lived realities that may or may not include access to their rights, the Nike Foundation conducted interviews and focus groups with girls in the Global South and asked girls about the challenges they face surrounding these topics. Girls in the study largely focused on education, health, marriage choice, bodily integrity, and economic empowerment, and how they saw these issues as interwoven with each other and with the larger social and cultural contexts of their communities. They called for multi-faceted solutions that fuse increasing their economic opportunities with expanding social acceptance so that their communities grant them access to needed resources. Instead, programs like the Girl Effect offer profit-driven solutions without addressing the inequalities experienced by girls such as those noted above. As these girls rightly state, the addition of funding for more schools, water sources, and health clinics will not ensure that women and girls actually experience more equal access to resources unless these services are coupled with major changes in the way families and communities view the role of women. Because the Nike Foundation was integral to researching and publishing these reports and because they launched the Girl Effect campaign specifically to address these issues, it is worth interrogating how the Girl Effect's public campaign differed from the messages of the study.

From Burdens to Breadwinners

In contrast to the human rights premise of the Nike Foundation research series, the Girl Effect public profile showcases how economically beneficial these programs are for investors, corporations, local governments, families, and girls. For example, both *Girls Count* and the Girl Effect address why it is important to highlight interventions for girls instead of girls *and* boys. The *Girls Count* series states that this is important because girls face much more severe discrimination than boys in terms of allocating family and community resources, gender violence, and access to basic rights, so girls' needs are more immediate than the needs of boys (Lloyd, 2009, p. 9). In contrast, a Girl Effect press release states that investing in girls is a better "return on investment" than investing in boys because "girls and women will reinvest 90 percent of their income back into their families, as compared to 35–40 percent for males" (Business Wire, 2008, para. 3).

When the *Girls Count* series addresses these ripple effects of investments in girls, the researchers state that investing in girls is important because educated girls experience "greater safety, enhanced social status, and better opportunities for self-actualization and empowerment" (Lloyd, 2009, p. 36). In addition to these immediate benefits to the girls themselves, educated girls are more likely to staff local health facilities and local schools, meaning that communities benefit from better and more frequent services (Lloyd, 2009, p. 47). In contrast, a Girl Effect "Smarter Economics" pamphlet published in 2011 shows how investing in girls will help corporations and governments that are currently losing money because of teen pregnancy and job inequality. It reads:

> Girls are the world's greatest untapped resource. Investments in girls have significant economic returns. These returns have the potential to uplift entire economies … With nearly four million adolescent mothers annually, India loses US$383 billion in potential lifetime income … If Ethiopian girls completed secondary school, the total contribution over their lifetimes is US$6.8 billion."
>
> *("Smarter Economics," 2012, p. 3)*

What this document fails to mention is that girls often have no say over when or under what conditions they get pregnant and give birth, nor does it account for the complex socio-economic structures that prevent women from being able to participate in paid labor markets both before, during, and after a pregnancy. Asking girls to bear the burden of solving complex economic inequalities further individualizes the neoliberal policy agenda that exacerbated much of this inequality in the first place. Yet, the document does go on to give this call to action: "Invest early so girls save money, build economic assets and move from burden to breadwinners" ("Smarter Economics," 2012, p. 7).

The idea that girls are burdens in their homes and communities appears in various forms throughout the *Girls Count* and Girl Effect materials. Whereas the *Girls Count* materials state that we must educate men and boys about girls' rights and inherent value, the importance of girls' health and education, and the importance of stopping sexual, emotional, and physical violence against women, the Girl Effect campaign states that men and boys will realize girls' value when investments in girls can lead to future financial gain for families and communities. The "Your Move" report, an 85-page document detailing why investments in girls are a good idea, states: "Families see little return on investing in a girls' education, without visible income for her in the future. There is little incentive ... to disrupt and transform her status quo, without the hope and prospect of something better" (Girl Effect, 2011c, p. 15). Once a girl can prove that she can support herself with paid labor outside the home, "Your Move" states, families and communities are more likely to support her choice to use her money for education:

> Suddenly she is viewed as a good investment. Someone who can generate prosperity for herself and her family. With that shift, other dominoes fall into place. Broader attitudes about girls change. Families become healthier and wealthier. The girl effect unfolds.
> *(Girl Effect, 2011c, p. 15)*

The Girl Effect suggests that the solution is simple: if girls are economically valuable, they will be valued as people.

The hyper-attention paid to encouraging individuals to self-govern and to view themselves as assets and commodities has occurred alongside a push for privatization and outsourcing that characterizes neoliberalism (Ouellette & Hay, 2008). Indeed, all choices, including choices about when and where to work, how to invest, and whether and when to marry, become choices amenable to a market rationality (Martin, 2002). Of course, these "choices" are limited by factors such as class and access to financial, social, and cultural resources. The rise in transnational business models has coincided with a push for companies to outsource labor, often choosing to manufacture goods in nations with low wages and few regulations. As employment instability increases and benefits decrease, the gap between the rich and the poor has increased worldwide, meaning that fewer and fewer people are able to contribute to the types of consumption demanded in the neoliberal model of personal lifestyle management (Conroy, 1998). Participation defined by a capacity to consume is especially alienating for marginalized communities because these groups have a more difficult time meeting the "challenges that become legible within historical and institutional particularities of neoliberalism" (Mukherjee & Banet-Weiser, 2012, p. 9).

Give a Girl a Cow

Despite the overwhelming amount of research stating that educational and economic investments will not lead to change unless they are coupled with changes to the social and political structures that enable unequal treatment of boys and girls[4] (Vavrus, 2003; Levine et al., 2008; Lloyd, 2009; Temin & Levine, 2009; Nussbaum, 2011), the Girl Effect continues to assert that change is "not that hard" (Girl Effect, 2011c, p. 7). Perhaps nowhere is this more apparent than in the online and social media content used to educate and mobilize individuals, non-profit organizations, corporations, and government entities to get involved. The social media arm of this campaign started by encouraging Facebook and Twitter users to like and share two YouTube campaign videos. As of September 2017, the two videos have amassed nearly 3.5 million views.

Although researchers call for systemic and multi-faceted changes to the ways that educational systems operate in the Global South, the Girl Effect's mobilization agenda encourages a simplistic form of online activism among users in the Global North that has little to do with on-the-ground changes in the Global South. These mobilization efforts include sharing and linking to the official YouTube videos (youtube.com/users/girl effect), website (girleffect .org), and the Facebook page (facebook.com/girleffect). Similar to the two Girl Effect reports, "Your Move" and "Smarter Economics," the online videos suggest the solution to gendered intergenerational poverty is simple. The campaign's namesake video (distributed via YouTube in May 2008) and the subsequent "The Clock is Ticking" video (first shown in September 2010) pair text-only messages written in English with music that gives the textual message a lighthearted feel.

"The Girl Effect" video states that "the world is a mess," but shuns the Internet, science, government, and money as potential solutions. Instead, the solution is ensuring that girls living in poverty stay in school. After asking viewers to "imagine a girl living in poverty," the word GIRL appears on the screen along with several smaller texts of the word FLIES. The flies begin to buzz around the word "girl," and the words "husband," "baby," "hunger," and "HIV" begin to stack on top of the girl text. This image constructs girls in the Global South as "Other"—as dirty, helpless, and dependent on wealthy, powerful Westerners to help them. Patricia Hill Collins (2000) argues that constructing dichotomous relationships—such as the relationship between people of color who are constructed as less than human and their white saviors —contributes to "the political economy of domination that characterized slavery, colonialism, and neocolonialism" (p. 78). Indeed, this video contrasts the unequal access to resources between women in the Global North and Global South, and uses constructions of the latter to justify corporate interventions aided by the social media crowdsourcing of the former.

The video then encourages viewers to "pretend you can fix this picture" and claims that through this act of pretending, girls living in poverty now have a chance:

> Let's put her in a school uniform and see her get a loan to buy a cow and use the profits from the milk to help her family. Pretty soon, her cow becomes a herd. And she becomes a business owner who brings clean water to the village, which makes the men respect her good sense and invite her to the village council where she convinces everyone that all girls are valuable ... Which means the economy of the entire country improves and the whole world is better off ... Invest in a girl and she will do the rest.
>
> *(man vs. magnet, 2008)*

Thus, girls are required to lift themselves out of poverty while men, corporations, and governments stand idly by, waiting for the moment when girls prove themselves valuable using the model set out by the kind-hearted corporations. Through this imagery, "the Girl Effect encourages viewers to systematically divorce girlhood 'from any serious relationship to structural systems' and to instead more securely attach girlhood to notions of individual choice and responsibility" (Bent, 2012, p. 57). Ideal girl recipients, in this model, do not use their personal wealth to invest in themselves, to vie for power, or to challenge the system that oppresses them. Instead, they use it to invest resources into the community that those already in charge have failed to prioritize. The idea that investing in girls by giving them money and then standing back while they "do the rest" on their own is counter to what scholars inside and outside the Nike Foundation suggest. Despite our many efforts to solve systemic problems with individualized solutions or "pick yourself up by your bootstraps" campaigns, decades of research show that, at best, these strategies lead to temporary Band-aids for small numbers of aid recipients, and at worst, they exacerbate inequalities by allowing corporations to continue operating in ways that exploit those at the bottom and then blame those at the bottom for not getting ahead (Edwards, 2008; Richey & Ponte, 2011).

The second video was released two years later at the Clinton Global Initiative meeting in September 2010, and it was accompanied by a revamped girleffect.org website and a short-lived Girl Effect Twitter account. Called "The Clock is Ticking," this video paints a more urgent picture, beginning with the line, "We have a situation on our hands and the clock is ticking." The video informs viewers that after age 12, girls living in poverty are viewed as women in their community, which puts them at increased risk for teen marriage, pregnancy, death during childbirth, forced prostitution, and "contracting and spreading HIV." Again, "the good news is there's a solution." The video states that if a girl stays in school through her teen years, by age 18 she will be able to financially support herself with a job and make decisions for her own life. The video states that this simple intervention will allow her to make several key decisions, including avoiding HIV and having control over when she marries and becomes pregnant (Girl Effect, 2010c).

This assumes that women and girls have access to knowledge about sexual and reproductive health—knowledge many women lack because of community taboos around speaking openly about sex (Greene et al., 2009). However, even when girls have knowledge about dangers such as HIV and increased mortality rates for adolescent childbirth, many lack the power to enact their knowledge. A 17-year-old married mother interviewed in the *Girls Count* reports discusses how she negotiates these issues with her polygamist husband, stating:

> He refused me to take any precautions against pregnancy ... Every time I have sex with him I fear HIV/AIDS ... He also moves around with other girls so my health is at stake but I have no option since I am solely dependent on him so I just brush my fears off.
>
> *(Greene et al., 2009, p. 26)*

Throwing money at girls' education and suggesting they can then help themselves will not solve these complicated issues.

Stickers as Activism

To reach the target demographic of women in the Global North, then, the Nike Foundation relied on the same tools they used in disseminating the viral videos: they distributed content via Facebook, linked frequently to sources on girleffect.org, and provided toolkits that helped consumers in the Global North take the next step in their involvement. As I will show, the deep concern for the humanity of girls in the Global South found in the Nike Foundation research reports is replaced with simplistic messaging about girls' economic value to parent corporations and with commentary that encourages consumers in the Global North to feel good about "helping."

The Girl Effect "Toolkit" (Girl Effect, 2011c) and "Plan an Event" guides offer all the materials one would need to raise awareness about the campaign. Despite the goal of educating people around the world about the importance of gendered intergenerational poverty, these campaign materials suggest that creating shirts, stickers, and parties is enough to start a revolution. The Toolkit is an 18-page guide that provides three main paths for spreading the word about the Girl Effect: a "talk it up" section with videos and sample PowerPoint presentations; a "make stuff" section that provides do-it-yourself templates for making buttons, posters, stickers, and T-shirts; and a "put on an event" section that provides ordered checklists for people wanting to plan a Girl Effect fundraiser, party, or club ("Toolkit," 2011). Alternatively, potential activists are encouraged to think of their own ways to spread the word. The Toolkit promotes several exemplars, including the Smith family, who traveled around the world in their private plane emblazoned with a Girl Effect logo on the rear.

Additionally, suggesting that parties and art exhibits are the impetus of a global restructuring that eradicates gender discrimination and poverty both minimizes the roles of political institutions that create and perpetuate inequalities and glorifies the impact of consumer-based involvement. Instead of fighting against institutions that perpetuate trade and labor inequalities, including corporations such as Nike, these examples show that activism is relegated to learning about the plight of the other and engaging in consumption-oriented activities—neither of which asks that "activists" interrogate their privilege or think critically about the issues.

The Girl Effect social media accounts also amplified certain related campaigns, success stories, and visions of campaign involvement using status updates. Some of the material for Facebook status updates included stories and statistics taken directly from other research and promotional materials. For example, a post from September 18, 2010, highlights the story of Juthika, a girl who moved "from BURDEN to BREADWINNER" by growing vegetables and raising ducks (Girl Effect, 2010a). Her story and photograph are also included in the "Your Move" report. Juthika's father's deteriorating health prevented him from working, and her mother's job outside the home did not pay enough for her entire family to survive. Instead of accepting her fate, Juthika took out a microfinance loan with BRAC, an official partner of the Girl Effect campaign, to finance the purchase of the ducks and seeds she needed to start her small farm. She uses the surplus from her $37 daily income to take care of her family.

Users are not encouraged to ask why the work Juthika's mother performed outside the home did not bring in enough money to support the family or how Juthika's father's health deteriorated to the point that he could not work. These exclusions make girls like Juthika particularly valuable to corporations, which benefit when supporters are actively discouraged from thinking about why Juthika's family might be impoverished in the first place. Additionally, Juthika's success is uncommon in the region. As noted, many microlending organizations have been under criticism for charging high interest rates, exaggerating the number of women who repay their loans in full, and failing to account for the number of women who take out new loans to repay existing loans ("Bangladesh," 2011; "BRAC," 2014).

The campaign's status updates also "amplify" several ways that citizens of the Global North have gotten involved in the campaign. In addition to spreading the word through sharing photographs, the moderators encouraged activism through creating and sharing consumer-based products. A post dated December 7,

2010, stated, "Sometimes spreading the Girl Effect only takes a little flour and eggs," and the accompanying photo depicted square sugar cookies decorated with the Girl Effect logo. The comment section included a link to the bakery where users could purchase the cookies (Girl Effect, 2010b). Similarly, the page featured a photo of a supporter's water bottle covered with Girl Effect stickers. The accompanying text read, "Sometimes all it takes to spread the word are a few stickers and a little H2O" (Girl Effect, 2011a). When a man asked where he could buy similar stickers for his daughter's water bottle, the moderator offered a link to the DIY sticker creation template available on the Girl Effect's "Mobilize" page.

Moderators are not just involved in social media campaigns; the Girl Effect Facebook page also highlights the offline work followers in the Global North were doing to raise awareness, such as one group's project to raise awareness and funds for girls' education in Cambodia. Participants "painted cardboard boxes and camped out in them on the school's football field to increase visibility for their cause. They raised over $8,000—and had some fun at the same time" (Girl Effect, 2011b). An accompanying image shows the group smiling amidst a village of cardboard boxes painted with slogans such as "everything happens for a reason." Another shows the girls watching a video on a large projection screen near the football stadium concession stands. Commenters offer glowing endorsements of this form of activism, and the Girl Effect lauds the group as heroes. The project's aim was to empower women in this group to create positive change by giving voice to the plight of impoverished girls in Cambodia.

While the above is certainly an altruistic investment of time and energy, none of the commentary addresses the problematic aspects of having fun masquerading as residents of cardboard slums in Cambodia. Safely nestled inside a secure football stadium, the masquerade limits the girls' exposure to the dangerous health conditions, threats of physical and sexual violence, and feelings of hunger commonly found in such slums and replaces it with a vision of poverty that allows them to raise money and "[have] some fun at the same time." As bell hooks (1992) argues, this form of imperialist nostalgia allows white cultural consumers to temporarily inhabit the lives of Others in ways that are void of the historical, social, and political roots of inequality, and thus they need not confront their privilege or the ways they use marginalized groups in their quest for self-actualization (p. 25).

These individual and group interventions come from a genuine desire to make a difference in a world with increasing inequality, but they also are carefully selected forms of activism constructed from a narrow range of opportunities encouraged by and supported through the materials the Girl Effect made available to followers. Therein lies some of the most difficult aspects of this brand of neoliberal activism: the well-intentioned desire to make a difference is co-opted by a corporate-driven system that asks activists to engage in interventions that are not especially threatening to the established order.

The Girl Effect after Nike

In September of 2015, the Nike Foundation relinquished its control of the Girl Effect by spinning the campaign into its own nonprofit organization. The organization is now partnered with a number of funders, and they have shifted the focus of its message considerably. Instead of focusing on gimmicky videos and toolkits to keep girls in the Global North talking about the campaign, the new efforts focus on empowering girls in the Global South to help break down the invisible barriers that keep them from experiencing their rights. The new Girl Effect website makes reference to this change, stating that the Girl Effect has moved "beyond single issues" and understood that providing access to services is "only part of the answer" (Girl Effect, 2017b, para. 9).

Instead of highlighting girls' lack of economic value in the family structure, the new Girl Effect materials show how not seeing the value of girls is a powerful and multifaceted barrier that results in girls' absence from decision-making structures, failure to receive familial support, and a collective failure to listen to girls when they express their ideas (Girl Effect, 2017a). Most notably, the campaign launched a new online video that pairs Nigerian poet Bassey Ikpi's performance of "Invisible Barriers" with an animated video "which dramatises the Invisible Barriers that are holding girls back" (Girl Effect, 2017a, para. 2). The video makes reference to earlier efforts to build schools, but notes that the schools alone were not enough to solve the multifaceted problems girls face. The poem declares: "It is not enough for us to build the rooms … we must encourage communities to hear the language girls speak." However, with 12,000 views, this video and new campaign are considerably less funded and visible within the media sphere.

These changes are not without their own neoliberal bent. For example, Ikpi's poem also asserts that economies will depend on the survival and livelihood of girls, and mentions that girls themselves will have to step out of the spotlight for change to happen. Thus, although the focus moved from encouraging girls in the Global North to "save" those in the Global South to one that at least acknowledged cultural barriers, the campaign still aligns with neoliberal ideology in a number of ways. For instance, the campaign conceptualizes an empowerment that does not threaten the established order. While the new campaign materials teach about the pervasiveness of invisible barriers facing girls, there is no mention of the reasons these systemic barriers are in place, and few ideas for removing the barriers themselves. Instead, the goal seems to be to encourage girls to rise up despite these barriers by encouraging them to find and value their own voice. To achieve these goals, the Girl Effect has worked with teens in targeted communities in the Global South to create mega youth brands, including mobile technology, print magazines, and a variety of girl-centered and branded products that girls can consume that encourage empowerment. While these empowerment materials reach millions of girls in Ethiopia, Rwanda, and Malawi (Girl Effect, 2017a), the quest for empowerment without the simultaneous discussion about systemic causes of and barriers to inequality results in what Koffman et al. (2015) refer to as "selfie humanitarianism" (p. 158). This version of philanthropic work divorces humanitarianism from the political causes and implications of such work, resulting in "the simultaneous depoliticisation, corporatization and neo-liberalisation of both humanitarianism and girl power" (p. 157).

Conclusion

This chapter questions the logic of investment philanthropy, highlighting how it spreads neoliberal ideas of citizenship that are especially damaging to women and girls. In this model, women and girls in the Global North believe it is their responsibility to "save" the distant Others they see in YouTube videos, a notion problematic for several reasons. First, this idea inaccurately places the burden of change on individuals, and not the corporations, institutions, and governments responsible for causing and perpetuating these problems in the first place. Second, it reinforces a vision of philanthropy in which consumers in the Global North inaccurately believe they know what is best for populations whose lives in no way resemble their own. Interventions supported by those with little knowledge about the complex factors impacting poverty and educational access often fail to account for differences in culture, societal structures and local economics, which means they also regularly fail to lead to sustainable changes (Stiglitz, 2006; Buffett, 2013). Third, "helpers" in the Global North are not encouraged to consider their own privilege during the helping process, which both contributes to the therapeutic feeling of this type of distant caregiving and enables corporations to capitalize on the positive associations consumers have with the project and the brand. These individualized therapeutic acts of caregiving are significant in that they perpetuate a neoliberal vision of citizenship in which a genuine desire to engage in activism that makes life easier for women and girls who lack access to basic human rights is individualized and commodified. The media construct systemic problems in individual terms and encourage women and girls to get involved through acts they perform from the comfort of their home or shopping center. Such involvement deflects attention away from solutions that entail collective action or systemic changes, and instead offers individuals a way to feel that they are uniquely qualified to make a difference via their isolated acts.

This profit-oriented approach to global philanthropy contributes to the rise of "education as panacea" (Vavrus, 2003). In this model, educational intervention serves as a safe and popular public policy intervention because it fits neatly with both human rights rhetoric and economic promises about return-on-investments.

Additionally, attempts to remedy unequal access to education are likely to garner media coverage that rarely (if ever) questions the ways that corporate-driven neoliberalism has increased social and economic disparities (Vavrus, 2003). As development researchers have shown, investments in education will not solve inequalities unless they are accompanied by major shifts in national and global economic policies advocated in the *Girls Count* studies.

Notes

1 Following the work of Mohanty (2003), I use Global North and Global South here to distinguish between "affluent, privileged nations and communities, and economically and politically marginalized nations and communities" (p. 226). Mohanty goes on to describe this geographic distinction, stating:

> While these terms are meant to loosely distinguish the northern and southern hemispheres, affluent and marginal nations and communities obviously do not line up neatly within this geographical frame ... An example of this is Arif Dirlik's formulation of North/South as a metaphorical rather than geographical distinction, where 'North' refers to the pathways of transnational capital and 'South' to the marginalized poor of the world regardless of geographical distinction.
>
> *(pp. 226–227)*

2 These reports focus entirely on the *systemic* discrimination facing women and girls in the Global South. It is important to note that systemic discrimination impacts women and girls throughout the globe, including wealthy nations such as the United States. Large poor populations exist within these wealthy countries, and men and women must make tragic choices between competing basic necessities such as food, healthcare, and education (Nussbaum, 2011).
3 This shift replaces the liberal discourse of economics with the liberal discourse of rights. Though both have been used in imperialist models of development, the latter is a more inclusive vision that foregrounds humanity over economics. Thus, the shift is an important intervention in models of development that frequently ignore problems that will not create profit for investors.
4 Here I distinguish between the economic work and the cultural changes girls hope to see, but I do not mean to state that economic and social changes are mutually exclusive. This distinction I make underscores the Nike Foundation's exclusive emphasis on economics and its pivot away from addressing social issues such as access to reproductive health information and care, to name just one issue important to girls in these regions.

References

Aizenman, N. (2016, November 1). Can microloans lift women out of poverty? *NPR*. Retrieved from www.npr.org/sections/goatsandsoda/2016/11/01/500093608/you-asked-we-answer-can-tiny-loans-lift-women-out-of-poverty

Bangladesh: Microfinance institutions pushed loans, admits major NGO. (2011, April 20). *Irin News*. Nairobi, Kenya. Retrieved from www.irinnews.org/report/92528/bangladesh-microfinance-institutions-pushed-loans-admits-major-ngo

Bent, E. (2012). (Re)Thinking the girl effect: A critical analysis of girls' political subjectivity and agency at the United Nations 54th session of the commission on the status of women (CSW 54). NUI Galaway. Retrieved from https://aran.library.nuigalway.ie/…/EBENT%20POST-VIVA%20October%2026%20201

Bigge, D. M. (2004). Bring on the bluewash: A social constructivist argument against using Nike v. Kasky to attack the UN Global Compact. *International Legal Perspectives*, *14*, 6–21.

BRAC. (2014). *BRAC FAQ*. Retrieved from www.brac.net/content/faq-0#.U6eAspSwLrQ

Bradford, W. (2012). Beyond good and evil: The commensurability of corporate profits and human rights. *Notre Dame Journal of Law, Ethics & Public Policy*, *26*, 141–280.

Buffett, P. (2013, July 26). The charitable-industrial complex. *New York Times*. New York, NY. Retrieved from www.nytimes.com/2013/07/27/opinion/the-charitable-industrial-complex.html

Business Wire. (2008). Former President Clinton announces World Bank, Nike Foundation, Denmark and Liberia CGI commitment to unleash economic opportunity for adolescent girls in Liberia. *Business Wire*. Retrieved from www.lexisnexis.com/hottopics/lnacademic

Carella, A. (2011, January 4). So now we have to save ourselves and the world, too? A critique of "the girl effect." *AidWatch*. Retrieved from http://aidwatchers.com/2011/01/so-now-we-have-to-save-ourselves-and-the-world-too-a-critique-of-%E2%80%9Cthe-girl-effect%E2%80%9D/

Conroy, M. (1998). Discount dreams: Factory outlet malls, consumption, and the performance of middle-class identity. *Social Text*, *16*(1), 63–83.

Edwards, M. (2008). *Just another emperor?* New York, NY: Demos.

Esty, K. (2014, January 6). The impact of microcredit on womens lives in Bangladesh. *Global Citizen*. Retrieved from: www.globalcitizen.org/en/content/the-impact-of-microcredit-on-womens-lives-in-bangl/

Girl Effect. (2010a, September 18). From BURDEN to BREADWINNER [Facebook status update]. Retrieved from www.facebook.com/girleffect

Girl Effect. (2010b, December 7). Girl Effect fun fact of the day [Facebook status update]. Retrieved from www.facebook.com/girleffect

Girl Effect. (2010c). *The clock is ticking*. Nexus Productions. Retrieved from www.youtube.com/watch?v=1e8xgF0JtVg

Girl Effect. (2011a, August 26). Sometimes all it takes to spread the word are a few stickers and a little H20 [Facebook status update]. Retrieved from www.facebook.com/girleffect

Girl Effect. (2011b, March 11). Heroes week: Meet Emily, high school hotshot with a big heart [Facebook status update]. Retrieved from www.facebook.com/girleffect

Girl Effect. (2011c). Toolkit. The Girl Effect. Retrieved from www.facebook.com/girleffect

Girl Effect. (2011d). Your move. Nike Foundation. Retrieved from https://novofoundation.org/wp-content/uploads/2012/07/Girl_Effect_Your_Move.pdf

Girl Effect. (2017a). Breaking through invisible barriers. Retrieved from www.old.girleffect.zone-preview.co.uk/about-us/breaking-through-invisible-barriers/

Girl Effect. (2017b). Our purpose. Retrieved from www.girleffect.org/our-purpose/

Greene, M. E., Cardinal, L., & Goldstein-Siegel, E. (2009). *Girls speak: A new voice in global development*. International Center for Research on Women. Retrieved from http://coalitionforadolescentgirls.org/wp-content/uploads/2014/02/Girls-Speak-A-New-Voice-In-Global-Development.pdf

Harvey, D. (2005). *A brief history of neoliberalism*. Oxford, UK: Oxford University Press.

Hill Collins, P. (2000). *Black feminist thought: Knowledge, consciousness, and the politics of empowerment*. New York, NY: Routledge.

hooks, b. (1992). *Black looks: Race and representation*. Boston, MA: South End Press.

ICAI. (2012). *Girl hub: A DFID and Nike Foundation initiative* (No. 5, pp. 1–20). Independent Commission for Aid Impact. Retrieved from www.oecd.org/derec/49963464.pdf

Koffman, O., Orgad, S., & Gill, R. (2015). Girl power and "selfie humanitarianism." *Continuum: Journal of Media & Cultural Studies, 29*(2), 157–168.

Kylander, N. (2011). *The Girl Effect brand: Using brand democracy to strengthen brand affinity* (pp. 2–9). Harvard University Hauswer Center for Nonprofit Organizations. Retrieved from www.hks.harvard.edu/hauser/role-of-brand/documents/girleffect.pdf

Levine, R., Lloyd, C. B., Greene, M. E., & Grown, C. (2008). *Girls count: A global investment & action agenda* (p. 87). Washington, DC: Center for Global Development.

Littler, J. (2009). *Radical consumption shopping for change in contemporary culture*. Berkshire; New York, NY: Open University Press. Retrieved from http://site.ebrary.com/id/10274026

Lloyd, C. B. (2009). *New lessons: The power of educating adolescent girls* (p. 151). Population Council. Retrieved from www.popcouncil.org/uploads/pdfs/2009PGY_New Lessons.pdf

man vs. magnet. (2008). *The Girl Effect*. Curious Pictures. Retrieved from www.youtube.com/watch?v=WIvmE4_KMNw

Martin, R. (2002). *Financialization of daily life*. Philadelphia, PA: Temple University Press.

McChesney, R. W. (2008). *The political economy of media: Enduring issues, emerging dilemmas*. New York, NY: Monthly Review Press.

Mohanty, C. T. (2003). *Feminism without borders: Decolonizing theory, practicing solidarity*. Durham; London: Duke University Press.

Mukherjee, R., & Banet-Weiser, S. (2012). *Commodity activism: Cultural resistance in neoliberal times*. New York, NY: New York University Press.

Nussbaum, M. C. (2011). *Creating capabilities: The human development approach*. Cambridge, MA: Belknap Press of Harvard University Press.

Ouellette, L., & Hay, J. (2008). *Better living through reality TV: Television and post-welfare citizenship*. Malden, MA: Blackwell Pub.

Pool, L. (2011). *First run features*, documentary. Pink Ribbons, Inc.

Reagan, R. (1981). Remarks at the annual meeting of the national alliance of business. Presented at the National Alliance of Business Annual Meeting, Washington, DC. Retrieved from www.reagan.utexas.edu/archives/speeches/1981/100581a.htm

Richey, L. A., & Ponte, S. (2011). *Brand aid: Shopping well to save the world*. Minneapolis, MN: University of Minnesota Press.

Schowalter, D. (2012). Financialization of the family: Motherhood, biopolitics, and paths of power. *Women & Language, 35*(1), 39–56.

Nike Foundation. (2012). *Smarter economics: Investing in girls*. Retrieved from www.educategirls.ngo/pdf/GirlEffect_Smarter-Economics-Investing-in-Girls.pdf

Stiglitz, J. E. (2006). *Making globalization work* (1st ed.). New York, NY: W.W. Norton & Co.

Temin, M., & Levine, R. (2009). *Start with a girl: A new agenda for global health* (p. 97). Washington, DC: Center for Global Development.
Vavrus, F. K. (2003). *Desire and decline: Schooling amid crisis in Tanzania*. New York, NY: P. Lang.
World Bank Group Archives. (2006). World Bank group historical chronology. World Bank Group Archives. Retrieved from http://siteresources.worldbank.org/EXTARCHIVES/Resources/World_Bank_Group_Historical_Chronology_19944_2005_.pdf

4

NEOLIBERALISM AND WOMEN'S RIGHT TO COMMUNICATE

The Politics of Ownership and Voice in Media

Carolyn M. Byerly

The breaking news about media mogul Harvey Weinstein's sexual harassment of women in the *New York Times* on October 5, 2017, seemed to represent a watershed moment in journalism history (Choksi, 2017). The Weinstein revelations pervaded the news nationally and internationally, opening the floodgates over the next months for women across the United States to tell similar stories of harassment and assault by one prominent man after another.[1] In the late months of 2017, news audiences learned about the sexual misdeeds of many well-known journalists and news executives in the very companies now reporting on these latest instances of harassment and assault. Indeed, the U.S. and global media seemed to have given women a microphone to tell about the personal, damaging experiences they had endured at the hands of renowned men who worked there and, in many instances, were their bosses.[2]

It is important to emphasize, however, that neither the news coverage of the allegations, nor the #MeToo movement it spawned, has yet to impact the gendered relations of power within media ownership or regulation that allow powerful men to control those companies where the sexual violations occurred. In other words, the structures that marginalize women's ability to control the operations and policies of those companies remain in the hands of men. This raises the question of whether the fact of news abundance or even organizing that is focused on men's bad behavior will alter women's fundamental and longstanding structural relationship to the news and entertainment media. As will be discussed in this chapter, that relationship is characterized by women's lack of access to employment and decision-making roles in the industries, as well as their underrepresentation and misrepresentation in content. Whether and to what extent the current extensive coverage of women's abuse provides a turning point for improvement remains an empirical question at this point in history. What seems clear, however, is that the lack of women's access to power and voice in the form of access to and ownership of the media has been – and likely will remain – a factor in their abuse until such time as women gain greater control over media ownership and content. Equally clear is that neoliberal policies to deregulate media have exacerbated the inequities in media ownership and access.

In this chapter, I briefly track women's historical marginalization within and by media, place the problem within a theoretical framework of women's right to communicate and feminist political economy, and then show that the problem of access to media has worsened for women under neoliberal communication policies and corporate practices. The scope of my concern is primarily my own nation, the United States, within whose borders the world's largest media conglomerates are headquartered. However, I will also recognize neoliberal media policies' impact on women in other nations' media as well, where possible, in order to show the global nature of the problem. The discussion will end with a discussion of the recently enacted neoliberal policy concerning net neutrality and a brief exploration of how feminist scholars and political activists might approach policy decisions such as this to develop remedies.

Women's Voice Matters

The broader question of women's relationship to news is bounded by the politics of women's voice – that is, their collective *public* voice, as seen and heard through contemporary media in this era of neoliberalism. Voice matters, and, in fact, an effective public voice is crucial to the legitimacy of modern democracies (Couldry, 2010, p. ix). Couldry (2010), a critical media scholar, argues that we are presently experiencing a *crisis* of voice across political, economic and cultural domains where neoliberalism has been growing over the last three decades and thereby has come to dominate public policy. Neoliberalism, as defined by Harvey (2005), is a theory of political and economic practice based on principles of strong private property rights, free markets, and trade, with the role of the state being to create and preserve an institutional framework that maintains such rights (p. 2). Noting that neoliberal communication policy has enabled deregulation resulting in concentrated media ownership under a few huge corporations, Couldry (2010) emphasizes that in looking to the media to find our voice (or perhaps a representation of our voice), we are likely to find instead an amplification of the corporate voice (p. 73).

Byerly (2013) has pointed out that neoliberal policy, as found in national-level communication policies, has led to a privileging of male corporate power and a dominance of men's voices, ideas, and economic power. And the news is not the only medium of concern. Though roles for strong women have expanded in recent years, data show that they also are under-represented in

Hollywood films, which are viewed all over the world (Hunt et al., 2017). Regional studies show that women's voices and images are similarly marginalized in traditional as well as digital media formats of both developed and developing nations (Byerly, forthcoming).

When women do gain voice and visibility – as they have through the #MeToo movement – it is most likely to be those who already hold social stature who speak up, take action, and get media coverage. Class and race enter decidedly into both the problem of sexual harassment at work and the news coverage of that harassment. Women in low-wage jobs may be unable to speak up about the abuse they experience at work because they face unemployment or threats of retaliation, and though #MeToo was started by Black and Brown women, some say that women of color have been particularly overlooked by that movement (Burke, 2017; Lockhart, 2017). Keeping the intersectional issues of gender, race, and class in mind is key to fully understanding the relations of power that structure media industries and the content they disseminate.

The Long Struggle for Access: Under-Representation in Media Content

For those of us who track women's relationship to media, this recent abundance of news about women's abuse by rich and powerful men would seem to represent a feminist breakthrough, a sign that the news industry has finally turned a corner and expanded women's ability to tell their stories in growing numbers. And yet, both practitioners and scholars would recognize that sexual harassment and abuse stories meet many of the traditional "news values" determining newsworthiness when those stories concern the rich and/or powerful. The news values of particular relevance in the recent spate of allegations are prominence, impact, unusualness, conflict, number of people affected, and titillation (School Video News, 2017). Also useful to remember is the fickle nature of the news business, which guarantees that this news moment, too, will be replaced by other breaking news.

There is also the matter of what research reveals. If the monitoring of media content over the last 40 years has shown anything, it is that women's ability to be seen and heard through news has not progressed at the same rate as their real-life roles or level of participation. Since the 1970s, women have benefited from women's liberation movements and taken ever greater leads in business, education, politics, and public life. They have struggled for a more egalitarian family life and have worked to end abuse and harassment. Yet, they are still limited in their ability to speak in their own self-interest in the news media of most nations – as concerned citizens, expert sources, or leaders. Gallagher (2015) observed that in the latest report of the Global Media Monitoring

Project (GMMP, 2015), which has been carried on every five years since 1995, the findings are troubling:

> At 24% of the total, there has been no change in women's share of news-making roles in the traditional media (newspapers, radio, television) since 2010, and indeed almost none since 2005 when women were 23% of newsmakers. The new digital media (Internet and Twitter news) offer little comfort. Here too, women were only 26% of people in the news in 2015. Across all media, women were the central focus of just 10% of news stories – exactly the same figure as in 2000.
> (Gallagher, 2015, p. 6)

Gallagher was referring to the GMMP global aggregate findings from print, electronic and online news stories in 114 nations in 2015. In the United States, GMMP researchers found slightly better results, with women being the subjects or sources of news in 37% of the 502 stories examined. Similarly, there had been an uptick in the number of female reporters, from 29% in 2010 to 40% in 2015. But even so, those women reporters remained locked in health and science reporting, with men dominating political and economic news (GMMP-USA, 2015, pp. 7–9).

Gallagher (2015) also noted that while this most recent round of the GMMP showed women slightly less likely to be portrayed as victims or identified by family status in the news, they were "still two to three times more likely than male newsmakers to be portrayed or identified in those ways" (p. 6). This figure was identical for the U.S. sample, which found women three times as likely as men to be presented as victims of violence or discrimination (GMMP-USA, 2015, p. 13). What is clear, however, in the current spate of stories about Weinstein and many other prominent men in the media industry, is that this is journalism that fits squarely in the "woman-as-victim" genre, with substantial attention to the details of and harms from the abuses (e.g., loss of promotion or employment, fear of not being believed, and feelings of unworthiness, among others).

The exact frequency and extent to which women in the current spate of stories have been shown as victors rather than victims, or able to articulate a pro-feminist position (or analysis), cannot be known until researchers begin to publish their findings from systematic analysis. We do know from previous work (Byerly & Hill, 2012) that the *New York Times* and other news outlets began to adopt feminist-generated language for abuse by the mid-1970s, after the National Organization for Women's state-by-state campaign for rape and sexual assault legal reforms made progress, and as feminist analyses on the subject began to be published. Thus, feminist-generated terms like sexual abuse, acquaintance rape, domestic violence/abuse, wife battering, and sexual harassment entered public discourse via the news and today are widely used (Byerly & Hill, 2012). However, what we also know from feminist media scholarship is that, more typically, the news presents a masculine narrative with women thwarted in their ability to speak in their own self-interest or to articulate pro-feminist opinions (i.e., opinions that might challenge a system of male supremacy). Rakow and Kranich (1991) found that female sources in the television news stories they examined were allowed to serve as the sign of a problem or social issue but not allowed to offer an opinion on or analysis of it from a woman's perspective. The salient research question to be posed by those who conduct detailed research on the Weinstein, et al., sexual misconduct stories will be to what extent feminist analyses of male supremacy and men's violence against women have been included in these stories, and whether those analyses also address matters of race and class.

Women at the Structural Level

Civil rights and feminist activism in the early- to mid-1970s had helped to expand women and minority access to broadcast ownership, only to see setbacks by the late 1970s through right-wing political backlash. The backlash was motivated by a resurgence of pro-corporate values that made its way into the political economy by way of well-organized legislative campaigns and a public discourse which echoed loudly through the U.S. news media. The era of neoliberal philosophy, which dominates through the present time, has edged out the gains by women and racial minorities who had benefited from legal advances in laws and court decisions in the 1970s and 1980s (Byerly & Valentin, 2017). The present situation is one of severe under-representation by women and people of color at both ownership and governance levels of both traditional media and new media corporations.

Research indicates that women remain prevented from entering governance and other decision-making levels, both within news and entertainment sectors (Byerly, Park, & Miles, 2011; Hunt et al., 2017; Lauzen, 2017; Ross & Padovani, 2017; Vega, 2012). As Table 4.1 illustrates, few women advance into the top levels of policy-making on boards of directors in large digital media conglomerates (Byerly, forthcoming). Digital companies provide both the infrastructure and content for global communication systems. Those who own those companies are extremely wealthy, and with that wealth, they also exercise enormous political and social influence. As Table 4.1 indicates, the great majority of corporate policy makers are also male. Other research indicates that they are also predominantly white in their racial and ethnic make-up (Byerly, 2013).

Situating Women in Media Conglomeration

Media conglomeration characterizes the great majority of the world's communication systems today, with women marginalized at every level. The conclusion to draw is that women are peripheral to both the control of and the benefits

TABLE 4.1 Women at the Macro Level: Ownership, Worth and Gender Representation on Boards of Digital Media Companies.

Digital media company	What is owned (example of brands)	Market value (in billions)	Number of women on board
Alphabet Google (USA)	YouTube, Android, Chrome, Nexus, Pixel, Blogger, Zagat, Google Search (& Gmail, Hangouts & other apps), Chrome, Nest, Verily, Waze	$553	1 (of 13) 8%
Amazon.com, Inc. (USA)	Amazon Prime (& Cloud Drive, Web Services, Marketplace, Echo, Fire TV), Kindle, Audible, Twitch.tv, Washington Post	$388	3 (of 10) 30%
Facebook, Inc. (USA)	Facebook, WhatsApp, Instagram, Oculus, Facebook Messenger, Internet.org	$371	2 (of 8) 25%
AT&T, Inc. (USA)	AT&T, DirecTV, Cricket Wireless, U-verse, YP.com (aka Yellowpages.com), Sky Brasil	$227	4 (of 13) 31%
Verizon Communications, Inc. (USA)	Verizon Wireless, Fios, AOL, Huffington Post, Engadget, TechCrunch, Terremark	$198	4 (of 12) 33%
Walt Disney Co. (USA)	ABC News, ESPN, Disney Channel, Walt Disney Studios, Pixar, Marvel, Lucasfilm, Disneyland and other parks and resorts	$151	4 (of 12) 33%
Comcast Corp/ NBC Universal (USA)	Xfinity, NBC Network, MSNBC, CNBC, Telemundo, Bravo, USA Network, Universal Pictures, Universal Studios and other parks and resorts	$146	2 (0f 12) 17%
Time Warner, Inc. (USA)	CNN, HBO, Warner Brothers Entertainment (also Records, Motion Pictures), TBS, TNT, NCAA.com, TMX.com, DC Comics	$68	2 (of 9) 22%
BCE (Canada)	Cable TV stations, specialty channels (Bravo, Canal D, Book TV, etc.), Bell Broadcast Radio group, wireless technologies.	$64	4 of 13 (31%)
Grupo Televisa (Mexico)	Broadcast TV stations, radio stations, Videocine film, Editorial Televisa publishing, Televisa Digital (Internet), Televisa Musica, football teams, Aztec stadium	$15	0 of 19 (0%)

Source: Byerly, C. M. (forthcoming), Gender, Media, Oligopoly: Connecting Research and Action. In N. Benequista & S. Abbott (Eds.), *International Media Development: Historical Perspectives and New Frontiers.* New York: Peter Lang Publishing. (Data gathered from company websites in 2017.)

from the world's communication technology companies and what they provide. Access to media is a pre-requisite for full social participation in the democratic process. Therefore, conglomeration is clearly a woman's concern (Byerly, 2014).

Feminist scholars have paid less attention to macro-level concerns such as media ownership than to women's representation in media content. As a result, there is little research to date on whether and to what extent gender equality figures into national-level communication policy. Male scholars have avoided the subject of gender for the most part, and both feminist scholars and activists have given it only minor attention (Gallagher, 2014). Feminist legal scholar Crichton (2014) and feminist media scholars Byerly and Valentin (2016) are among a small number who have examined U.S. policies, including court decisions, regarding women's equality in media policy and practice, concerning media employment and ownership. Ross and Padovani (2013) have begun to examine corporate and governmental policy for gender equality within the 28 European Union states. However, despite the passage of international documents like the Beijing Platform for Action in 1995,[3] with its Section J calling for gender equality in the media, or the Convention for the Elimination of Discrimination against Women (CEDAW),[4] there has been little movement toward placing gender and media concerns on the international agenda (Gallagher, 2011, p. 459).

Theorizing Women's Structural Relationship to Media: Women's Right to Communicate

Current research shows women continue to be thwarted in exercising their right to communicate in the United States, a nation that prides itself on its freedom of press and expression. The right to communicate has been defined and established at both national and international levels. Democratic nations have typically recognized free expression in speech and press as a *citizen's* right, as, for example, in the First Amendment of the United States Constitution. That right was expanded to the international level in Article 19 of the Universal Declaration of Human Rights, proclaimed by the United Nations in 1948, thereby elevating "the right to freedom of opinion and expression" to a *human* right:

> Everyone has the right to freedom of opinion and expression; this right includes freedom to hold opinions without interference and to seek, receive and impart information and ideas through any media and regardless of frontiers.
>
> *(Article 19)*

Women's specific right to communicate has been addressed within this framework by feminists who participated in the campaign for Communication

Rights in the Information Society (CRIS), launched in 2001 at the UN-sponsored World Summit on the Information Society (WSIS) in Porto Alegre, Brazil.[5] Grassroots organizations joined that movement at the World Social Forum in 2005, calling attention to what participants called the growing divide between "have" and "have nots" in terms of access to media technology. McIver, Birdsall, and Rasmussen (2003) are among those who recognize that communication, human rights and technology are inextricably linked, and it follows that access to communication technology is the basis and means for exercising freedom of expression.

The United Nations Educational, Scientific and Cultural Organization (UNESCO) has similarly noted that gender inequality has remained prevalent in both access to information communication technologies (ICTs) and the development of online news. The agency has called for policies conducive to women's ability to use ICTs for personal expression and connectivity and has taken steps to create an environment for nations to consider how to enact such policies (UNESCO, 2014).

In the U.S. context, it is possible to situate women's interests within the current struggles for both traditional (print, broadcast) and digital (Internet-based) policy that serves women and men of all income levels equally. The Federal Communications Commission represents the crucible where these gender, race and class politics have been played out. However, it is important to first establish the theoretical importance of technology in the right to communicate. Taking an intersectionality approach, Collins and Bilge (2016) have followed current understandings that the information technologies of social media (e.g., Facebook, Twitter, and Snapchat), and a shift on the Web from top-down distribution of knowledge to a network of broad-based knowledge creators, enables new dialogs that have potentially important effects on democracy (p. 164). These feminist scholars observe that the formation of critical consciousness in the broader public is reliant on access to new technologies. Proceeding from their recognition that democracy and neoliberalism are both theories of power, we can make direct application to how women or other disenfranchised groups might bring fresh new ideas about criminal justice, education, health care, war and other matters of broad public concern into political discourse.

Neoliberalism, Women and the Internet

The neoliberal communication policies advanced by wealthy male owners of the large media corporations can be seen in the struggle over network ("net") neutrality in the United States that has been waged for more than a decade. Net neutrality is the principle that the Internet should be maintained as a resource equally accessible to all. But the matter of Internet regulation has been highly politicized, with powerful media industries pitted against public interest in general, something that specifically affects women's and other citizens' groups. In 2015, during Democratic President Obama's administration, the Federal Communications Commission, with a Democratic Party majority of 3–2, took a public interest position and classified the Internet as a "communication service" that should be regulated like other services.[6] Adopting a principle of net neutrality, the commission assured that, like other utilities that served a broad, diverse public, it would be operated with equal access to all users, including equitable pricing. In December 2017, under Republican President Trump, and a Republican Party majority of 3–2 in the FCC, the commission revisited the matter, declaring the Internet to be an "information service" and allowing open competition among providers as to terms of services and charges. The new regulation enables companies that offer Internet service to charge according to the way that customers use their service, but also potentially to block some websites, and give higher-paying customers faster, more reliable service (Fung, 2017). Critics have pointed out that the largest telecommunication giants, including Verizon and Comcast, had invested more than $100 million in campaign contributions to candidates of both parties in order to assure a favorable pro-industry policy environment (Soha, 2017).

Women and racial minorities in the United States have also raised fears about the censoring of groups and individuals who espouse views contradictory to those in power. In fact, there is precedent for such. In 2007, the Verizon corporation refused to allow the National Abortion Rights Action League (NARAL) to use its network for a promotional text message program, citing its own right to block "controversial or unsavory" content (Boboltz, 2017). Feminist media advocacy groups have also spoken out about the potential harm to women under the new rule. The Boston-based Women, Action & the Media (2017) group observed that women already face structural inequality in media access and that ending net neutrality would threaten women's and girls' voices online:

> Especially affected by these structural inequalities are women & girls of color, trans women, queer women, and indigenous women (to name a few), who are regularly attacked and objectified by major media while simultaneously being erased from our screens and speakers. Having rich White men in charge of media and media policy has only made major media richer, whiter, and full of men – shocker. Now they want to add the internet to their domain.
>
> *(WAM, 2017)*

The New York-based Women's Media Center (2017) factored social class and race into a gender analysis of why net neutrality matters:

For low-income communities, for women, for people of color, when all web-based content is treated equally, and two-way communication over the Internet is free from discrimination, these historically underserved communities are empowered and our voices are heard. Without a free and open Internet, #BlackLivesMatter, and the organizations that represent these communities, would not have been able to launch a movement with a single hashtag exposing police brutality and social injustices within communities nationwide.

(Women's Media Center, 2017)

In California, the Oakland-based Center for Media Justice's (2017) executive director, Malkia Cyril, put the matter of net neutrality into a civil rights framework, saying that:

A Net Neutrality repeal would remove one of the very few most important first amendment protections communities of color have today, at a time when free speech protections are more important than ever. The right to speak and be heard; the ability to seek opportunity, stay connected, and protest injustice – these are core civil rights. In a digital age, protecting core civil rights means enforcing, not repealing, Title II Net Neutrality.

(Center for Media Justice, 2017)

Conclusion

There is not a single solution to the social injustice represented by women's and people of color's lack of access to media technology, to media ownership, or to the process that establishes communication policy which defines these. Rather, it is useful to consider a configuration of activities that together might begin to reshape federal communication policy in the United States. The following recommendations draw on the activist policy-related work that my colleagues and students at Howard University have undertaken and published in recent years, most particularly the article "Race-and Gender-conscious Policies: Toward a More Egalitarian Communications Future" (Byerly et al., 2011).

First is the matter of re-establishing a legal definition for "public interest," something that had been established in the FCC's "1960 Programming Policy Statement." Demonstrating true neoliberal ideology, the FCC began to chip away at the notion of public interest in the 1980s under then Republican President Ronald Regan, first by eliminating the 14 "major elements of public interest and then ending the requirement that broadcast stations (radio and television) keep program logs and certain other files previously available to the public" (Byerly et al., 2011, p. 430). The present dominance of digital media would require a rethinking of what public interest should mean today and how it might be measured. However, the setting of definitions and standards, as well as giving the public access to records, would better enable public interest groups to determine whether today's media perform in women's and the broader public interest.

Second is the need for the FCC to adopt rules bringing all media under its authority to conform to a public-interest oriented policy. While communication policy in the U.S. has historically focused mainly on those media using the public airwaves (i.e., broadcast media), there is nothing inherently wrong with policy requiring digital-based companies that are owned by the same parent companies as broadcast stations to also conform. One aspect of a public-interest model would be the incorporation of a "localism principle," that is, the requirement for television and radio stations (whether cable or broadcast) to include a percentage of locally-oriented content in their programming. Both scholars and activists should examine media policy nation-by-nation to identify models for such policy and let it guide their own agenda development.

Third is the matter of conglomeration and how to end it. One goal would be to articulate demands for more rigorous anti-trust enforcement by state attorneys general and federal authorities. This and any other recommendations contained in this discussion will require the work of many. In fact, there is already an active media justice environment, formed by multiple groups representing people of color, women, immigrants and others on the social margins arguing against the present communication policy that allows a single company to own almost unlimited numbers of media outlets. These groups include: The Women's Media Center; National Organization for Women; Women, Action & Media; Free Press; Multicultural Media Telecommunication Council; Center for Media Democracy; Common Cause; Georgetown Law Center's Institute for Public Representation; Operation Push; Public Knowledge, the Communications Office of the United Church of Christ, and other groups. Collectively, they comprise a growing, well-organized grassroots movement seeking to liberalize communication policy through both federal law and regulatory policy.

Fourth, is the need to push for measures that would stimulate women's media ownership. Technical and financial assistance at the organizational level, such as incentives and supports for the employment and advancement of women and people of color within both traditional and digital companies, would help them develop the skills needed for ownership and management.

Fifth, is the need to expand scholarship that focuses on the problems and possibilities discussed in this chapter. There has never been a more compelling moment in U.S. history for scholarship in the service of democratic media policies. Because those policies must incorporate gender, race, and other aspects of equality, so must scholarship take an intersectionality approach in its questions and research designs. It naturally follows that such scholarship should be made widely available to activist groups who can use it in the front lines of media policy work.

Notes

1 To be fair, it should be acknowledged that one allegation against a female also surfaced in the timeframe considered. Andrea Ramsey, a Democratic candidate for a congressional seat in Kansas, ended her bid in December 2017 after a former male subordinate alleged she had sexually harassed him years earlier (Rosenberg, 2017).
2 These included NBC Today host Matt Lauer, ABC reporter Matt Halperin, NPR board chairman Roger LaMay and news chief Michael Oreskes, PBS and CBS host Charlie Rose, New York Times White House reporter Glenn Thrush, and PBS host Tavis Smiley, to name a few (List of men in media accused of sexual misconduct, 2017). In addition, in 2015, Fox news anchor Gretchen Carlson filed a sexual harassment suit against her company's founder and chairman Roger Ailes, with similar allegations against Fox program host Bill O'Reilly by other women to follow within two years' time. Both men were fired, and expensive settlements were arranged for the accusers by the company (List of men in media accused of sexual misconduct, 2017).
3 The Beijing Platform for Action contains the resolutions and work adopted by official delegates to the Fourth United Nations Conference on women, held in Beijing, China, 1995. For more information, see www.un.org/womenwatch/daw/beijing/platform/
4 The Convention on the Elimination of Discrimination Against Women (CEDAW) was adopted by the United Nations General Assembly in 1970. In 30 articles, the document defines what constitutes discrimination against women and prescribes a national action to end discrimination for states that sign onto it. For more detail, see www.un.org/womenwatch/daw/cedaw/
5 For a longer history of the CRIS campaign, see http://cdn.agilitycms.com/wacc-global/Images/Galleries/RESOURCES/COMMUNICATION-RIGHTS/Assessing-Communication-Rights.pdf
6 The Federal Communications Commission is a quasi-independent regulatory agency with five commissioners chosen by the president of the United States. The party in power has the majority number in any given year. The regulations, rules and processes governing media ownership and a range of other things, adopted by the commission, must comport with established law.

References

Boboltz, S. (2017, December 14). How net neutrality repeal could silence women and people of color. *Huffington Post (Online)*. Retrieved from www.huffingtonpost.com/entry/how-net-neutrality-repeal-could-silence-women-and-people-of-color_us_5a32c000e4b0ff955ad11f10

Burke, T. (2017, November 9). #MeToo was started for black and brown women and girls. They're still being ignored. *Washington Post (Online)*. Retrieved from www.washingtonpost.com/news/post-nation/wp/2017/11/09/the-waitress-who-works-in-the-diner-needs-to-know-that-the-issue-of-sexual-harassment-is-about-her-too/?utm_term=.c1eeb16f9b1e

Byerly, C. M. (2011). *Global report on the status of women in news media.* Washington, DC: International Women's Media Foundation. Retrieved from www.iwmf.org/resources/global-report-on-the-status-of-women-in-the-news-media/

Byerly, C. M. (2013). Women and media control: Feminist interrogations at the macro level. In C. Carter, L. Steiner & L. McLaughlin (Eds.), *The Routledge companion to media and gender* (pp. 105–115). Abingdon, UK: Taylor & Francis/Routledge.

Byerly, C. M. (2014, April). Media conglomeration and women's interests: A global concern (commentary). *Feminist Media Studies, 14*(2), 322–326.

Byerly, C. M. (forthcoming). Gender, media, oligopoly: Connecting research and action. In N. Benequista & S. Abbott (Eds.), *International media development: Historical perspectives and new frontiers.* New York, NY: Peter Lang Publishing.

Byerly, C. M., & Hill, M. (2012, December). Reformulation theory: Gauging feminist impact on news of violence against women. *Journal of Women and Gender.* www.academia.edu/2247510/Reformulation_Theory_Gauging_Feminist_Impact_on_News_of_Violence_Against_Women

Byerly, C. M., Park, Y. J., & Miles, R. (2011). Race and gender-conscious policies: Toward a more egalitarian communications future. *Journal of Information Policy, 1,* 425–440.

Byerly, C. M., & Valentin, A. (2016). Women's access to media: Legal dimensions of ownership and employment in the United States. In R. Lind (Ed.), *Race and gender in electronic media: Challenges and opportunities* (pp. 267–292). New York, NY: Routledge.

Byerly, C. M., & Valentin, A. (2017). Women's access to media: Legal dimensions of ownership and employment in the United States. In R. A. Lind (Ed.), *Race and gender in electronic media* (pp. 267–292). New York, NY: Routledge.

Center for Media Justice. (2017). Center for Media Justice (online). Retrieved from http://centerformediajustice.org/category/articles-speeches-and-publications/

Choksi, N. (2017, October 5). Actresses respond to Harvey Weinstein's accusers: "I believe you." *New York Times.* Retrieved from LexisNexis Academic www.lexisnexis.com.proxyhu.wrlc.org/hottopics/lnacademic/

Collins, P. H., & Bilge, S. (2016). *Intersectionality.* Malden, MA: Polity Press.

Couldry, N. (2010). *Why voice matters: Culture and politics after neoliberalism.* Los Angeles, CA: Sage Publications.

Crichton, S. N. L. (2014). The incomplete revolution: Women journalists – 50 years after Title VII of the Civil Rights Act of 1964, we've come a long way baby, but are we there yet? *Howard Law Journal, 58*(1), 49–112.

FCC. (2017, May). *Third report on ownership of commercial broadcast stations.* Washington, DC: US Federal Communications Commission. Retrieved from www.fcc.gov/media

Fung, B. (2017, November 22). FCC moves to end net neutrality standard. *Washington Post,* p. A1.

Gallagher, M. (2011). Gender and communication policy: Struggling for space. In R. Mansell & M. Raboy (Eds.), *The handbook of global media and communication policy* (pp. 451–466). Malden, MA: Wiley Blackwell.

Gallagher, M. (2014). Media and representation of gender. In C. L. Carter, L. Steiner & L. McLaughlin (Eds.), *The Routledge companion to media and gender* (pp. 23–31). Abingdon, UK: Routledge Taylor & Francis.

Gallagher, M. (2015). Foreword. In *Who Makes the News? Global Media Monitoring Project 2015* (pp. vi–vii). Toronto, Canada: World Association for Christian Communication. Retrieved from http://cdn.agilitycms.com/who-makes-the-news/Imported/reports_2015/global/gmmp_global_report_en.pdf

Global Media Monitoring Project (GMMP). (2015). *Who makes the news 2015 reports*. Retrieved from http://whomakesthenews.org/gmmp/gmmp-reports/gmmp-2015-reports

Harvey, D. (2005). *A very brief history of neoliberalism*. Oxford, UK: Oxford University Press.

Hunt, D., Ramón, A.-C., Tran, M., Sargent, A., & Díaz, V. (2017). *Media diversity report: Setting the record straight*. Los Angeles, CA: University of California Los Angeles (Bunche Center for African American Studies). Retrieved from https://bunchecenter.ucla.edu/wp-content/uploads/sites/82/2017/04/2017-Hollywood-Diversity-Report-2-21-17.pdf

Lauzen, M. (2017). *The celluloid ceiling: Behind the scenes employment of women on the top 100, 250, and 500 films of 2017*. San Diego, CA: San Diego State University (Center for the Study of Women in Television & Film). Retrieved from https://womenintvfilm.sdsu.edu/research/

List of Men in Media Accused of Sexual Misconduct. (2017, November 30). *St. Louis Post-Dispatch*. Retrieved from LexisNexis Academic www.lexisnexis.com.proxyhu.wrlc.org/hottopics/lnacademic/

Lockhart, P. R. (2017, December 19). Women of color in low-wage jobs are being overlooked in the #MeToo moment. *Vox (Online)*. Retrieved from www.vox.com/identities/2017/12/19/16620918/sexual-harassment-low-wages-minority-women

McIver, W. J., Birdsall, W. F., & Rasmussen, M. (2003). The Internet and the right to communicate. *First Monday*, 8(12). Retrieved from http://firstmonday.org/ojs/index.php/fm/article/view/1102/1022

Rakow, L. F., & Kranich, K. (1991). Woman as sign in television news. *Journal of Communication*, 41(1), 8–23.

Rosenberg, E. (2017, December 15). Female congressional candidate leaves race after sexual harassment allegations resurface. *Washington Post (Online)*. Retrieved from www.washingtonpost.com/news/powerpost/wp/2017/12/15/female-congressional-candidate-leaves-race-after-sexual-harassment-allegations-resurface/?hpid=hp_no-name_hp-in-the-news%3Apage%2Fin-the-news&utm_term=.abae449a35b7

Ross, K., & Padovani, C. (2013). *Advancing gender equality in decision-making in media organizations*. Vilnius, Lithuania: European Institute for Gender Equality (EIGE).

Ross, K. & Padovani, C. (Eds.). (2017). *Gender equality and the media: A challenge for Europe*. London, UK: Routledge.

School Video News. (2017). Twelve factors in newsworthiness. Retrieved from http://schoolvideonews.com/Broadcast-Journalism/Twelve-Factors-in-Newsworthiness

Soha, M. (2017, December 15). What losing net neutrality means for democracy. *Huffington Post (Online)*. Retrieved from www.huffingtonpost.com/entry/what-losing-net-neutrality-means-for-democracy_us_5a3422a4e4b0e1b4472ae62e

UNESCO. (2014). *World trends in freedom of expression and media development*. Paris, France: United Nations Educational, Scientific and Cultural Organization.

Vega, A. (Ed.). (2012). *Communication and human rights*. Mexico City: National Autonomous University of Mexico.

Women, Action & the Media. (2017). Open letter: We must take action now to preserve net neutrality and protect women's and girls' voices online. Retrieved from http://womenactionmedia.org/net-neutrality/

Women's Media Center. (2017). The status of women in the US Media 2017. *Women's Media Center (Online)*. Retrieved from www.womensmediacenter.com/reports/the-status-of-women-in-u.s.-media-2017

PART III
Responsibility and Choice

5

NUMINOUS FORTUNE AND HOLY MONEY

Dave Ramsey's Cruel Optimism

John Ike Sewell

Proselytizing for neoliberal capitalism has become an American cottage industry. Such cheerleading for neoliberalism is often guised as the "straight talk" of "just plain folks" circulated via mass media. Scores of media personalities and self-appointed pundits have attained quasi-celebrity by advising their readers, listeners and viewers on budgeting, wealth management and lifestyle strategies. Simply put, financial self-help is Big Business in and of itself.

Dave Ramsey is one such straight-talking pundit—and a rich and influential one, at that. A prophet of austerity-to-prosperity, Ramsey is among America's most successful financial self-help personalities. The flagship of the Ramsey Solutions media conglomerate, "The Dave Ramsey Show," is a syndicated talk radio program that airs on more than 550 stations, claiming a listenership of more than 12 million (By The Numbers, 2016). Ramsey's show promotes a faith-based system of money/debt-management for its predominately middle-class (and presumably white) listeners. For Ramsey and his acolytes, "Financial Peace" is realized through strategies of austerity and self-discipline, taking on additional work to repay debts, abstaining from using credit and, eventually, amassing wealth.

The Ramsey Solutions media empire includes "The Dave Ramsey Show," book publishing, live events, classes, podcasts, audio and televisual recordings, a newspaper column and Financial Peace University, a nine-week training program hosted (at no cost to Ramsey's organization) by churches. Ramsey's materials implicitly and explicitly promote neoliberal ideology through discourse linking the broad, populist appeals of Christianity, Western democracy, "free markets," familial duty, patriarchy, patriotism, and notions of capitalism's naturalness and inevitability.

This essay is an ideological analysis of Dave Ramsey's best-selling book, *The Total Money Makeover*, to parse how its messages implicitly and explicitly promote neoliberal ideology. It is argued that Ramsey persuades by melding the bootstrap narrative, the appeal of American "givens," and a self-presentational style akin to Lakoff's (2002) "strict father" model, delivering an oversimplified message to an audience desirous of "straight talk." Ramsey's rhetoric supports neoliberal ideology by overlapping popular American mythologies and motifs to deliver a message of virtuous independence that is attained, quite simply, by (first) paying one's bills and (then) amassing wealth. Building wealth is a virtue, and the wealthy are the virtuous.

Ideological Criticism

Ideologies are rarely overtly stated. Most often, ideological messages are implicit in texts that are—ostensibly at least—*not even about ideology*. This is to say that the ideologies of a given culture are embedded in its cultural artifacts. Through incessant repetition of embedded ideological messages, we come to understand ideologies as natural, inevitable and of essence.

This essay uses the method of ideological criticism, a type of rhetorical criticism used "to discover and make visible the dominant ideology embedded in an artifact" (Foss, 2004, p. 243) to understand why Ramsey's message supports neoliberalism and how he makes himself credible for his followers. With more than 5 million copies in print since its first publication in 2003 (By The Numbers, 2016), Ramsey's *The Total Money Makeover* is the best-selling of his numerous self-help books on lifestyle and personal finance. Hence, the book is a paradigmatic example of Ramsey's teachings. Ideological critics examine artifacts to determine the nature of the ideology it explicitly or implicitly promotes and to detect the rhetorical strategies that persuade the audience to accept the ideology (Foss, 2004, pp. 244–245). First, the critic examines the artifact to ascertain which beliefs and values of a culture are made valid in the artifact and which are elided and/or invalidated. Whose worldview is promoted and whose is suppressed? Then, the critic's task is to understand the rhetorical strategies used to persuade for the identified ideology.

Data analysis for this study consisted of a three-step process of: (1) data management; (2) data reduction; and (3) concept development. The first step of this study was to make a close reading of the entire text while meticulously taking notes. From the notes, I created a list of recurrent terminology. Next I used an open coding system (Lindolf & Taylor, 2002, p. 219) to develop a set of high-inference categories with which to establish running themes from the text. Conclusions from the data analysis were made through a process of analytic induction (Atkinson, et al., 2003, pp. 143–144). This schema provides a cogent procedure to unveil the ideological underpinnings and to explain the persuasive strategies of *The Total Money Makeover*.

Defining Neoliberalism and Neoliberal Ideology

The meaning of neoliberalism continues to evolve semiotically. Neoliberalism is generally understood as designating *laissez-faire* economics, globalization, deregulation, privatization, and free trade (Chomsky, 1999; Giroux, 2011, 2015; Kotz, 2015; Ong, 2006). Hardt and Negri (2009) suggest that neoliberalism is the exploitative action of transnational corporations to privatize public services and commonly held wealth, such as natural resources (pp. 137–138). With deregulation, neoliberalism has established unimpeded momentum that is impervious to government control. Enjoined in a transnational network, local and national economies are dominated by global, neoliberal economic forces—and, thus, global neoliberal practice becomes the de facto setting of all micro-economies connected within this network (Castells, 2009, p. 424). As such, the impact of local politics and local economies on corporate sovereignty is all but erased (Giroux, 2015, p. 133).

Neoliberalism is a condition/syndrome, a heuristic and an ideology. Ideology functions as a way of convincing people to accept their lot—that "how it is" is made to seem natural, normal and inevitable. As ideology, neoliberalism sustains itself through connections or perceived connections with longstanding, often unquestioned "givens" of Western culture, such as consumerism, capitalism, democracy and individualism. Berlant (2011) contends that neoliberalism, much like any institution and/or structure of power, perpetuates itself through the production of a certain subjectivity. For Berlant, neoliberalism fosters a sense of economic autonomy and self-determining agency that only *feels* like empowerment (p. 15). As such, neoliberalism functions as a heuristic: individuals "learn," through an experience of "self-discovery," that predatory practice yields independence and agency. All the while, these seemingly "empowered" subjects are speeding the momentum of a greater transnational force that will eventually exhaust, outmode and disempower them. In this way, neoliberalism motivates a "false notion of freedom which it wraps in the mantle of individualism and choice, and in doing so reduces all problems to private issues" (Giroux, 2015, p. 127). However fictive these ideas and associations may be, such appeals to notions of freedom, individualism and choice continue to reinforce neoliberalism's ideological staying-power and coherence.

Ramsey's Audience

So, who exactly is Ramsey's audience? Ramsey's website provides figures for his audience's demographic breakdown, including gender (51 percent male/ 49 percent female), education (25 percent high school graduates, 51 percent college graduates and 20 percent post-grad), household income (21 percent $30,000 or less, 31 percent $30,000–$50,000, 30 percent $50,000–$75,000, and 18 percent $75,000+), marital status (71 percent married) and age (85 percent between the ages of 25 and 54)[1] (Demographics, 2016). There is no mention of how Ramsey's organization obtained these figures. And as per Ramsey's information, *none* of his audience is childless.[2] In addition, the racial/ethnic breakdown, perhaps tellingly, is elided entirely.[3] Still, Ramsey's information, provided it is accurate, suggests that his audience is primarily lower middle class—or thereabouts, with 52 percent of households earning $50,000 or less annually.

Dave Ramsey's Riches-to-Rags-to-Virtuous-Riches Backstory

Dave Ramsey's story is an archetypal American narrative of (more or less) sin and redemption—a redemption that is followed by ample success. A real estate broker, Ramsey built a net worth of over $4 million by age 26, all the while "living large," beyond his means. "I was good at real estate, but I was better at borrowing money," he explained (Ramsey, 2013, p. 3). Predictably, Ramsey's prosperity façade fell apart after a major creditor's bank was sold to a larger corporation. Ramsey was audited, foreclosed upon and bankrupted in 1986.

By 1992, Ramsey recast himself as a financial self-help expert, self-released the first edition of his best-selling financial self-help book, *The Total Money Makeover* (*TMM*), and launched The Lampo Group, LLC, the parent corporation for all of Ramsey's companies. Ramsey's media and financial counseling enterprise has mushroomed into an empire with over 550 employees (About Us, 2016). He has written or co-authored 15 books, with a combined sales total of around 10 million. His radio show is broadcast by 575 affiliate stations. Ramsey writes two newspaper columns ("Dave Says" and "Dave Ramsey's EntreLeadership") published in 450 newspapers worldwide. As of early 2017, Ramsey holds an estimated net worth of around $55 million (Dave Ramsey Net Worth, 2017).

With these riches and notoriety comes the power of influence, or vice versa. Is Ramsey rich and famous *because* he is influential, or is Ramsey influential *because* he is famous and rich? Power equates with money, which for the most part equates with fame. So, while the abovementioned quandary is in its way unfathomable, it is still quite telling inasmuch as it bolsters the claim that hegemonic power perpetuates itself, a foundational premise of this article.

Indeed, millions upon millions of people have purchased or at least been exposed to Ramsey's products and services. Ramsey's influence is probably most profound for those who enroll in his educational programs: over 4.5 million in Ramsey's Financial Peace University, over 2 million high school students in his Foundations High School Program, over 90,000 college students in the Foundations in Personal Finance College Program, and over 25,000 users of the Foundations in Personal Finance Homeschool Edition (By The Numbers, 2016). For these people, his "students," Ramsey is a powerful man indeed—a household name and trusted advisor.

As Ramsey tells his story, excess and hubris led to a fall. That fall was followed by a period of contemplation, a redefinition—or perhaps a rebranding—of the self, a program of self-discipline/austerity, and a subsequent ascendancy to a heightened plane where virtuous actions yield real money. And, for those who stay the path of righteousness, both the money and the quality of virtue multiplies exponentially. Ramsey's thesis doesn't always correspond with today's economic and mathematical realities. But Ramsey's acolytes are the faithful. They are the plain-talking Everymen, the True Believers. And when appeals to faith, spirituality, plain talk and common sense are invoked, it is easier for those perceiving themselves as the faithful, plain-talking and commonsensical to overlook the numbers. It is also easier to see the world as a level playing field where anyone can achieve success through self-discipline and righteousness.

Ramsey's Neoliberal Ideology

Ramsey is an influential individual whose message functions as ideological indoctrination delivered as "straight talk." Quite often, ideological messages are guised as, or inscribed in, "common sense" narratives about mundane, day-to-day practices. Ideological messages are most effective when embedded in texts that seem to be about something else. "Ideology never says 'I am ideological'" (Althusser, 2005, p. 86). In *TMM*, Ramsey tacitly delivers a neoliberal message that articulates faith, economics and optimism to form a "common sense" narrative that presupposes and construes a historically contingent neoliberal Truth.

Throughout *TMM*, Ramsey continually reminds his readers that his ideas are simply good judgment and Everyman's gumption. In *TMM*'s introduction, Ramsey opines that his maxims "are common sense, which isn't so common anymore" (p. xi). Ramsey then leads his readers through a series of seemingly commonsensical premises toward the certain conclusion that anyone can pay their way out of debt and into prosperity—given the necessary discipline and resolve, that is.

Ramsey's discourse is an amalgam of quintessentially American attitudes, archetypes and motifs supporting neoliberal Truths. This essay will explain how the neoliberal messages of *TMM* are interwoven in and inseparable from the rhetorical strategies used in their delivery. This is to say that the book's incessant barrage of running themes and archetypes are so mired in cliché that their use precipitates a style of delivery—and vice versa. The common themes and archetypes of the book summon up a kind of kneejerk cognitive connection with certain ways of expression where the theme/archetype predetermines its style of delivery—just as the styles of delivery both summon and bolster the embedded Truths of the themes and archetypes. As such, I will identify the running themes of *TMM* that bolster neoliberal ideology individually and in tandem with the analysis of the rhetorical strategies used in their delivery to avoid redundancy. Finally, an assessment of how the identified themes and rhetorical strategies work together in service of the catch-all neoliberal ideological message that underpins the book will be offered in this essay's conclusion.

Authoritative Voices: "Straight Talk," Strict Father Morality and Prosperity Ministry

Ramsey portrays himself as wise, but ever so curmudgeonly, much similar to the personas used by actor Wilford Brimley and TV psychologist Dr. Phil. While he boasts his own expertise,[4] Ramsey is, nevertheless, dismissive of intellectuals and the academy, both of which he paints as elitist. Such anti-elitism is a hallmark of the speech of political conservatives and religious fundamentalists. Ramsey uses simple language to convey that he, too, is Everyman. Tellingly, Ramsey's use of "Everyman" as an epicene term denoting both male and female or as a catchall for "everyone" underscores the patriarchal basis of his narrative. Both tacitly and implicitly correspondent with the hierarchic structuring of fundamentalist Christianity and capitalism itself, Ramsey's family unit is led by men who make financial decisions for the family. Thus, the Everyman narrative exemplifies how Ramsey's discourse excludes or at least marginalizes women.

Simplistic speech that regularly alludes to "plain folks" is one of the seven common propaganda devices defined, famously, by the Institute for Propaganda Analysis. This "plain folks" rhetorical strategy works best when "members of society's political or social elite court the public by appearing to be just ordinary folks and therefore wise and good" (Sproule, 1997, p. 135). Ramsey continually evokes "plain folks," all the while eliding that he himself is both rich and powerful, and, as such, a member of the elite he condemns.

The family metaphor is a longstanding trope of political conservatives and religious fundamentalists. Here, the nation-state is cognized as a family. Conservatives and fundamentalists use this metaphoric scheme so incessantly because both collectivities are patriarchal hierarchies whose political ends are best served through rhetorical strategies evoking the family structures they so revere. Lakoff (2002) terms the conservative family metaphor the "Strict Father model" (p. 13). With the Strict Father model, leadership is male, or at least *gendered* male. Here, an authoritarian leader (the Strict Father) mentors his "children" (the citizenry) using a leadership style presuming that "the exercise of authority is itself moral; that is, it is moral to reward obedience and punish disobedience" (p. 67). In tone and style, Ramsey takes on what is more or less a Strict Father role: he admonishes his "children" (listeners/readers) when they err and praises them when they righteously stay the path.

> Some of you are so immature that you are unwilling to delay pleasure for a greater result. If you will make the sacrifices now that most people aren't willing to make, later on you will be able to live as those folks will never be able to live.
>
> *(Ramsey, 2013, p. 5)*

Here, Ramsey's paternalistic "straight talk" frames paying one's debts as a path to freedom, spurring his readers to stay the course and tacitly bolstering neoliberal ideology.

Through the Strict Father role, Ramsey summons the voice of patriarchy, not only referencing and in service of the traditional, heteronormative family, but also referencing and in service of a greater hierarchy—the patriarchal relationship between God and man.[5] Ramsey positions himself as the Strict Father and, by proxy, as the conduit or voice of God. And who is more authoritative than God himself?[6]

Ramsey is not an evangelist per se, but he openly acknowledges his ideas' bases in Christian faith. With appeals to optimism and independence, Ramsey's message is quite similar to the proselytizing of well-known prosperity ministers such as Joel Osteen, T. D. Jakes, and Paula White. Prosperity ministers proffer a straightforward formula for success where religious faith is a precondition for power and affluence. Faith is the precursor that functions to externalize the internal, thereby yielding physiological health, social capital, success, and fortune (Bowler, 2013, p. 7). In other words, making money is, effectively, the outward manifestation or transubstantiation of immaterial faith in the form of material wealth. In this view, the faithful are certain to succeed financially. Neoliberal capitalism is understood as a meritocracy with a moral hierarchy. "If you are a good person, it is your spiritual duty to possess riches for the good of mankind" (Ramsey, p. 198).

Ramsey (2013) confidently offers a "proven plan to win" (p. xi). Ramsey's message of empowerment emphasizes individual responsibility, all the while eliding the inbuilt and very real structural inequalities of U.S. neoliberal capitalism. Ramsey's post-millennial variant of prosperity ministry sermonizes a privatization of faith (Comaroff & Comaroff, 2001). With God's help, individuals find autonomy to provide for themselves. As Ramsey posits, disciplined individuals of faith who work hard and persevere will eventually and inevitably prosper in a free market economy. A champion of privatization and deregulation, Ramsey urges the worldview that autonomous individuals, empowered by faith, take full responsibility for their health and welfare in a cruelly competitive—but also natural and inevitable—market economy.

> This is the real world where sad old people eat Alpo! Please don't be under the illusion that this government, one that is so inept and dim-witted with money, is going to take care of you in your golden years.
>
> *(Ramsey, 2013, p. 51)*

Ramsey holds out the promise that with the knowledge he imparts on his shows and in his books, people can indeed pay off their debts—and thrive, even. In this way, an individual's failure to prosper is not the fault of an inequitable system—it's the fault of the individual for not having the enabling faith and discipline necessary to prosper *within* the system. If a virtuous populace shoulders its own financial burdens, there is no need for the social safety net of government. "Those who are worried about polarization, about the widening gap between the haves and the have-nots, need not look to the government to solve the problem; just call for a national Total Money Makeover" (Ramsey, 2013, p. 48). In this way, Ramsey's individualist message bolsters the neoliberal ideology that free market capitalism is a just and natural system. Ramsey's appeal to Western individualism thus reinforces allegiance to the "innate moral equilibrium of the marketplace" (Bowler, 2013, p. 226) and reaffirms the existing socioeconomic order.

The strategy of intermeshing elements of faith, independence, American optimism and a notion of responsible business practice to deliver a populist, "common sense" message is a common tactic of prosperity ministers. In *TMM*, Ramsey positions himself as a plain-talking realist whose quasi-mystic teachings reveal The Truth, which is realized/enabled *through practice*. "What I do is help people understand and act on time-honored truths about money that will truly change their lives. … The stuff I teach is the truth" (Ramsey, 2013, pp. xiv–xviii). Ramsey counterpoints "myth" and "truth" as a structuring conceit for the book, going so far as to use the dichotomized pairing as a bold print subheading a total of 34 times. Throughout, Ramsey evokes faith, God and the Christian Bible[7] to bolster this Truth, including directly citing various translations of the Bible 11 times. Ramsey's Truth is simply worded and doesn't necessarily *seem* esoteric. But in practice, Ramsey's "straightforward" counsel yields a complex entanglement of attachments to and entailments with long-standing religious, cultural and economic forces. This intermeshing imbricates the individual's money management actions into a complex set of transnational interactions. In this way, Ramsey's acolytes are hailed, indoctrinated into and ensnared by neoliberal ideology.

Ramsey conflates notions of responsible citizenship, faith, wealth and virtue to function, mutually, as doctrine, an aggregation of ideas that define right and wrong and provide direction in blunt and oftentimes oversimplified ways. Doctrinal speakers like Ramsey order their narratives to first bolster familiar, seemingly secure ideas, such as God and family, then to introduce some form of peril—in Ramsey's discourse, these threats are insolvency, debt, and bankruptcy—and, finally, to suggest a course of action that reaffirms the espoused doctrine (Hart, 1971, p. 253)—in this case, a doctrine and ideology of "Financial Peace."

Through repeated exposures, we become conditioned to respond to certain evocative terms, mottoes, and catchphrases. Ideological and doctrinal language is typified by idioms and adages that operate as "ideographs," culture-bound, high order abstractions that operate as Truths. Rhetors use ideographic terminology such as "right of privacy" and "freedom of speech" (McGee, 1980, p. 6) —or "free market economy" and even "truth," as Ramsey often does—as a means of *circumventing* persuasion. Ideographs, which Ramsey frequently invokes, spur immediate associations that limit our analytical/interpretive capabilities by "prohibit[ing] our appreciation of an alternative pattern of meaning" (p. 9). In other words, Ramsey's rhetoric is steeped in the ideographic dialect of hegemonic power, a vocabulary of seemingly simple terms whose use may drive the foreclosure of meaning(s).

At its core, Ramsey's ideological message is a message of optimism that is (yet again) similar to those espoused by prosperity ministers. "This book [*TMM*] has given [readers] hope to win, and that hope has caused them to take action and claim ultimate victory over their financial struggles and worries—and to actually *win!*" (Ramsey, 2013, p. xi). For prosperity ministers and Ramsey, optimism breeds its own momentum: Those who are optimistic set higher goals that are realized through ardent discipline. "The cheerfulness and optimism which the prosperity gospel called for were *cultivated* habits that had to be worked at but which would lead to success in every realm, including the economic" (Bowler, 2013, p. 232). Still, this urged optimism might be, or at least function as, a way of convincing the "Common Man"[8] not only to accept that his lot is natural and inevitable, but to be happy about it. Such convincing is the goal of neoliberal ideology.

Ramsey's Cruel Optimism

"Success" is never quite so simple. To aspire to something is to forge a connection with it. We aspire to social statuses, jobs, knowledge, material goods, anything that is denotative of exchange power (i.e. money) and, even, to the political itself. To desire or aspire to something necessarily requires a sense of optimism(s). As Berlant (2011) explains, to aspire to something impels not only the cognitive attachment to a desired object or goal, but a series of obligational entanglements. "When we talk about an object of desire, we are really talking about a cluster of promises we want someone or something to make to us and to make possible for us" (p. 23). But obtaining an object of desire is more than a simple *quid pro quo*. We become attached not only to a sought-after object and/or status, but also to the complex set of relational interactions through which the object of desire is acquired. If we lose or can never acquire an object of desire, we mourn not only the loss of or the inability to acquire the object itself, but also the loss of the associations that our foreclosed ambitions entailed. Sometimes we want what we don't need—and when we get it, there are unanticipated, negative repercussions.

Other times we don't get what we want—and, even if we didn't really need what we thought we wanted, the loss of the perception of opportunity is, nevertheless, devastating. Our attachment to the object of desire provides us a way of defining ourselves and our lives. Berlant defines these entanglements as "cruel optimism," "the condition of maintaining an attachment to a significantly problematic object [of desire]" (p. 24). Here, Berlant's concept explains why someone might grieve the loss of a conquered addiction, or stay in an abusive relationship or continue to amass debts—or to remain, steadfastly, on a journey toward Financial Peace, for that matter.

TMM, which Ramsey frames as a challenge to America's dominant ideology of debt, might also be understood as supporting the dominant ideology of neoliberal capitalism. Ramsey's teachings, which he claims offer "biblically based, common sense education and empowerment that give HOPE to everyone in every walk of life" (About Dave, 2016), might also be termed cruel optimisms because: (1) they urge debtors to stay in the system and, thus, on the proverbial treadmill; (2) they enmesh and/or conflate preexisting, dominant U.S. ideologies of Christianity, capitalism and patriarchy in ways that mutually support all three constructs, thereby perpetuating multiply interrelated structures and systemic inequalities of power as status quo; (3) they serve to ensnare followers in a host of entailments, such as unrealistic workloads and staying obligated to debts with exponential interest rates,[9] that may not, in fact, yield the desired results of Financial Peace; and (4) Ramsey's purportedly universal plan for Financial Peace is most effective for people with high income. The lower one's income, the less leverage/agency they will have to affect the desired change. In other words, a person with a large debt who makes a lot of money can pay off their debts and thereby "buy" Financial Peace, whereas someone with a low income and a comparatively small debt may not be able to *ever* pay their debts and acquire Financial Peace—no matter how tenacious, disciplined, virtuous and faithful they may be. And for those who can't afford to buy themselves out of debt, Ramsey's buoyantly stern Strict Father admonitions to pay off debts, no matter what, are cruel optimisms, indeed.

Testimonials and Number-Crunching

The testimonial is a common figure of ideological persuasion (Sproule, 1997, p. 135). *TMM* is generously peppered with accounts of people achieving Financial Peace under Ramsey's tutelage to bolster the book's "Everyman" narrative and attest to the program's efficacy—to "prove" that Ramsey's plan works for everyone, as promised. These accounts, however, are as telling for the information they omit as for the information they provide. There is much talk of dollar amounts saved—but no mention of the incomes of those making the testimonials. One family claims to have paid off a $57,000 debt and given

$7,000 to their church in just six months (p. 6). A married couple claims to have paid off $58,000 in debt and saved $18,000 for an emergency fund in 10 months (Ramsey, 2013, p. 82). And yet another family claims that its sole, predictably male, breadwinner accepted a $4,000 per month reduction in pay to pursue another, more interesting career (p. 110). This begs the question of how much would one have to be making to accept a $4,000 reduction in monthly pay, all the while paying off debts and affecting a Total Money Makeover. Throughout *TMM*, Ramsey uses the testimonials of people who claim to have paid off debts in a year that are equal to or greater than the total yearly incomes of over half of his audience.[10] These examples suggest that Ramsey cherry-picked the testimonials of more affluent followers for their ability to quickly pay off debts,[11] thus "proving" the informal fallacy that if X is true for A and X is true for B, then X will be true for all: if these prosperous, virtuous people can do it, then you can, too.

Neoliberal Strategies Yield Ramsey Solutions

Ramsey is, for all intents and purposes, a preacher for neoliberal capitalism whose business model unsurprisingly mirrors neoliberal practice. A consummate salesman and evangelizer of his own cause, Ramsey liberally fills his literature and shows with plugs for his other books and other shows. And when Ramsey is not hawking his own wares, he's quoting someone else doing it. In one testimonial, David Jarrett, a Ramsey follower, says he bought multiple copies of *TMM* to give to friends as a way of sharing the wealth. "I ordered twenty copies of *The Total Money Makeover* and have enjoyed giving them to my coworkers so they, too, can experience what it's like to be debt free" (Ramsey, 2013, p. 43).

Ramsey's business practices are remarkably similar to neoliberal strategies—especially in terms of infrastructure. Most of his seminars and training sessions, such as Financial Peace University—which is *not* free to attend—are held in churches or religious schools. Likewise, Ramsey' s organization commonly recruits clergy and church members to teach his courses.[12] A brochure targeted toward churches touts that by offering Ramsey's courses, churches can build a stronger base of tithers, increase donation revenues, and "raise a culture of generosity by helping your people beat the debt that keeps them from giving" (Information Guide, 2016). Here, Ramsey has streamlined the common neoliberal strategy of outsourcing. Effectively, he has conscripted free labor and secured free venues. With evangelical fervor, Ramsey converts followers to his cause as a community outreach. And these followers carry the proverbial torch by then zealously promoting Ramsey's products and classes to others. In this way, Ramsey's message of austerity, discipline, optimism and faith yields him big profits.

Debits and Credits: Summing Up

Ramsey's common sense worldview finds its basis in the amorphous religiosity of just plain folks and cruel optimism. Melding common sense narratives of populism, patriarchy, and patriotism is a time-honored persuasive strategy of preachers and politicians alike that Ramsey has maximized to fullest potential. He pushes these familiar appeals a step further, however, through a bit of rhetorical sleight of hand. Ramsey deftly straddles the tangible, lived world of economics and the intangible world of the spiritual by positioning himself as *neither* a prophet nor an expert, *either* a prophet or an expert, and as being *both* a prophet *and* an expert—whichever of these argumentative positions works best, given the exigencies of a particular utterance. Ramsey paints himself as a rebel who mounts his opposition from within the system: He is a rich capitalist who defies lenders and America's culture of debt; he is suspicious of academics and avowedly anti-elitist; the personal finance strategies he advocates are framed as nonconformity, nevertheless promoting the system and ideology of the existing economic order. *TMM*'s packaged rebellion yields a contingent neoliberal Truth that is *anything but* emancipatory for the lower-middle class readers Ramsey claims as over half of his audience. Given economic and mathematical realities, only those with high incomes are truly able to instantiate Ramsey's virtuous vision. For the rest, Ramsey's cruel optimism only serves to perpetuate a system of axiomatic "givens" whose end result is to keep plain folks endlessly on the treadmill, in endless thrall of numinous fortune and holy money.

Notes

1 Ramsey's figures overlap. There is no explanation as to whether someone with an annual income of $30k would be classified as "$30k–$50k" or as "$0–$30k," for example.
2 The "number of children" figure is another example of bad math, accounted as follows: one child—23 percent, two children—41 percent, three children—22 percent, and four+–14 percent. Oddly, there is no accounting of people without children.
3 The 33 photographs in *TMM* may provide clues as to the racial/ethnic breakdown of Ramsey's audience. Of the photos, 28 (almost 85 percent) are of Caucasian families, 3 (just over 9 percent) are of families of color, and two (just over 6 percent) are indeterminate.
4 In *TMM*, Ramsey says, "I seldom list my formal academic credentials because, honestly, I don't think they are important" (2013, p. xvii).
5 Here, I deliberately used the epicene "man" as denotative of all people to illustrate the pervasiveness of patriarchy.
6 Here I use sexist/exclusivist language that defines God as male, just as Ramsey does, to illustrate my point.
7 All of these evocations function as ideographs.
8 Ramsey's speech and writing often include similar sexist/exclusivist, patriarchal terminology.

9   An alternative not mentioned by Ramsey, but which might be useful for some of his followers, would be filing for bankruptcy and thus erasing the debt.
10 As per Ramsey's breakdown, 52 percent of his audience make $50,000 or less per year (Demographics, 2016).
11 A more cynical interpreter might even conclude that the testimonials are not real.
12 Ramsey Solutions calls the instructors of Financial Peace University sessions "advisors." Financial Peace University advisors are not paid. They are not exclusively clergy or church members, but most are.

References

About Dave. (2016). Retrieved on February 25, 2016 from www.daveramsey.com/careers/about-dave/
About Us. (2016). Our story. Retrieved on February 25, 2016 from www.daveramsey.com/careers/about-us
Althusser, L. (2005). Ideology and ideological state apparatuses: Notes toward an investigation. In M. G. Durham & D. M. Kellner (Eds.), *Media and cultural studies: Keyworks* (pp. 79–88). Hoboken, NJ: Wiley-Blackwell.
Atkinson, P., Coffey, A., & Delamont, S. (2003). *Key themes in qualitative research: Communities and change.* New York, NY: Alta Mira Press.
Berlant, L. (2011). *Cruel optimism.* Durham, NC: Duke University Press.
Bowler, K. (2013). *Blessed: A history of the American prosperity gospel.* New York, NY: Oxford University Press.
By The Numbers. (2016). General statistics. Retrieved from www.daveramsey.com/pr/fact-sheet/
Castells, M. (2009). *Communication power.* New York, NY: Oxford University Press.
Chomsky, N. (1999). *Profit over people: Neoliberalism and global order.* New York, NY: Seven Stories Press.
Comaroff, J., & Comaroff, J. L. (2001). Millennial capitalism: First thoughts on a second coming. In J. Comaroff & J. L. Comaroff (Eds.), *Millennial capitalism and the culture of neoliberalism* (pp. 1–56). Durham, NC: Duke University Press.
Dave Ramsey Net Worth. (2017). Retrieved on January 9, 2017 from www.therichest.com/celebnetworth/celeb/tv-personality/dave-ramsey-net-worth/
Demographics. (2016). Retrieved on March 6, 2017 from https://cdn.ramseysolutions.net/media/pdf/listener_demo.pdf
Foss, S. (2004). *Rhetorical criticism: Exploration and practice.* Long Grove, IL: Waveland Press.
Giroux, H. (2011). *Zombie politics and culture in the age of casino capitalism.* New York, NY: Peter Lang.
Giroux, H. (2015). *Dangerous thinking in the age of the new authoritarianism.* New York, NY: Routledge.
Hardt, M., & Negri, A. (2009). *Commonwealth.* Cambridge, MA: Belknap Press.
Hart, R. P. (1971). The rhetoric of the true believer. *Speech Monographs, 38*(4), 251–260.
Information guide. (2016). PDF received via email on March 7, 2017 upon request from http://daveramsey.com
Kotz, D. M. (2015). *The rise and fall of neoliberal capitalism.* Cambridge, MA: Harvard University Press.
Lakoff, G. (2002). *Moral politics: How liberals and conservatives think.* Chicago, IL: University of Chicago Press.

Lindolf, T. R., & Taylor, B. C. (2002). *Qualitative communication research methods* (2nd ed.). Thousand Oaks, CA: Sage Publictions.

McGee, M. C. (1980). The "ideograph": A link between rhetoric and ideology. *Quarterly Journal of Speech, 66*(1), 1–16.

Ong, A. (2006). *Neoliberalism as exception: Mutations in citizenship and sovereignty*. Durham, NC: Duke University Press.

Ramsey, D. (2013). *The total money makeover: A proven plan for financial fitness*. Nashville, TN: Nelson Books.

Sproule, J. M. (1997). *Propaganda and democracy: The American experience of media and mass persuasion*. New York, NY: Cambridge University Press.

6

FROM HOMO ECONOMICUS TO HOMO SACER

Neoliberalism and the Thanatopolitics of The Meth Project

Michael F. Walker

Presenting a challenge to the governance of our ostensibly free and democratic society, intoxication, like sex, is a sphere of human experience and interaction that can be both terribly fun yet fraught with peril for the individual and the state. It can be disruptive, and core values of liberal democracies—such as concerns for personal liberty and privacy—conflict with desires for public health and safety, social stability, and, above all, economic productivity. Since at least the temperance movement, intoxicant use in the United States has been bound up in a scripted performance of value with ideal citizens engaging in socially sanctioned forms of use while savage deviants are said to flout these norms to the detriment of all.

In the neoliberal rationality that permeates the United States, human beings are constructed as citizens with a political/economic subjectivity that is "free to choose"—what we say, who we vote for, where we live, where we work, what we own. We are what Foucault (2008) describes as an entrepreneurial version of *homo economicus*—rational actors who are expected to maximize our economic potential as we enact a market-based freedom. As such, we are empowered to make decisions about our conduct and are held accountable for the choices we make. We can be handsomely rewarded for "making good choices" and harshly penalized for "bad decisions" (Harvey, 2005; Nadesan, 2010). Those unable or unwilling to exercise their freedom in ways that meet the needs of capital are "allowed to die"; they are simply cut off from the means of life (Foucault, 1990, pp. 138–139).

Throughout the late 1990s and early 2000s, rising methamphetamine (or meth)[1] use provoked a great deal of angst and prompted numerous efforts by state and non-state actors to curtail use of the drug. Among these was The Meth Project (TMP), a multi-media prevention campaign that deploys graphic public service announcements (PSAs) to dissuade potential methamphetamine users from using the drug. The PSAs are "fall from grace" narratives wherein a "good subject"—generally coded as white and middle class—uses or has used methamphetamine and is thereby transformed into a "meth addict," a diseased criminal who should be expelled from the polis and "allowed to die."

Using The Meth Project as a case study in the governance of a particular drug, I conduct a rhetorical analysis of these PSAs (along with websites, press releases, promotional material, and other secondary sources) to argue that TMP represents a biopolitical exercise seeking to "conduct the conduct" of neoliberal citizens. Through a thanatopolitical discourse—a set of rhetorical acts defining despised forms of life that can, and even should, be allowed to die—TMP promises certain addiction, monstrous transformation, and expulsion from the white middle class into destitution for those who violate its abstinence-based norms and use methamphetamine even a single time.

The Millennial Meth Crisis: Contextualizing the Meth Project

An amphetamine derivative, methamphetamine is a central nervous system stimulant that had been legal in the United States until 1970, when increasing intravenous use prompted its outlaw (CSAT, 1999, pp. 6–7; Rasmussen, 2008). After its prohibition, the drug persisted as a regional phenomenon primarily confined to the West Coast, Southwest, and Hawaii. However, by 1998, a "methamphetamine crisis" was taking shape as use and manufacture of the drug spread into the Midwest and eastern United States (Office of National Drug Control Policy, 1998, qtd. in CSAT, 1999, p. 11). The spread and increase of methamphetamine use ushered in a host of difficulties, particularly in areas ill-equipped to deal with the drug. From 1995 through the early 2000s, treatment admissions for methamphetamine and "methamphetamine-related" emergency room visits were both rising quickly (SAMHSA, 2004, 2008). Child welfare services in several states reported notable rises in meth-related cases (Gonzales, Mooney, & Rawson, 2010, p. 392). Concurrently, law enforcement reported sharp increases in meth-related crime and meth lab busts, and jails reported larger percentages of arrestees testing positive for methamphetamine (National Association of Counties [NACO], 2005; Hunt, Kuck, & Truitt, 2006; Parsons, 2014, p. 162). While one can dispute the completeness, accuracy, and meaning of such data, this information served as the basis for various assertions, including those by TMP.

The rise in overall methamphetamine use, the introduction of the drug into regions previously unacquainted with it, and the turmoil methamphetamine left in its wake, spurred a wave of media hype reminiscent of the panic surrounding crack cocaine in the 1980s and 1990s (see Parsons, 2014, p. 122; Reinarman & Levine, 1997a, 2004). News reports often emphasized the drug's "highly addictive" nature while describing the most lurid details of methamphetamine's effects (Arizona Republic, 2005b, 2005c, 2006a, 2006b). Reporting was not the only means by which the sense of crisis was conveyed. Documentaries such as *Crank: Darkness on the Edge of Town* (Jarrell, 2007) provided a voyeuristic exploration of the "facts" of methamphetamine. Films such as the dark comedy *Spun* (Akerlund, 2002) and the neo-noir *The Salton Sea* (Caruso, 2002) used methamphetamine as a plot device and the "world" of meth users as a setting. More recently, the wildly popular and critically acclaimed television series *Breaking Bad* (Gilligan, 2008–2013) placed its character study of alienation and hubris within the underground economy of methamphetamine. Though the forms vary, all these mediums share ideological content—chiefly, that methamphetamine is a purely destructive force that will inevitably have devastating consequences, not only for the people involved with it, but also for everyone around them.

The Meth Project emerged from within this context of rising use and media hype. TMP is a large-scale, multi-platform media prevention campaign that originated in 2005 as the Montana Meth Project (MMP). The MMP was a philanthropic effort spearheaded by Thomas Siebel, the founder of Siebel Systems (now part of Oracle) and was funded with a $25.8 million investment from the Thomas and Stacey Siebel Foundation (Siebel & Mange, 2009, p. 413). Based on its perceived success in Montana, several states adopted the program, which is now referred to simply as The Meth Project.[2] TMP approaches methamphetamine as a consumer product, and its goal is to "unsell meth" in order to reduce use among its target audience of teenagers and young adults (Siebel & Mange, 2009, p. 415). TMP's prevention campaign has been built around PSAs disseminated via print, billboards, television, radio, and websites, with its television spots serving as the flagship of its efforts. Over the course of its life, TMP has run 19 of these 30-second PSAs. All forms of the PSAs use graphic and disturbing imagery to target an audience between ages 12 and 17 (Siebel & Mange, 2009, p. 410).

Governmentality, Biopower, and Thanatopolitics

Governmentality is a theoretical and methodological application of Foucault's (2003a) description of governance as the "conduct of conduct"—the structuring of possibilities for individuals such that they "choose" to conform themselves to ideal forms of life (pp. 137–138). Building on this notion of the conduct of conduct, Rose (1999) points out that in liberal democracies, power "governs at a distance" and enlists the agency of subjects in their own self-regulation informed and shaped by mostly professionalized, knowledge-discourses of normalization (pp. 1–11). Miller and Rose (2008) note that "power is not so much a matter of imposing constraints upon citizens as of 'making up' citizens bearing a kind of regulated freedom" (p. 53; see also Dean, 2010, p. 18). In this sense, governmental power guides, rather than dictates; the goal of power in a "free" society is not to engage in acts of force to secure compliance. Ideally, people choose conformity and are often rewarded for it. At the same time, we should remain aware of the state's prerogative to use force to secure compliance.

Governance (that is, the conduct of conduct) of issues such as intoxicant use should be understood as exercises in what Foucault (1990, 2007) described as biopower. As opposed to the sovereign use of force, biopower is concerned with the management and fostering of life toward ends that increase the power and prosperity of the state. While sovereign power was, and is, most concerned with securing the compliance of the population to the wishes of the king or state, biopower represents those efforts to organize and even nurture the population to maximize its productive capacities, while minimizing internal and external threats to those capacities.

Biopolitical governance functions through norms created (mostly) by formal knowledge discourses of the human sciences, policed by various apparatuses of security such as social workers, probation officers or public health officials (Foucault, 2007). Norms establish borders between preferred and despised forms of life (Foucault, 1984; see also Rose, 1999). Norms also set aspirations —people can measure their merit or progress and claim membership in a larger community of people like themselves. In this sense, norms serve as the basis for individuals to surveil, judge, and modify their own behavior through various "technologies of the self" (Foucault, 2003b, p. 146). These self-governing citizens remain relatively free from blatantly coercive exercises of power and gain access to cultural goods. Norms also establish deviance and identify "unruly subjects." Those who cannot or will not govern themselves within given norms can become objects for more or less direct applications of a state (sovereign) power. Court-ordered 12-step meetings, drug testing, and incarceration are all examples of treatment, surveillance, and disciplinary technologies to which people who step outside norms of intoxicant use in the United States are subjected (Foucault, 1984, pp. 196–197; Nadesan, 2008, p. 5). If the question of sovereign power is "whom do you serve?" then the question of biopower is "of what use are you?"

Concomitant with the desire to foster and control the mechanism of life is the power to "disallow [life] to the point of death" (Foucault, 1990, p. 139). This is not an exercise of the power to kill per se; rather, it speaks to a focus on managing life that society can also "allow to die"—either by design or neglect—in the name of protecting or fostering preferred forms of life. When we examine the parameters that define preferred forms of life articulated in artifacts such as TMP, we can also discern the borders outside of which life is allowed to wither away and die. These discursive borders constitute the thanatopolitics —the politics of passive death—of the phenomenon. Subjects caught on the wrong side of the biopolitical/thanatopolitical border are reduced to the status of *homo sacer*, or "bare life" (Agamben, 1998).

Bare life can be thought of as "life not worthy of being lived" (Agamben, 1998, pp. 136–143) and lacks full political and material subjectivity. To be *homo sacer* is to have access to the means of life blocked or denied—the uninsured worker relying on emergency rooms to treat a chronic illness, the heroin addict risking disease from a dirty needle, and the teen banished from the family into homelessness because of methamphetamine use are all *homo sacer*. This status is justified in neoliberal discourses through various mythological/ ideological constructs such as meritocracy, rugged individualism, the self-made man, boot-strapping narratives and the like that place onus for success or failure squarely on the individual while rendering invisible structural impediments to a self-actualized life. The decisions people make dictate the circumstances of their lives; ergo, those who constitute bare life have only themselves to blame.

Articulating the Norm: A Choice of Life and Meth

Biopolitical government is always engaged in some effort to cultivate, guide, mold, browbeat, or punish human beings in the service of *something* (Dean, 2010, p. 17). Whether this *something* can be considered noble, such as the extension of legal rights to historically marginalized groups, or monstrous, such as genocides designed to purify a race, the ultimate end of such endeavors is to achieve an ideal form of life. For TMP, this *something* is a world where people are not only meth-abstinent, they do not try methamphetamine even a single time—hence the tagline "Not Even Once." In true neoliberal fashion, TMP constructs methamphetamine use as a rational choice, with potential users conceptualized as consumers who approach methamphetamine as they would any other consumer product—they decide to use or not use after a cost/benefit analysis. As an exercise in the conduct of conduct, TMP seeks to couch the command "not even once" in the form of an exhortation to make a rational, individual choice. Instead of issuing orders (Don't use meth!), TMP offers facts that make it obvious meth use is a "bad choice" (Why on Earth would you ever want to use meth?!?).

On TMP's account, much of the meth crisis arose from a dearth of accurate information on meth's hazards that made it seem both attractive and only slightly risky, leading people to choose poorly, try the drug, and end up addicted. To tip the scales back toward people making the right choice, TMP decided to convey to teens that "methamphetamine is the most addictive illicit drug in the world and that [teens] should fear using the drug because of its effect on them and those around them" (Siebel & Mange, 2009, p. 410). TMP seeks to influence the thinking of audiences along several lines, including increasing perceived risk, decreasing perceived benefits, and stigmatizing use

(Siebel & Mange, 2009). In this way, TMP attempts to align the free choices of people with larger public health and public safety goals (see Nadesan, 2008; Rose, 1999).

The addictive qualities of methamphetamine play a prominent role in supporting TMP's abstinence telos. Within TMP, methamphetamine is problematized—that is, made intelligible and actionable (see Nadesan, 2008; Rose, 1998, p. 25)—as a pharmacological determinant (Reinarman & Levine, 1997a, pp. 8–9). TMP describes meth as "powerfully addictive" (MPF, n.d.a), and one of the "most highly addictive substances" (MPF, 2013c), or "one of the most addictive substances known" (MPF, 2013a). The PSAs of TMP are unambiguous about the inevitability of addiction, which is portrayed as a swift and certain outcome of using methamphetamine even a single time. For example, in the PSA *That Guy*, the protagonist insists that he will snort meth "just once" before using the drug. Following this initial surrender, we witness him rush from snorting, to smoking, to injecting methamphetamine. Each time, he protests that he will take this next step "just once" before immediately moving to the more stigmatized, and presumably more dangerous, form of use. This rapid progression signifies growing addiction which sprang instantly from the first use. Emphasizing methamphetamine abstinence, each PSA in TMP ended with the campaign tagline "Not Even Once." Thus, while not stated explicitly, within the web of signifiers generated by the PSAs of TMP, addiction is not merely probable, it is all but certain if a person succumbs to temptation and uses the drug "even once."

To validate its assertions, TMP harnesses multiple knowledge discourses put forward by experts "embodying neutrality, authority and skill in a wise figure operating according to an ethical code 'beyond good and evil'" (Miller & Rose, 2008, p. 69). For instance, all TMP websites provide access to a video on the neuroscience of methamphetamine supplied by the University of California Los Angeles Integrated Substance Abuse Program (MPF, 2013b). Similarly, one of the answers to "What is Meth-Induced Psychosis?" is a segment from the A&E documentary "A Question of Life or Meth" (MPF, 2013d). Here, a credentialed expert (a psychiatrist) working "in the trenches" provides a first-hand account of the hallucinations his methamphetamine-using patients experience. TMP also provides an extensive list of sources, many from government agencies and peer-reviewed journals (MPF, n.d.b). For a casual reader, or perhaps even a more sophisticated researcher, this combination of volume and apparent quality serves to establish that TMP has "done its homework."

Within TMP's epistemology, the root of all meth-related problems is the poor personal choice to use methamphetamine, which leads to addiction which causes significant harm to the polis. For instance, TMP notes that:

> Methamphetamine's effects cost the U.S. between $16.2 and $48.3 billion per year. Meth is one of the most addictive substances known and its use

imposes a significant disproportionate burden on individuals and society in money spent on treatment, healthcare, and foster care services, as well as the costs of crime and lost productivity.

(MPF, 2013a)

Here, TMP lists several macro-level harms—healthcare, child abuse, crime, and lost productivity—and frames them in terms of economic loss. These macro-level threats to economic well-being are linked to the micro-level threat of individual addiction. This statement also reveals both TMP's orientation to pharmacological determinism and its indictment of individual users: by taking such an addictive drug, "they" (people who choose to use this highly addictive substance) cost "us" (taxpayers, consumers, business owners, etc.) money.

As we can see, TMP constitutes an exercise in biopower. More concretely, the campaign conveys a concern with managing the health of a population through a biopolitical discourse focused on meth use as a threat to the general health, welfare, safety, and economic prosperity of the population. The program articulates norms of behavior supporting an ideal form of life based on methamphetamine abstinence that also serves to identify "bad subjects"—people who use methamphetamine even a single time. To conduct the conduct of ideal citizens, TMP threatens good subjects thinking of violating its abstinence norm with certain addiction and dissolution into a loathsome meth addict.

TMP constructs the meth addict through an exclusionary narrative that follows "normal" teenagers as they fall from the safety of the middle class into methamphetamine addiction. The PSAs construct the meth addict as an object to be despised and feared by creating close connections between this person's addiction and crime, disease, and madness. Portrayed as an Other who descends into a debased state, the meth addict lives either in squalor or on the streets, thus completing the symbolic transformation from *homo economicus* to *homo sacer*.

Crime

Moral entrepreneurs have long associated substance use with criminality in their efforts to promote a given regimen of government, such as personal abstinence or state prohibition, targeted at intoxicant use. This criminalization of various intoxicants was often interwoven with racist, classist, sexist, and xenophobic narratives. (Humphries, 1999; Musto, 1999; Pegram, 1998; Provine, 2007; Reinarman & Levine, 2004; White, 1998). Consistent with Nadesan's (2008) observation that biopower creates zones of exclusion and oppression, these crusades drew on substance use to keep particular groups of people under control.

TMP both reproduces and extends this connection by constructing meth addicts as sources of crime and violence. As with addiction, crime in TMP mythology is an inevitable consequence of a person's voluntary choice to use methamphetamine, even once. For example, in *Just Once*, we witness the protagonist, a young woman, stealing from what we may assume is her mother's purse and then prostituting herself after she progresses from snorting methamphetamine to smoking the drug. In *Junkie Den*, a group of meth addicts congratulate a young man on his first use of methamphetamine by describing the fun they will have, which includes stealing together. These representations solidify the construct of the meth addict as a dangerous element in society who needs to be feared and controlled. Moreover, the crimes of TMP are petty, brutal, degrading, and often victimize loved ones and innocents. For example, in *Boyfriend*, a young woman is prostituted by her high school sweetheart; in *Laundromat*, the protagonist terrorizes a mother with young children (including a frightened, screaming baby) as he commits his crime; and in *Mother*, a young man assaults his mother when she attempts to stop him from stealing her purse. These are crimes that inspire outrage rather than awe, illustrating that meth addicts not only generate crime, but also have devolved into a particularly loathsome type of criminal.

TMP's drugs-and-crime narrative symbolically transitions people from "decent citizen" to "meth addict." In the greater methamphetamine narrative by which TMP is informed, and to which it contributes, the meth addict serves as a conventional folk-devil, a stereotyped deviant and cultural scapegoat who solidifies, reproduces, and extends longstanding tropes surrounding substance use and more generally despised behaviors (Goode & Ben-Yehuda, 1994, pp. 28–29; see also Cohen, 1972). By linking methamphetamine use to various social ills, the meth addict emerges as an "Other" suitable for exclusion and punitive treatment. As a source of crime, the meth addict also is a source of fear, which as Altheide (1996) notes, "often leads people to look for fear-reducing solutions, usually involving the state's use of force" (p. 69; see also Altheide, 2002, 2006). Thus, the creation of the meth-addicted Other serves to coalesce the community behind calls for increased surveillance and disciplinary actions, such as pre-employment drug screens, court-ordered rehabilitation or incarceration to curb the disruptive consequences of drug use.

Madness

After criminality, another characterization of the fall into the monstrosity of addiction are the associations the TMP makes between methamphetamine use and madness. The link is not entirely without reason. As Room (2005) notes, at least part of the stigma surrounding intoxicant use stems from the tendency of certain drugs to lower inhibitions and cause alterations to perception, which can make people appear irrational and/or behave unpredictably (p. 150). However, this tendency toward unpredictability is reconstructed as an absolute propensity for mayhem in anti-drug discourses. For example, not only was cocaine said to produce violent sexual appetites in black men, it was also said to have such a powerful effect that "cocaine crazed negroes" were virtually immune to bullets, which prompted police to upgrade their weaponry (Musto, 1999, p. 7; Provine, 2007, p. 77). The discourse on methamphetamine is also peppered with fearsome and grotesque tales of sleep-deprived meth users who commit violent acts: "A father beheading his 14-year-old son, a cop shooting down two of his colleagues, a mother stabbing her child more than 150 times" (Arizona Republic, 2005a).

As with the meta-discourse on methamphetamine, TMP frames the drug as having the power to drive people insane and then turn on the people they care about. This is reflected in *Mother* as the protagonist storms about his house in a frenzied search for money, strikes his mother as she attempts to stop him, and then strides off without even glancing back at the damage he has caused. The crazed meth addict is a particularly powerful signifier in *Parents*, wherein the out-of-control protagonist is pounding and kicking the door to his parents' house while he threatens to kill them if they do not let him in. In both these PSAs, the insanity of the situation is brought into further relief by a voiceover of the protagonist calmly discussing the good relationship he has with his parents. The discordance between the visual and aural narratives not only accentuates the chaos of the situation, it may also be interpreted as a look inside the disordered mind of the narrator; these meth addicts are so out of touch with reality that they interpret these violent situations as part of the ongoing and caring relationships they have with their families.

Disease

Disease imagery also plays a significant role in TMP's construction of meth addicts as monsters. Discourses of disease, whether as actuality or metaphor, can activate moral denunciation and demarcate exclusion by creating angst and dread, and serve to mark individuals or groups as threatening, disgusting, and degenerate (Gilman, 1988; Sontag, 1990). In TMP, disease signifiers are pervasive and vivid. Vomit, blood, sweat, runny noses, greasy hair, darkened "raccoon" eyes, and open sores on the face and body all signify the physical decay brought on by methamphetamine addiction. In *Just Once* and *That Guy*, we witness the protagonists' physical deterioration as they progress through various stages of addiction. Each of the characters begins with unblemished faces and bodies that become ever more "diseased" as their addictions progress. In other cases, the health of abstinence is contrasted with the disease of addiction. In *Everything Else*, a healthy young woman who is curious, asks to try methamphetamine at a party is shown all the future horrors that will result from this decision, including a mirror that shows her sore-covered "meth-face." In *Bathtub*, the female protagonist reacts to a stream of bloody water going down the shower drain, turns around, and is confronted by her sore-covered, meth-addicted future self who pleads with her, "Don't do it." Here one is presented with a stark contrast between the healthy (unblemished) non-user and the diseased (blemished) user.

Disease signifiers serve as a semiotic "glue" that binds together meth use with crime and madness. The further the protagonists in the PSAs move into addiction and its linked deviances, the more obviously their bodies show the ravages of their failure to make good choices. Physical degeneration signifies moral degeneration as TMP taps into longstanding associations between the physically grotesque and the morally bankrupt. Iris Marion Young (1990) reminds us that—as with racist narratives—this scaling of the body as "ugly" (i.e., diseased) provides a basis to establish the Other as one who is to be "feared, hated, or avoided" (p. 123). The diseased bodies of meth addicts not only serve as markers of deviant behavior, but also demarcate them as excluded Others.

Fall and Banishment

TMP lacks overtly coercive means to impose its will. Therefore, it uses rhetoric to persuade people of the dangers meth poses so they choose abstinence, and implicitly recommends a course of action for those affected by meth users' poor decisions. The threat of addiction and the degeneration of "normal" people into insane, diseased criminals manifestly promise both material and existential consequences for those ignoring TMP's abstinence injunction and succumbing to the temptation of methamphetamine. The subtext of these narratives is that people who use meth represent "bad subjects" who ought to be banished and allowed to die.

The fall from the middle class is generally signified by transformations in the bodies of meth addicts as well as the environments in which they dwell. These transformations involve the move from cleanliness to filth and from order to chaos, violating what Young (1990) describes as a "bourgeois respectability": middle-class norms focused on cleanliness, order, and moderation that apply to control of both the body and the environment (pp. 136–137). Maintaining respectability requires ablution of both body and dwelling by banishing dirt, odors, chaos, and pollution. The signifiers of what could be called class status in TMP conform to these ideas of respectability. Before "the fall," the homes of the protagonists are single-family dwellings (as opposed to apartments or other multi-family dwellings), and the interiors appear to be both clean and orderly. Cars are neither overly expensive nor falling apart. The clothing and grooming of the protagonists (before they start using) are both clean and moderate—there are no obvious signifiers of rebellion, deviance, or sexual immodesty. In short, the protagonists begin as what one might call "good kids from good homes."

During the fall, we witness drastic changes in the users and their surroundings. Previously clean bodies and clothes become visibly dirty. Markers of disease—sweat, sores, matted hair—serve double duty as signifiers of poor hygiene while clean, well-ordered homes degenerate into garbage-strewn flops. As Linnemann and Wall (2013) note in their critique of the Faces of Meth (FOM) campaign:

> Documenting transformation of abject bodies from pure to polluted, clean to unclean, ... focuses the power of the image and the power to punish on marginalized, subordinate, and stained "white trash." Symbols of pure irrationality and abjection, FOM locates meth users outside community, outside law, outside reason, outside bourgeois conventionality.
>
> *(p. 323)*

As in FOM, these signs of decay signify the degraded class status of the newly minted meth addicts, physically marking them as objects of punitive exclusion.

In TMP's narrative, it is addiction, triggered by the intake of methamphetamine, that serves as the mechanism of this transformation, and here is where banishment is both implied and manifest. For instance, the filthy protagonists of both *Crash* and *Jumped* are in dingy rooms with torn up walls and garbage on the floors. It is not an unreasonable assumption that the fledgling meth addicts are now homeless or squatting. *Junkie Den* is set in a grimy room in what appears to be an abandoned house and the denizens of the den are uniformly dirty and diseased-looking. As they welcome the protagonist into their inner circle, it is clear this will be his "new home" and they will be his new family. The healthy, well-groomed protagonist of *That Guy* is reduced to a quivering, sore- and sweat-covered mess living in an alleyway next to a dumpster, symbolically becoming "white trash."

For women, banishment includes the punishment of sexual degradation and the marginality of being a "bad mother." As Linnemann, Hanson, and Wall (2013) note, images of threatened sexuality in TMP break along distinct gender lines—threats to sexual performance for men and threats of rape or sex work for women. This paternalistic concern over white female sexuality has a long history in anti-drug discourses with fears articulated over white women having sexual desires for, being forced into prostitution by, or being raped by non-white men. This gendered aspect of TMP is brought into relief in the PSAs *Just Once, Sister,* and *Boyfriend*, in which white, middle-class teens are "reduced" to prostitution to obtain methamphetamine. The prostitution in TMP is distinctly classed with lascivious and/or unkempt Johns purchasing sex from young, white meth addicts outside a party, at a truck stop bathroom, and in a seedy motel room, further demonstrating how far these young women have fallen.

While threats to white female sexuality dominate TMP's gendered messages, the program also invokes the specter of "crack mothers" from the 1990s: Women (typically portrayed as poor and African-American) whose craving for crack cocaine was so strong that they continued to use the drug even when pregnant. Importantly, this narrative justified attempts to prosecute these women for child abuse and even to jail them preemptively in order to keep them drug-free through their pregnancies (Cherry, 2007; Humphries, 1999; Reinarman & Levine, 2004; see also Meyers, 2004). The crack mother narrative is echoed in the PSA *Everything Else* when the protagonist is presented with her "meth baby." Just as with crack mothers in the 1990s, Linnemann, Hanson, and Williams (2013) observe that the meth panic of the 2000s also sparked moves to enact harsher child welfare laws that would disproportionately impact women, once again making drug-tainted motherhood a site of discipline and punishment.

The narrative of methamphetamine use presented by TMP differs from past drug panics in that it does not draw on an external, racialized threat against whom the white middle class can marshal. Whereas past drug scares have created external, racialized threats to white middle-class security, TMP creates a class-based, internal threat that must be neutralized. This internal threat can be described as the threat of degeneration into social marginalization that drug use presents to members of the white middle class, embodied in TMP by the construct of the meth addict as "white Other"—a member of a white underclass referred to in the colloquial as "white trash." In their analysis of that particular slur, Annalee Newitz and Matt Wray (1997) note this pejorative:

> Names that which seems unnamable: A race (white) which is used to code "wealth" is coupled with an insult (trash) which means, in this instance, economic waste. Race is therefore used to "explain" class, but class stands out as the principle term here.
>
> *(p. 8)*

For Newitz and Wray, "white trash" serves to identify a subgroup of whites who have not succeeded economically. This brings into relief certain contradictions in notions of white superiority.

As Willoughby-Herard (2007) notes, the presence of poor whites in a society undermines narratives of white supremacy by exposing that whiteness "in and of itself guarantee[s] nothing" (p. 492). In other words, the existence of a white underclass makes it difficult, if not impossible, to position whites as inherently superior. At the same time, the lack of a guarantee that Willoughby-Herard references goes beyond destabilizing constructs of racial superiority/inferiority. At the least, it points to the specter of economic deprivation that haunts whites and non-whites alike in the United States. As Linnemann and Wall (2013) observe, "we might also see the emaciated, stained faces of meth using 'shadow people' as a spectral haunting of ignored, dismissed marginalized whites and a reminder of the frail and precarious social and economic position of whiteness" (p. 327). In TMP's narrative, the meth addict as "white trash" confronts members of the white middle class with the precariousness of their membership in a privileged social group. Situated at the intersections of whiteness, poverty, and social stigma, methamphetamine is, in the mythology of TMP, positioned as a gateway drug to a life as white trash.

A telling example of symbolic exclusion from the middle class is shown in the aforementioned *Parents*. The home the young man is trying to break into has the markers of respectability. Through the picture window of this single-family dwelling we see a clean, well-ordered living room. The house is decorated with lights and a Christmas tree, a signifier of a time reserved for family. As the protagonist pounds on the door and threatens to kill his father, his parents hug and comfort each other. Finally, behind the relative safety of a locked door, they turn off the lights and leave the protagonist to his impotent rage. This image is not simply of a family trying to cope with a drug-enraged child. Rather, keeping the meth addict locked out of the house and turning off the lights on him at Christmas sends a clear message—the meth addict has been banished.

This symbolic banishment reveals a significant, yet unstated, goal of TMP. While the explicit goal of TMP is the reduction of meth use as a public health aim, TMP is also a means to regulate and discipline neoliberal subjects. While numerous individual disciplinary interventions exist in the larger methamphetamine control effort, in TMP, the meth addict serves as the disciplinary intervention. By linking a single use of methamphetamine with a slide into criminality, madness, and disease, TMP associates a willful misbehavior with the inevitable collapse of a stable subject into a state of social inferiority and zone of exclusion, thereby threatening one's physical, social, and mental security. This possibility of becoming a meth addict serves as a screen and a mirror for both individual and collective projected anxieties (see Linnemann et al., 2013). The exclusion promised to the meth addict is an ontological threat created by the promise of expulsion from normalcy (Gilman, 1985, p. 20). Thus, TMP attempts to manage life by moving people toward the goal of methamphetamine abstinence by using the threat of transformation into a meth addict. To the extent that it secures individual compliance, TMP protects the white middle class from the various hazards posed to it by methamphetamine.

Conclusion

A close exploration of the discursive structure of its PSAs reveals that in its effort to educate audiences about the negative consequences of methamphetamine use,

TMP draws from deep and longstanding associations of intoxicant use with crime, madness, and disease, painting a picture of methamphetamine users as both dangerous and disgusting. TMP shows a penchant for punishing, by way of exclusion, those who violate its norm of abstinence. Through its choices about how to unsell methamphetamine, TMP extends and contributes to an understanding about populations that use certain intoxicants that has long served as a justification for punitive state and non-state actions excluding drug users from significant aspects of public life. Not only does TMP assert "this is what could happen to *you*," it also states, "this is how *they* are." Moreover, through its narrative of banishment, it says "and this is what must be done about *them*." The meth addicts of TMP symbolically join the ranks of those Young (1990) would describe as marginalized—the mentally ill, the outsourced workers, the homeless veterans, the disenfranchised parolees, the immigrants dying of thirst in the Arizona desert. These are people deemed extraneous to the needs of neoliberal capitalism. Yet, their existence embarrasses us by exposing our contradictions and frightens us by reminding us of our own precariousness.

In the narratives constructed by TMP, methamphetamine is the threat that promises marginalization if consumed. It is through the construct of the meth addict that TMP seeks to tame the threat. The meth addict serves as a point of condensation for angst springing not just from the perils of methamphetamine, but from middle-class precarity as well. Whereas TMP's narratives of crime, madness, and disease are all manifest consequences of succumbing to the temptation of methamphetamine, the neoliberal subtext running through TMP is that people who use methamphetamine have abused their citizenship by making "bad choices" and therefore should fall from the middle class into destitution. Like other marginals, in the thanatopolitics of TMP and the larger war on drugs, the meth addict is a threat to order, is of no use, and therefore can be allowed to die.

Notes

1 Throughout the text, I use the terms "methamphetamine" and "meth" interchangeably.
2 Each of the various state programs kept the convention of: The (State Name) Meth Project (e.g., The Arizona Meth Project, Georgia Meth Project, etc.)

References

Agamben, G. (1998). *Homo sacer: Sovereign power and bare life*. Stanford, CA: Stanford University Press.
Akerlund, J. (Director). (2002). *Spun* [Motion picture]. USA: Sony.
Altheide, D. L. (1996). *Qualitative media analysis*. Thousand Oaks, CA: Sage.
Altheide, D. L. (2002). *Creating fear: News and the construction of crisis*. Hawthorne, NY: Aldine de Gruyther.
Altheide, D. L. (2006). *Terrorism and the politics of fear*. Lanham, MD: AltaMira Press.

Arizona Republic. (2005a, February 7). Meth mess: Our stand: This drug breeds ugly dangers and death in our city. *The Arizona Republic*, p. B6. Retrieved from ProQuest database.

Arizona Republic. (2005b, November 14). Proposed steps against meth make good sense: Our stand: Fighting drug abuse worth inconvenience to law-abiding public. *The Arizona Republic*, p. 6. Retrieved from ProQuest database.

Arizona Republic. (2005c, December 4). Put meth to death: Our stand: Public should demand tough new laws. *The Arizona Republic*, p. V4. Retrieved from ProQuest database.

Arizona Republic. (2006a, November 28). Shooter suspects dodging blame. *The Arizona Republic*, p. A1. Retrieved from ProQuest database.

Arizona Republic. (2006b, December 14). Man gets 25 years for stabbing death of ASU official: Sentence also includes earlier knifing that put second man in hospital for four months. *The Arizona Republic*, p. B2. Retrieved from ProQuest database.

Caruso, D. J. (Director). (2002). *The Salton Sea* [Motion picture]. USA: Warner Brothers.

Center for Substance Abuse Treatment (CSAT). (1999). *Treatment for stimulant disorders.* Treatment Improvement Protocol (TIP) Series: No. 33. DHHS Publication No. (SMA) 99–3296, Rockville, MD: Substance Abuse and Mental Health Services Administration.

Cherry, A. L. (2007). The detention, confinement and incarceration of pregnant women for the benefit of fetal health. *Columbia Journal of Gender and Law, 16*(1), 147–197.

Cohen, S. (1972). *Folk devils and moral panics: The creation of the mods and rockers.* Oxford, UK: Martin Robertson.

Dean, M. (2010). *Governmentality: Power and rule in modern society* (2nd ed.). Thousand Oaks, CA: Sage.

Foucault, M. (1984). The means of correct training. In P. Rabinow (Ed.), *The Foucault reader* (pp. 188–205). New York, NY: Pantheon.

Foucault, M. (1990). *The history of sexuality: An introduction* (Vol. 1). R. Hurley (Trans.). New York, NY: Vintage.

Foucault, M. (2003a). The subject and power. In P. Rabinow & N. Rose (Eds.), *The essential Foucault: Selections from the essential works of Foucault 1954–1984* (pp. 126–144). New York, NY: The New Press.

Foucault, M. (2003b). Technologies of the self. In P. Rabinow & N. Rose (Eds.), *The essential Foucault: Selections from the essential works of Foucault, 1954–1984* (pp. 145–169). New York, NY: The New Press.

Foucault, M. (2007). *Security, territory, population: Lectures at the College De France 1977–1978.* M. Senellart (Ed.), G. Burchell (Trans.). New York, NY: Picador.

Foucault, M. (2008). The birth of biopolitics. *Lectures at the College De France 1977–1978.* M. Senellart (Ed.), G. Burchell (Trans.). New York, NY: Picador.

Gilligan, V. (Creator). (2008–2013). *Breaking Bad* [Television series]. USA: American Movie Classics (AMC).

Gilman, S. L. (1985). *Difference and pathology: Stereotypes of sexuality, race, and madness.* Ithaca, NY: Cornell University Press.

Gilman, S. L. (1988). *Disease and representation: Images of illness from madness to AIDS.* Ithaca, NY: Cornell University Press.

Gonzales, R., Mooney, L., & Rawson, R. (2010). The methamphetamine problem in the United States. *Annual Review of Public Health, 31*(1), 385–398.

Goode, E., & Ben-Yehuda, N. (1994). *Moral panics: The social construction of deviance.* Oxford, UK: Blackwell.

Harvey, D. (2005). *A brief history of neoliberalism*. New York, NY: Oxford University Press.
Humphries, D. (1999). *Crack mothers: Pregnancy, drugs and the media*. Columbus, OH: Ohio State University Press.
Hunt, D., Kuck, S., & Truitt, L. (2006). *Methamphetamine use: Lessons learned* (Document # 209730). Cambridge, MA: ABT Associates Incorporated.
Jarrell, T. (Producer & Director). (2007). *Crank: Darkness on the edge of town* [Documentary]. USA: Independent Television Service.
Linnemann, T., Hanson, L., & Wall, T. (2013). "With scenes of blood and pain": Crime control and the punitive imagination of The Meth Project. *British Journal of Criminology, 53*(1), 605–623.
Linnemann, T., & Wall, T. (2013). This is your face on meth: The punitive spectacle of "white trash" in the rural war on drugs. *Theoretical Criminology, 17*(3), 315–334.
Meth Project Foundation. (2013a). About us. Retrieved from http://foundation.methproject.org/About-Us/index.php
Meth Project Foundation. (2013b). Brain and behavior. Retrieved from http://foundation.methproject.org/Our-Work/brain-and-behavior.php
Meth Project Foundation. (2013c). Meth info. Retrieved from http://foundation.methproject.org/Meth-Info/index.php
Meth Project Foundation. (2013d). What is meth-induced psychosis? Retrieved from www.methproject.org/answers/what-is-meth-induced-psychosis.html#Mind-Games
Meth Project Foundation. (n.d.a). Methamphetamine facts. Retrieved from http://foundation.methproject.org/documents/Fact%20Sheet_Methamphetamine.pdf
Meth Project Foundation. (n.d.b). References. Retrieved from http://methproject.org/common/documents/methprojectorg_research_sources.pdf
Meyers, M. (2004). Crack mothers in the news: A narrative of paternalistic racism. *Journal of Communication Inquiry, 28*(3), 194–216.
Miller, P., & Rose, N. (2008). *Governing the present*. Malden, MA: Polity Press.
Musto, D. F. (1999). *The American disease: Origins of narcotics control* (3rd ed.). Oxford, UK: Oxford University Press.
Nadesan, M. H. (2008). *Governmentality, biopower, and everyday life*. New York, NY: Routledge.
Nadesan, M. H. (2010). *Governing childhood into the 21st century*. New York, NY: Palgrave-MacMillan.
National Association of Counties (NACO). (2005). *Two surveys of U.S. counties: The criminal effect of meth on communities, the impact of meth on children*. Washington, DC: Author.
Newitz, A., & Wray, M. (1997). Introduction. In M. Wray & A. Newtiz (Eds.), *White trash: Race and class in America* (pp. 1–14). New York, NY: Routledge.
Parsons, N. L. (2014). *Meth mania: A history of methamphetamine*. Boulder, CO: Lynne Reinner Publishers, Inc.
Pegram, T. R. (1998). *Battling demon rum: The struggle for a dry America, 1800–1933*. Chicago, IL: Ivan R. Dee.
Provine, D. M. (2007). *Unequal under law: Race in the war on drugs*. Chicago, IL: University of Chicago Press.
Rasmussen, N. (2008). *On speed: The many lives of amphetamine*. New York, NY: New York University Press.
Reinarman, C., & Levine, H. G. (Eds.). (1997a). Crack in context. In *Crack in America: Demon drugs and social justice* (pp. 1–17). Berkeley, CA: University of California Press.

Reinarman, C., & Levine, H. G. (Eds.). (1997b). The crack attack: Politics and media in the crack scare. In *Crack in America: Demon drugs and social justice* (pp. 18–51). Berkeley, CA: University of California Press.

Reinarman, C., & Levine, H. G. (2004). Crack in the rearview mirror: Deconstructing drug war mythology. *Social Justice, 31*(1), 182–199.

Room, R. (2005). Stigma, social inequality and alcohol and drug use. *Drug and Alcohol Review, 24*(2), 143–155.

Rose, N. (1998). *Inventing ourselves: Psychology, power, and personhood.* Cambridge, MA: Cambridge University Press.

Rose, N. (1999). *Governing the soul: The shaping of the private self* (2nd ed.). New York, NY: Routledge.

Siebel, T. M., & Mange, S. A. (2009). The Montana Meth Project: "Unselling" a dangerous drug. *Stanford Law and Policy Review, 20*(2), 405–416.

Sontag, S. (1990). AIDS and its metaphors. In *Illness as metaphor and AIDS and its metaphors* (pp. 93–183). New York, NY: Doubleday.

Substance Abuse and Mental Health Services Administration. (2004). *Amphetamine and methamphetamine emergency department visits, 1995–2002.* The DAWN Report. Rockville, MD: Author.

Substance Abuse and Mental Health Services Administration. (2008). *Geographic differences in substance abuse treatment admissions for methamphetamine/amphetamine and marijuana: 2005.* The DASIS Report. Rockville, MD: Author.

White, W. L. (1998). *Slaying the dragon: The history of addiction treatment and recovery in America.* Bloomington, IL: Chestnut Health Systems.

Willoughby-Herard, T. (2007). South Africa's poor whites and whiteness studies: Afrikaner ethnicity, scientific racism, and white misery. *New Political Science, 29*(4), 479–500.

Young, I. M. (1990). *Justice and the politics of difference.* Princeton, NJ: Princeton University Press.

Young, J. (1999). *The exclusive society.* Thousand Oaks, CA: Sage.

7
AS AMERICAN AS CAPITALIST EXPLOITATION

Neoliberalism in *The Men Who Built America*

Christopher M. Duerringer

Scholars of protest and social movements have long written about the significance of civil religion—that durable reservoir of national ideology, which, especially in times of tumult, serves as touchstone, codex, and compass for U.S. culture. Operating like any other religion, civil religion offers beliefs, value hierarchies, celebrations, and rituals to comfort and inspire the faithful. Public memories of the lives and words of presidents and military officers serve quasi-messianic functions: fallen soldiers are honored as martyrs; celebrations of achievements and victorious battles unify and model important values; anniversaries of tragic defeats and losses are, likewise, converted into days for remembrance of American values and behavior; and mass pledges, singing, and salutes offer the same kind of comfort as genuflection, recitation of prayers, or counting rosary beads. And as the pull of organized religion weakens (Lipka, 2015), the religious qualities of "Americanism" have only become more important in sociological interpretations of life in the United States. However, it is also clear that the principles steering much of U.S. public discourse and policy have shifted beneath our feet. The shift to the zealous defense of free markets rather than free people (i.e., the shift from liberalism to neoliberalism) is, likewise, clearly reflected in the production of cultural texts that revise civil religion.

This project offers a critical rhetorical analysis of one particularly notable example of the new civil religion: *The Men Who Built America*, a four-part set of docudramas about famous robber barons[1] of the late nineteenth and early twentieth century who, the History Channel opines, "almost single-handedly laid the foundation for the America[2] we now know and love." In the first portion of this chapter, I explicate the concept of civil religion as developed by sociologist Robert Bellah, which I then reconfigure for life under neoliberalism. Next, I trace the plot of *The Men Who Built America*, as the series retells the history of the United States through the lens of private enterprise. Ultimately, I argue that the series preaches a neoliberal civil religion by articulating America and Americanism with capitalism; offering tidy "rags-to-riches" narratives that support the myth of "bootstrap individualism" so important to neoliberalism's denunciation of the significance of class, racial, ethnic, and sexual identities; and by the near complete effacement of the millions who worked, built, and fought for the nation that made these men's fortunes possible.

Review of Literature

Civil Religion

"While some have argued that Christianity is the national faith," Robert Bellah (1967) wrote, "few have realized that there actually exists alongside of and rather clearly differentiated from the churches an elaborate and well-institutionalized civil religion in America" (p. 1). Although not expressly proper to any particular religion, "common elements of religious orientation that the great majority of Americans share," expressed in the words and actions of the Founding Fathers, "have played a crucial role in the development of American institutions and still provide a religious dimension for the whole fabric of American life, including the political sphere." Bellah located American civil religion in "a set of beliefs, symbols, and rituals" that includes the inauguration of the president, the commemoration of fallen soldiers on national holidays, and the conduct of rituals like the Pledge of Allegiance.

Bellah's initial concept attracted a great deal of interest and debate. Mathisen (1989) noted that scholars have differed in terms of their definition, description, and attempts to historicize American civil religion. His bibliography of hundreds of those works demonstrates the breadth and depth of the scholarly conversation that Bellah incited. Summarizing the consensus of Bellah's adherents, Roger Chapman (2009) defined the concept as "the intertwining of religion and patriotism ... [that] promotes social cohesion and promotes moral courage during times of national testing" (p. 20). Bellah pointed to such intertwining at numerous points in the early days of the republic: the Declaration of Independence assigns responsibility for rights to the Creator rather than the state; Washington was inaugurated by placing his hand on the Holy Bible; inaugural addresses seem to take the form of a sermon; during the Civil War, biblical themes of sacrifice and rebirth were attached to the nation; and insofar as his death is the price he paid for reviving the nation, Lincoln emerges as a Christ figure.

American civil religion has been said to be episodic, sometimes flowering and sometimes fading (Marty, 1976; Wilson, 1979). Mathisen (1989) regarded the waning of American civil religion in the 1970s and early 1980s as a lagging indicator of the failure of the Carter administration to strike the right balance between the prophetic and secular after the great failures of Vietnam and Watergate. Perhaps more importantly, Mathisen's essay reflects the essential recognition that American civil religion is continuously restored and renovated, with varying degrees of success. In this essay, I suggest that American civil religion has been undergoing another change. The religious feeling remains but, increasingly, our national religion is as much about capitalism as it is about democracy.

Neoliberalism

Neoliberalism ranks with postmodernism and affect among the most popular yet hazily defined academic buzzwords in recent memory. One might hear the term used to describe a school voucher plan; our nation's military adventures in the Middle East; a home improvement show on television; a personal security device; a t-shirt bearing an activist message, and the politics of Emmanuel Macron, Mitt Romney, or Hillary Clinton. Clearly then, the term does not belong to a political party or a discrete domain of objects.

As I employ the term, neoliberalism signals an alarming transformation in politics and culture wherein the values of liberalism (i.e., individualism and self-governance) are superseded by the values of "free market"[3] capitalism. It is a "theory of political economic practices that proposes that human wellbeing can best be advanced by liberating individual entrepreneurial freedoms and skills within an institutional framework characterized by strong property rights, free markets, and free trade" (Harvey, 2005, p. 2). In practice, neoliberalism manifests itself as "an array of market oriented principles" (Chomsky, 1999, p. 19), imposed upon populations to varying degrees, that purport to "encourage private enterprise and consumer choice, reward personal responsibility and entrepreneurial initiative, and undermine the dead hand of the incompetent, bureaucratic and parasitic government" (McChesney, 1998, p. 7).

In a sense, neoliberalism signals a bizarre kind of inversion—an instance of "affirming the consequent"[4] at the macro level—in which a limited set of the products of liberal democracy are now taken as its substitutes: civil liberties, the rule of law, toleration and other felicitous features of liberal government are now supposed to be synonymous or even produced by the economic regimes that grew out of them in the nineteenth and twentieth centuries. This describes the position taken by Milton Friedman (1962) in his influential work, *Capitalism and Freedom*. For Friedman and the legions who followed him in the 1980s and 1990s, economic freedom (defined in laissez-faire terms) is productive of political and legal freedoms.[5] For this reason, one hears of U.S. efforts to guarantee free markets, deregulation of industries, or the privatization of public utilities in the developing world with more regularity than U.S. sacrifices for the causes of representative democracy, civil liberties, or free speech.

This shift in principles is evident in reviewing U.S. military actions over the last century. While it joined the First and Second World Wars in defense of its sovereignty and on behalf of its allies, the United States waged wars in Korea and Vietnam for free markets more than free people. It has propped up client states and knocked down others when the needs of free market capitalism, not civil liberties, were at stake. And in the aftermath of the terror attacks of September 11, 2001, the Bush administration's advice to concerned citizens was simple—do your part and go shopping:

> As we work with Congress in the coming year to chart a new course in Iraq and strengthen our military to meet the challenges of the 21st century, we must also work together to achieve important goals for the American people here at home. This work begins with keeping our economy growing. … And I encourage you all to go shopping more.
> (New York Times, 2006)

In the neoliberal state, the freedom to buy and sell is a fair substitute for the freedom to speak.

Domestically, we glimpse the neoliberal impulse in policies that would strip regulation, privatize public treasure, and look to markets to solve public problems. Where the welfare state once looked after the poor, the sick, and young and aged, the neoliberal state delegates that work to the free market. School voucher proposals would hand state revenues back to private citizens, on the basis of the logic that individual economic actors will choose the best schools and let lousy ones bleed out. Public utilities were deregulated on the basis of a similar faith: there would be no need for the state to ensure the public's welfare because capitalist competition would surely require airlines, cable companies, and wireless carriers to treat their customers like kings or lose their business.

As a governing philosophy, neoliberalism has produced a number of noteworthy effects. The first and most obvious is staggering economic inequality and suffering. Increasingly freed of bothersome regulation, capital has crushed labor power, laid waste to the environment, and begun consolidating power in nearly every industry. Renowned economist Thomas Piketty (2014) finds that economic inequality is now more pronounced than at any point in the previous century. More distressingly, Piketty's data suggests that our current situation is more or less normal for capitalist economic activity, and that the "Golden Age" of modern capitalism between 1910 and 1950, when wages rose alongside economic output in Organization for Economic Cooperation and Development (OECD) countries, was less a result of any economic policy or tendency of capitalism towards equilibrium than the convenient side-effect of disruptions created by the World Wars and technological advancement (p. 20). And he shows that where it has spread in the developing world, where neoliberal policies have been rigorously imposed by the International Monetary Fund (IMF) and the World Trade Organization (WTO), capitalism has created and further deepened economic inequality. And worst of all, Piketty finds that the world economy is trending more and more in the direction of "patrimonial capitalism"—an economic situation in which economic gain via accumulated capital significantly outstrips that available through labor. That is, it will be far more profitable to own things than to sell one's labor. Under such conditions, the only predictable way of becoming wealthy is to be born that way. Those lucky few who are born rich are more likely to see their wealth grow and grow. In light of these developments, it is difficult for any serious person to contend that our neoliberal policies have produced freer people.

As Harvey (2005) contends, perhaps the most damning evidence against neoliberal policies is that the most orthodox neoliberal policies are almost never implemented where their advocates reside (i.e., in the United States or Germany). In order to receive financial assistance from the International Monetary Fund, for example, developing nations have been required to implement Structural Adjustment Programs that neoliberalize their economies—opening their markets to foreign capital, reducing "unnecessary" regulation, and slashing government spending on public goods like education and welfare (Kay, 1993). Given the enormous disparities between industrialized and developing economies, these reforms tend to turn their host nations into treasure chests of raw materials and low-cost labor, which are looted by enterprising corporations and venture capitalists. In Africa, where such Structural Adjustment Programs have been widely deployed, Palast (2012) reports that total income has declined by 23%. And when, after the global financial meltdown of 2009, the nations of Ireland, Spain, and Greece found themselves unable to pay their foreign debts, the people of those countries were subjected to harsh austerity measures. U.S. investment banks and bond traders created the complicated and risky asset backed securities and collateralized debt obligations that eventually wiped away a fifth of the entire planet's annual economic output (Conway, 2009), but it would be average Spaniards, Greeks, and Irish who would pay the price.

Even within the most industrialized economies, neoliberal reforms disproportionately target the jobs and fortunes of working people. In the United States, for example, there has been enormous pressure to privatize public education, to undermine labor unions, and to deregulate all manner of formerly public goods. But there has been no equivalent effort to deregulate the regulatory apparatus that grants companies like Apple, Google, Pfizer, Merck, Samsung, and Google the right to use patents, trademarks, and copyrights to corner markets and engage in rent-seeking activities; to end the massive subsidies that prop up U.S. petrochemical, automobile, and agriculture firms; or to end the continuous flow of bailouts, restructurings, and quantitative easing that keeps many corporations healthy while their workers and customers struggle. In practice, Gore Vidal (as quoted in Chang, 2012) reflected, neoliberalism has meant "free enterprise for the poor and socialism for the rich."

Second, one finds that the neoliberal reforms that were supposed to produce freer people actually tend to get in the way of political and legal freedom. After the Second World War, the U.S.'s international priorities shifted to the protection of national economic interests and the world capitalist system (Haines, 1989). Noam Chomsky (1992, 1999, 2004, 2007) has been particularly vocal in chronicling the costs of this shift. In addition to our involvement in the Korean and Vietnam Wars—both of which were arguably more about protecting the interests of capitalism than democracy—the U.S. has acted to destabilize sovereign, often democratically elected, governments in Latin America and the Middle East. Conversely, the United States has made strange bedfellows with tyrannical regimes and extremists when those contacts appeared more likely to be friendly to American business interests abroad. To the extent that neoliberalism has resulted in our intervention in democratically elected states and, simultaneously, cozying up to some of the world's most brutal dictators, it is difficult to maintain that "capitalism with the gloves off" really produces more liberty for the people who live in those states.

Nonetheless, neoliberalism now enjoys such a position of hegemony that one struggles to find a U.S. politician who has not bought in to some degree. While Barack Obama successfully marketed himself as a change candidate in 2008, his politics were thoroughly neoliberal, as was the massive healthcare bill that came to bear his name. And although Republicans now oppose it, primarily on the principle that their political opponent passed it, the Affordable Care Act (typically known as Obamacare) is a prime example of the influence of neoliberalism in U.S. politics. Rather than carrying out the business of providing healthcare directly to citizens, the ACA entrusts the private sector, the laws of supply and demand, and markets with the task of providing affordable healthcare to millions of Americans. To the extent that Republicans have principled disagreements with the law (mostly, they have political points to score by opposing it), they only desire that it be *more* neoliberal.

As Jim Aune (2002) put it, hegemonic neoliberal economic and political theory have produced a rhetoric of economic correctness such that anyone who doubts the virtues of free markets and deregulation is subject to public shaming. What may be going on is more than just a rhetoric of economic correctness, but a transformation in American civil religion (or some kind of adjunct to it). This chapter attends to one particularly vivid example of how this important and dangerous transformation in U.S. politics and culture is represented and celebrated within the 2013 docudrama series, *The Men Who Built America*.

The Men Who Built America

Originally aired on the History Channel in 2013, *The Men Who Built America* is a four-part series spanning six hours of cable television. A loosely chronological dramatic narrative intercut with talking-head style commentary, the series retells of the story of the United States' rise to national greatness through the lives of five famous industrialists and robber barons: Cornelius Vanderbilt, Andrew Carnegie, John D. Rockefeller, J. P. Morgan, and Henry Ford. Along the way, the series narrates the expansion of the railroads, the industrial production of steel, the electrification of the nation, the rise of monopoly and oligopoly capitalism, and the automobile. For these, viewers will learn over and again, are the source of America's greatness.

The narrative begins with the death of Abraham Lincoln, depicting chaos and terror among those gathered as the fallen president is carried out of Ford's Theatre, where he had been shot. This event underscores the precarious position of the United States at the dawning of the modern era. Over a montage of scenes of the American heartland, the wreckage of the Civil War, and budding industry, the series narrator explains that the tragedy also clears the way for a new kind of American leadership:

> Just five days after the end of the civil war, President Abraham Lincoln is the final of the 600,000 deaths in America's bloodiest conflict. The country is divided. And the world looks at American democracy as a failed experiment. But what most don't realize is that a new era has dawned. The nation is entering an age of advancement. And from the void left by the death of perhaps the greatest statesman we will ever know, a new breed of leader will emerge.
>
> *(Palmer, White, & Magan, 2012)*

Throughout the series, the narrative flow is interrupted by "talking head" cutaway shots, featuring renowned business leaders who comment about the significance of the events unfolding in the story. In the first of these, advertising executive and television celebrity Donny Deutsch expounds on the significance of the men mythologized here, calling them "entrepreneurial rock stars ... who set the standard for the American dream." As scenes of the narrative to come are featured in a montage, the gravel-voiced narrator continues on this theme: "men of insight, innovation, and ingenuity the likes of which the world has never seen ... propelling the United States of America to greatness" (Palmer, White, & Magan, 2012). The second cutaway features former *Apprentice* star, then C-list celebrity and future president, Donald J. Trump, who avers: "These were great men with a vision that nobody else had. And that's why in the last half-century, that 50-year period, we built the world!" Now, the show is under way.

The opening credits feature highly stylized freeze frames of each of the robber barons, captioned with their last names, as a bawdy blues-rock sound track blares. The aesthetic is closer to that of an advertisement for the Dodge Ram pickup truck than a documentary. Although it will not be possible to describe in close detail all six hours of the narrative, the following vignettes from three of the five "great men" featured in the series offer a representative sampling of the mythology being crafted in each episode.

Vanderbilt

Vanderbilt's story begins in New York City in 1865. A slow-motion shot of the stern-looking middle-aged man walking purposefully through a dimly lit street is narrated:

> For the first time in the country's short existence, the man most capable of leading America is not a politician. He's a self-made man, who through sheer force of will turned a poor upbringing on the docks of New York harbor into an empire.
>
> *(Palmer, White & Magan, 2012)*

Typically, the series will introduce each robber baron at the height of his powers, flashback to his upbringing, and then demonstrate the influence of those formative experiences as the man makes his contribution to the building of America. Vanderbilt's tale is framed by way of a flashback to his late teens, where he is shown engaging in bare-knuckle boxing matches. During this display, the narrator tells the story of how, at the age of 16, Vanderbilt bought a ferry with a $100 loan from his mother and then developed a reputation as "a cutthroat businessman willing to do anything to get ahead." The same tenacity and brutality that won him boxing matches is shown to benefit him in the world of industry.

In case the symbolism of the boxing match was lost on anyone, the next cutaway features dotcom millionaire and owner of the Dallas Mavericks National Basketball Association franchise Mark Cuban, who waxes nostalgic for the good old days of free market capitalism:

> Back then, it was just pure competition—my brain against your brain; my effort against your effort. You just competed. That's the way they looked at business. ... It was just win or lose, and the best win.
>
> *(Palmer, White, & Magan, 2012)*

As Vanderbilt wins his boxing match, the narrative resumes: "His single ferry soon becomes a fleet of ships. ... Vanderbilt will become so synonymous with shipping that his nickname soon becomes, 'The Commodore.'" The next cutaway features Jim Cramer, of the television show *Mad Money*, attributing Vanderbilt's success to his great vision:

> Vanderbilt recognized that what was going to be important is transporting goods from one place to another. And he had this idea that required infrastructure, and not infrastructure that the *government* was going to provide, but that *he* was going to provide.
> *(Palmer, White, & Magan, 2012)*

So, the series explains, "over the next 40 years, Vanderbilt builds the largest shipping empire in the world."

The same vision that led Vanderbilt to become a shipping magnate leads him to abandon the industry. He sees that the establishment of cross-country railroad lines will undermine the importance of shipping and, therefore, sells off his holdings and invests his wealth into railroads. In another cutaway, former General Electric CEO Jack Welch claims that Vanderbilt had an element of success that not many possess: "the ability to see around corners" (Palmer, White, & Magan, 2012). As a train chugs into a picturesque frontier station, the narrator details the result of Vanderbilt's incredible vision: he becomes the richest man in America, amassing more than $68 million. But in the rough and tumble world of industrial capitalism, no one is safe for long.

Vanderbilt's attempts to build a railroad empire soon put him into several contests of wills with other railroad companies. His competitors believe that he has been weakened by grief over the death of his son and refuse to negotiate. In a quick cutaway, Donny Deutsche lectures the audience: "People are always rooting for very successful people to fail. The day people are not taking shots at you, it means that you are not on top anymore" (Palmer, White, & Magan, 2012). But Vanderbilt is not done yet. He stares icily out the window of a parlor. He unfurls a map of the railroads across a large desk, stares intently, and resolves, "If they want a war, I'll give them a war."

A speeding train grinds to a halt over a tall bridge. Meanwhile, Vanderbilt orders his remaining son: "I want you to close the Albany bridge" (Palmer, White, & Magan, 2012). Vanderbilt holds the city of New York hostage, refusing to allow his competitors access to the all-important city. As passengers are instructed to exit a stranded train, Vanderbilt chomps on the cigar and intones, "We're going to watch them bleed." Unable to deliver cargo to the most important destination in the country, Vanderbilt's competitors begin to fail. As the stock prices of those railroads tank, Vanderbilt bides his time playing poker. When the stocks hit bottom, he instructs his son to purchase every share available, staging a hostile takeover of his competitors. An animated map of the United States reflects a growing network of rail as the narrator describes this economic expansion in cultural terms: the railroads are "tying the country together in a way that just 15 years earlier was unimaginable." And better yet, they are "providing over 180,000 jobs." "Laying tracks," viewers learn, "becomes America's engine for unprecedented growth."

This turns out to be the zenith of Vanderbilt's time in the show's spotlight, for he is soon outsmarted by Jay Gould and Jim Fisk, who exploit a legal loophole to dilute the value of stock that Vanderbilt purchases, ultimately selling him more than $7 million in increasingly worthless paper. Vanderbilt knows he's beaten and turns his attention to the oil that will soon fill those railroad cars. In the process, he gives John D. Rockefeller his opportunity.

Rockefeller

As with Vanderbilt, the series makes the case for Rockefeller's work ethic and character by flashing back in time to show us his formative years. As young John watches thin soup being ladled into bowls in the kitchen of his working-class childhood home in Cleveland, Ohio, the narrator explains that "he hungers for something bigger, and he knows it isn't going to be handed to him" (Palmer, White, & Magan, 2012). Viewers next see the young Rockefeller slicing up fudge and selling the candy to his classmates in order to subsidize his family's meager budget. Next, John watches from the wings as his father "Devil Bill" Rockefeller, a small-time con man, hawks snake oil to a roomful of curious onlookers. Afterward, the man packs his things (including the few dollars young John had earned selling candy) and imparts one piece of worldly knowledge before abandoning the family: "Never trust anybody, son—not even me."

The story flashes forward to Rockefeller's mid-20s. The narrator explains the interim: "With his father gone, Rockefeller is forced to quit school and get a job to support his mother and siblings. His work ethic and intuition will become the building blocks for the American Dream" (Palmer, White, & Magan, 2012). In the next cutaway, U.S. Senator John D. Rockefeller IV describes his great-grandfather as "an absolutely brilliant businessman. ... And there's an ethic in the Rockefeller family of hard work." Back to the narrative, viewers see Rockefeller at his desk "stuck in a dead end job" and seeking a "big idea."

Rockefeller gets his big idea when his church service is interrupted by the sound of men outside striking oil. As he gazes upon the gusher, the voice of Mark Cuban narrates Rockefeller's insight: "I think entrepreneurs and certain businesspeople just look at life and look at things that are changing and are able to see those things and say, 'I can create a business out of that'" (Palmer, White, & Magan, 2012). "Rockefeller realizes oil has the potential to change the world," the narrator explains, "and make him rich in the process." Ultimately though, Rockefeller does not drill for oil (a risky enterprise) but decides to make his money refining oil. He invests his entire worth into building the first refinery.

When Vanderbilt offers Rockefeller a deal that will give him an enormous amount of business, he accepts it, even though he is aware that his refinery cannot live up to the terms of the contract. In the next cutaway, Donald Trump teaches:

> You have to be smart, you have to have vision, you have to have all of these different things. But the most successful people are the people that have the right idea but never, ever quit or gave up. The people that really succeed in life are those that don't quit.
> *(Palmer, White, & Magan, 2012)*

Rockefeller attracts investors by marketing his product on the basis of its purity and safety and, thereby, pumping up demand from a public concerned about the risk of fire.

Soon, Rockefeller's exclusive deal with Vanderbilt is not enough to fuel his business aspirations. He plays the railroads against each other and ultimately gets a far better rate for shipping his oil. He takes those profits and begins buying out his competitors. "His intent is simple," the narrator states. "He wants to own every refinery in the country. It's a concept that's been impossible to execute. Today, we know it as a monopoly" (Palmer, White, & Magan, 2012). Rockefeller's great-grandson returns for another cutaway: "Creating monopolies—crushing the opposition—part of me says he did that because it was there to be done, that he could do it better than anybody else, and he made a bloody fortune out of it." As Rockefeller strides purposefully toward the screen, the narrator summarizes the state of things: "By the time he's finished, Rockefeller controls 90% of the North American oil supply."

When Vanderbilt unites with his competitors to fight back against Rockefeller's growing power, the series intones, "the move is nothing short of war" (Palmer, White, & Magan, 2012). As he walks through his Cleveland refinery, Rockefeller is struck by inspiration. Rockefeller realizes that the pipes that transport the oil through his refinery could just as well be used to transport it over very long distances, thereby cutting the railroads out of his business entirely. As Rockefeller stares at a map of the region, another scene is edited in through a cross-fade: a laborer hurls a pick into the earth, a pair of hands roll a large pipe into a freshly dug trench, another pair turns a wrench. Viewers are witnessing the rollout of Standard Oil's pipeline. The series underscores the stakes of this audacious move: "The pipeline will require a massive investment and incredible risk. But if he gets it right, Rockefeller will be able to do what he loves to do most—win." Mark Cuban identifies this as a common feature in great businesspeople: "You're willing to do things that other people aren't willing to do. Everybody's got ideas and ambitions, but most people aren't willing to cross that line. And I think an entrepreneur that's successful—that's your nature." The music swells, the men building the pipeline freeze, and the shot is replaced with a black and white photograph of Rockefeller's completed pipeline. The narration focuses on the magnitude of the achievement: "Rockefeller's workers labor around the clock, blasting through the countryside and laying over a mile and a half of pipeline every day." Jack Welch returns to extract a lesson from the episode:

> Business, in the end, is understanding the playing field: who's on it, what their strengths are, what their weaknesses are, and what is your checkmate play to top'em and nail'em. And so you're always in that competitive game—you're looking at innovation, you're looking at leapfrogging, trying to get ahead of them. You're never complacent, you're semi-paranoid about what they're doing. That's what the game is all about.
> *(Palmer, White, & Magan, 2012)*

Carnegie

Carnegie's success begins with a flashback to his youth, where a 12-year-old Andrew is required to help support his family by working for a local railroad. He earns the favor of the company's president, Thomas Scott, and begins working as his personal assistant, couriering correspondence. Carnegie biographer H. W. Brands describes the genesis of Carnegie's success:

> He realizes fairly early on that he's smart. He discovers in himself an ambition, and when Andy Carnegie showed the intelligence, showed the nerve to take on some of the responsibilities, Scott realized that this was somebody to cultivate, somebody to nurture.
> *(Palmer, White, & Reams, 2012)*

As Carnegie and Scott stride through a rail yard, the narrator pushes the story along: Scott sees Carnegie's potential and swiftly promotes him through the company until he is the manager of the firm, overseeing its expansion into the western frontier.

As Scott's right-hand man, Carnegie is tasked with building a bridge across the mighty Mississippi River. Initially flummoxed, Carnegie is forced to innovate in order to build the mile-long structure. Although no one has ever built a bridge this large before, the narrator explains, "Carnegie knows there's no reward without risk. He invests everything he has into the bridge" (Palmer, White, & Reams, 2012). "Andy Carnegie stepped up," H. W. Brands agrees. "He decided he could do it. One striking thing about Carnegie—and this is true of the great entrepreneurs—they're willing to take risks." Carnegie and an employee stand in an office considering various options. None seem large or strong enough for the task. Their preferred design, a cantilevered construction, will not withstand the force of the current of the Mississippi. Carnegie stares out a nearby window, and then insists, "Nothing's impossible." In a cutaway, AOL founder Steve Case instructs viewers:

> You have to be patient, to have perseverance—having a sense of where you want to go, and having the passion to still believe in your idea even when everybody else is saying, "Why waste your time on this?"
>
> *(Palmer, White, & Reams, 2012)*

Walking through town, Carnegie comes upon a man hammering steel. He remembers the engineer's concerns about the need for stronger materials. A montage depicts Carnegie and his engineer deep in deliberation, the mechanical presses forging metal, and the hammering of iron. Carnegie's biographer describes his state of mind:

> He's looking into the future. He looks across the Mississippi and he sees a bridge. And he's able to see that future, and then willing to have enough confidence in his vision to put everything he's got into it. And he's willing to convince others that he knows what that future is going to be.
>
> *(Palmer, White, & Reams, 2012)*

Carnegie innovates—he travels to different mills, visits with chemists, and ultimately embraces Henry Bessemer's new manufacturing technology to produce a steel bridge that can span the mighty river. "At just 33," the series narrates, "Andrew Carnegie is poised to realize the impossible: building the first major bridge to span the Mississippi River, uniting America." Though beset by delays and cost overruns, Carnegie succeeds beyond his wildest dreams, becoming a steel magnate.

Analysis

Upon consideration, three recurring themes deserve critical attention: (1) the story's continual articulation of industrial capitalism and its products with America, American progress, and Americanism; (2) the moral training the story provides viewers for success in life—training that entirely effaces the significance of race, class, gender, sexuality, and all other collective identities; and (3) the near total erasure of labor, particularly of the armies of men and women who made these "great men" possible.

Articulating Industrial Capitalism with Americanism

The most significant ideological work done here consists in the way that *The Men Who Built America* conflates economic freedom (at least insofar as anyone can claim laissez-faire capitalism as a kind of economic freedom) with political and legal freedom. One might expect a discussion of the "men who built America" to include Thomas Jefferson, John Adams, or Benjamin Franklin. They and the other "founding fathers" drafted the Declaration of Independence and thereby set the United States on its course. Men like Martin Luther King, Jr., and John F. Kennedy might also be likely protagonists. But over and again, this series implies that what is important and enduring about the United States is not its insistence upon human rights or the rule of law, but capitalism and the products of our capitalist economy. Perhaps no one underscores this point more clearly than future President Donald J. Trump, who claims in the series premier that, in the last 50 years, the United States built the world. What Mr. Trump appears to mean is that, in the late twentieth century, the United States successfully exported precisely the kind of free market worldview celebrated here to vulnerable states around the globe.

From the outset, the narrative elevates these businessmen to the level of Abraham Lincoln, a democratically elected politician and one of the nation's greatest leaders. The show continually depicts these titans of industry pulling the nation into the future. Where one might hope for a nation united by its commitments to freedom and equality, fortified by its constitution, Bill of Rights, communities, and citizens, or mobilized by its ambitions and values, the neoliberal nation is sustained by capitalism. Vanderbilt's railroad empire unites it; Rockefeller's Standard Oil lights it; Carnegie's steel raises it up. And although this chapter doesn't examine the narratives of the two other "men who build America" depicted in the series, it makes clear that J. P. Morgan's electrification modernizes it, and Ford's car gives it mobility. In each case, the products of industrial capitalism stand in for the goods formerly produced by the state, the community, and the public itself. According to this narrative, to be a U.S. citizen is to have modern infrastructure, to have the conveniences provided by industrial capitalism, and to be gainfully employed in the production of these wondrous products. Who could ask for more?

The Myth of the Self-Made Man

Few popular culture texts function more didactically than *The Men Who Built America*. At every turn, the series draws practical and moral lessons from the lives of these industrialists. The viewer is continually coached to take the right attitude toward life: one must take risks, even to the point of jeopardizing one's entire financial wellbeing; one must be ambitious; one must be preternaturally confident in the value of one's ideas; one must be willing to work harder than other people, and do things that others simply will not.

Viewers also receive specific lessons in entrepreneurial capitalism. As entrepreneurs, they must constantly be working to see "around corners" in the market, as Rockefeller did; they must anticipate what the public will need. They must focus on emerging technology, like Vanderbilt and Carnegie. They must remember to carefully manage their public image as the face of the firm, lest they suffer consequences akin to those experienced by Carnegie when his company's handling of strikers earned him negative press. They must be able to persuade others to see the value of their products.

The series furnishes viewers with two durable metaphors for making sense of the business world: the competitive game; and the fight. Viewers are instructed to survey the playing field, anticipate future moves, and look for a checkmate play. When, for example, the series recounts, with a shocking lack of moral evaluation, J. P. Morgan's use of extortion and subsequent hostile takeover of the Westinghouse Electric Company in his pursuit of Nikola Tesla's intellectual property, it is abundantly clear that "winning" is the only criterion for greatness. Likewise, viewers see that success means fighting hard; it means being ruthless, pulling no punches; and it means perpetually watching one's back. Business, they see, is about the survival of the fittest. If they are ever to succeed like Vanderbilt, they will have to make their opponents bleed like he did.

More broadly, the series traffics in the myth of the self-made man who pulls himself up by the bootstraps. In describing the lives and achievements of these industrialists, the series consistently elides the significance of family, community, class, race, gender, and all other manner of collective and structural phenomena in its relentless focus upon the individual characteristics and behaviors that defined these men. As such, they suggest to viewers that success in America is about individual effort, intellect, and vision. As Dana Cloud (1996) has pointed out, stories celebrating "individual triumph over humble beginnings" pervade our culture, operating "in the service of an inegalitarian economic order buttressed by an ideology of individual achievement and responsibility" (p. 115). In their nearly total effacement of collective and structural barriers to success, stories like these operate in the service of neoliberal ideology, imagining that each of us is an isolated, autonomous economic actor; that the free market rewards those who are smartest and work hardest; and that the government ought to stay out of the fight.

This series is undoubtedly about a handful of men's lives, but it is also clearly about masculinity writ large. The vignette featuring a young Cornelius Vanderbilt as a bare-knuckled fighter is only the most blatant of a litany of romantic depictions of hegemonic masculinity. Capitalism is a fight, a war, or a contest of wills; the men in these stories are depicted as seasoned warriors—they play poker, talk little, drink a lot, are preternaturally stoic, and take no prisoners. Over and again, viewers are coached that success in capitalism requires that they be aggressive, rational, and ruggedly individualistic; that they must be perpetually watching their backs, pushing forward, never comfortable, and always hungry for more. While these traits may well characterize many of the men and women who sit at the top of our largest companies, they do not necessarily produce the kind of families, neighborhoods, communities, or nations that we deserve. Indeed, the same aggression, indifference to the suffering of others, and endless hunger for more wealth have been implicated in the environmental and human destruction caused by the capitalist economic activity celebrated in this series.

Erasure of Labor and Working People as a Class

For as much as the series focuses on the wonders of industrial capitalism, it is marvelous in its omission of the men and women who did nearly all of the work. Labor is, for the most part, entirely disappeared from the narrative. In the universe constructed by this retelling of U.S. history, these great men rise above the country on the basis, apparently, of willpower and ingenuity alone. In the series' retelling of Cornelius Vanderbilt's rise from a poor boy to a captain of the shipping industry, the figure of the laborer—the man who toils for Mr. Vanderbilt, who captains his ships, who loads his freight, and who collects his payments—is disappeared entirely. Likewise, the tale of John D. Rockefeller's oil pipeline includes labor only incidentally and only insofar as statistics about the marvelous rate of production are mentioned. The series announces with wonder that Rockefeller's men worked around the clock and managed to lay more than a mile and a half of pipeline a day. "A mile and a half, can you imagine that?" the series asks. It does not mention what became of those men who worked around the clock or what they were paid to earn Mr. Rockefeller his advantage over the railroads.

Only in Carnegie's tale does labor become a subject of any significant attention. Viewers are treated to a dramatic reenactment of the confrontation between the workers in his plant and the army of mercenaries hired by his right-hand man, Henry Frick. Viewers learn that Carnegie's employees are working 12 hours a day, six days a week, despite frequent workplace accidents. This, it is explained by the business experts, was just "the way it was back then," implying that such working conditions do not still characterize a great deal of work under U.S. firms. Besides, the series teaches, it was the cost of yanking America into modernity. When Carnegie cuts pay and decertifies the union in pursuit of further profits, the men strike. Frick puts the strike down with the aid of his hired mercenaries, leading to multiple murders. Ultimately, the lesson viewers are offered from this episode is not about the treatment of labor but about publicity. Carnegie's mistake, the experts explain, was in not correctly managing the public's perceptions of his firm.

By focusing on the owners standing atop the U.S. economy and disappearing almost entirely the figure of the actual worker, the series perpetuates one of the fundamental distortions of neoliberal ideology. As Stuart Hall (1986) explained, to speak of the false consciousness produced by an ideology is not necessarily to call it a total fabrication; typically, ideology works by distorting, simplifying, and omitting. Capitalism is about entrepreneurs to be sure; but it is hardly only about them.

By turning Standard Oil into John D. Rockefeller or U.S. Steel into Andrew Carnegie, the series erases the armies of men and women who labored under relations of exploitation and coercion in order to make their bosses filthy rich. This omission is necessary, of course, for anyone who would hope to call capitalism as it was configured back then or now any kind of economic freedom. It is necessary, as well, for a worldview that would pretend that any of us is an isolated, agent operating on her or his own. This erasure of labor is necessary, further, for the series to render the works of these industrialists as overwhelmingly positive. Viewers might not swell with as much pride at hearing about Vanderbilt's conquering of the railroads, or Rockefeller's ruthless streamlining of his monopoly, if they understood the enormous human costs of those profit-seeking behaviors. The structural unemployment, the layoffs, the collusion to undercut wages—all are swept out of the frame so long as the worker is not a part of the story. In the end, the real men and women who built the United States of America—who erected bridges, laid bricks, forged metal, paved roads, dug trenches, riveted parts—turn out to be unimportant to the story of U.S. capitalism.

Conclusion

This chapter has offered a critical analysis of *The Men Who Built America* on the basis of the recognition that the series operates not only as a look back at the origins of our national greatness, but a model against which audiences are invited to judge the present. A growing population of the world's richest country find themselves downsized, laid off, underemployed, or stuck in the "gig economy" trying to make ends meet. And in this series, they are offered personal and national salvation by way of a return to the American values of hard work, dedication, competitiveness, and toughness that used to guarantee success to the best and boldest. They are invited to enroll themselves into the rags-to-riches stories; to identify with the captains of industry; and, most frighteningly, to confuse capitalism with Americanism.

When he began theorizing American civil religion in the late 1960s, Robert Bellah suggested that it was in a state of decline. In the following decades, sociologists would recognize it as a phenomenon with ebbs and flows. A critical rhetorical perspective situates American civil religion as a hegemonic discourse that must be perpetually renewed to contain the most salient contradictions posed by the status quo. In this view, periods that seem to evidence a decline in civil religion may often be more productively understood as periods of transformation. Civil religion is not dying so much as it has been challenged and has subsequently changed its stripes in order to remain vital in our neoliberal age. If we have traded George Washington, Abraham Lincoln, and Franklin D. Roosevelt for Henry Ford, John Rockefeller, and J. P. Morgan, we still have our deities; and if we have traded "one nation under God" for "the freer the market, the freer the people," we still have a common faith.

Those concerned to fight the pernicious effects of neoliberalism must find ways to intervene in the production of neoliberal subjectivity—to demonstrate the exploitation and coercion that mark life under capitalism for most of its subjects; to insist upon the collective and structural features of life that never seem to be a problem for the protagonists of our rags-to-riches stories; and to articulate a conception of Americanism that does not depend for its vitality on wealth and the production of things. After all, the men and women who actually built the United States of America did so much more than that.

Notes

1 The term is a reference to medieval barons, who were known to charge outrageous prices to those traveling through their territories. Applied to early U.S. industrialists, the term refers to "a set of avaricious rascals who habitually cheated and robbed investors and consumers, corrupted government, fought ruthlessly amongst themselves in general carried on predatory activities" (Bridges, 1958, p. 1).
2 We ought to recognize the conflation of the United States of America with America as more than shorthand. When the show speaks of the building of America, it really means to address the people, culture, and history of the United States. To confuse the two is to act as though the peoples, cultures, and histories of the rest of North, Central, and South America are unimportant or non-existent. The show is hardly alone in this substitution: one hears of Americans and Americanism, the American Dream, and so forth. When I have traveled abroad, Europeans have always introduced me as an American, not a US American. Some truth is probably revealed in the substitution as well: the United States enjoys such wealth, power, and cultural hegemony that its citizens and representatives are often able to act as if it were half the world or, sometimes, the whole thing.
3 Robert Reich (2015) has pointed out that there has never been a free market. For as long as economies have been a matter of public concern, ruling classes and state authorities have established the parameters of economic production, consumption, and exchange.
4 Affirming the consequent is a fallacy of logic in which one confuses the observation of an outcome or effect for proof that one possible cause of that effect has occurred. The person who, having observed puddles on the ground, assumes that it has rained commits this kind of error since it is possible for water to puddle on the ground without any rain. The neoliberal mistakenly believes that the creation and maintenance of "free markets" is an indicator or guarantor of legal and social freedom.
5 Although Friedman was cautious to note that this relationship is not guaranteed (despotic governments have sometimes permitted private enterprise), his followers tend to simplify matters. Where Friedman would claim that economic freedom as imagined by laissez-faire economics is most conducive to political and legal freedom, policymakers and thought leaders have acted as if capitalism *is* freedom.

References

Aune, J. A. (2002). *Selling the market: The rhetoric of economic correctness*. New York, NY: Guilford Press.

Bellah, R. (1967). Civil religion in America. *Daedalus, Journal of the American Arts and Science, 96*(1), 1–21.

Bridges, H. (1958). The robber baron concept in American history. *The Business History Review, 32*(1), 1–13.

Chang, H. (2012, October 24). We must stop protecting the rich from market forces. *The Guardian*. Retrieved from www.theguardian.com/commentisfree/2012/oct/24/stop-protecting-rich-market-forces

Chapman, R. (2009). American civil religion. In R. Chapman & J. Ciment (Eds.), *Culture wars: An encyclopedia of issues, voices, and viewpoints* (pp. 20–21). London, UK: Routledge.

Chomsky, N. (1992). *Deterring democracy*. New York, NY: Hill and Wang.

Chomsky, N. (1999). *Profit over people: Neoliberalism and global order*. New York, NY: Seven Stories Press.

Chomsky, N. (2004). *Hegemony or survival: America's quest for global dominance*. New York, NY: Henry Holt and Company.

Chomsky, N. (2007). *Failed states: The abuse of power and the failure of democracy*. New York, NY: Henry Holt and Company.

Cloud, D. L. (1996). Hegemony or concordance? The rhetoric of tokenism in "Oprah" Winfrey's rags-to-riches biography. *Critical Studies in Mass Communication, 13*, 115–137.

Conway, E. (2009, August 8). IMF puts total cost of crisis at £7.1trillion. *The Telegraph*. Retrieved from www.telegraph.co.uk/finance/newsbysector/banksandfinance/5995810/IMF-puts-total-cost-of-crisis-at-7.1-trillion.html

Friedman, M. (1962). *Capitalism and freedom*. Chicago, IL: University of Chicago Press.

Haines, G. (1989). *The Americanization of Brazil: A study of U.S. cold war diplomacy in the Third World, 1945–1954*. Wilmington, DE: SR Books.

Hall, S. (1986). The problem of ideology: Marxism without guarantees. *Journal of Communication Inquiry, 10*(2), 28–44.

Harvey, D. (2005). *A brief history of neoliberalism*. Oxford, UK: Oxford University Press.

Kay, C. (1993). For a renewal of development studies: Latin American theories and neoliberalism in the era of structural adjustment. *Third World Quarterly, 14*(4), 691–702.

Lipka, M. (2015, May 13). A closer look at America's rapidly growing religious 'nones'. *Pew Research Center*. Retrieved from www.pewresearch.org/fact-tank/2015/05/13/a-closer-look-at-americas-rapidly-growing-religious-nones/

Marty, M. E. (1976). *A nation of believers*. Chicago, IL: University of Chicago Press.

Mathisen, J. A. (1989). Twenty years after Bellah: Whatever happened to American civil religion? *Sociological Analysis, 50*(2), 129–146.

McChesney, R. W. (1998). Introduction. In N. Chomsky, *Profits over people: Neoliberalism and global order* (pp. 7–16). New York, NY: Seven Stories Press.

New York Times. (2006, December 20). President Bush's news conference. Retrieved from www.nytimes.com/2006/12/20/washington/20text-bush.html

Palast, G. (2012, April 29). IMF's four steps to damnation. *The Guardian*. Retrieved from www.theguardian.com/business/2001/apr/29/business.mbas

Palmer, K., White, D. C. (Writers), & Magan, R. (Director). (2012, October 16). A new war begins [Television series episode]. In P. Cabana, S. David, & D. Hoogstra (Executive Producers), *The men who built America*. New York, NY: History Channel.

Palmer, K., White, D. C. (Writers), & Reams, P. (Director). (2012, October 23). Bloody battles [Television series episode]. In P. Cabana, S. David, & D. Hoogstra (Executive Producers), *The men who built America*. New York, NY: History Channel.

Piketty, T. (2014). *Capital in the twenty-first century*. Cambridge, MA: Belknap Press.

Reich, R. (2015). *Saving capitalism: For the many, not the few*. New York, NY: Knopf Publishing.

Wilson, J. F. (1979). *Public religion in American culture*. Philadelphia, PA: Temple University Press.

PART IV
Consumers and Advertising

8
AFFIRMATIVE ADVERTISING AND THE MEDIATED FEELING RULES OF NEOLIBERALISM

Rosalind Gill and Akane Kanai

> *I'm worth it, you're worth it, we're all worth it.*
> *(The Prince's Trust and L'Oréal Paris, 2017)*

"Positive" messages like the one above are ubiquitous in contemporary media. From advertising to smartphone apps, and greetings cards to Facebook walls, Western cultures have become suffused with exhortations to wellness, self-belief and defiance. Indeed, for anyone with even limited media exposure or participation, it is hard to go for very long without encountering injunctions to "choose beautiful," "be your best self" or "dance like nobody's watching."

In this chapter, we consider the contemporary multiplication of affirmative and inspirational messages across media through the lens of an interest in neoliberalism. Extending contemporary understandings of neoliberalism beyond the familiar focus upon economic and political power, we seek to demonstrate how it operates as an everyday sensibility that shapes modes of relating to the self and others. Moreover, we will argue that neoliberalism is undergoing a profoundly psychological turn, centered on cultivating the qualities, dispositions and feelings needed to survive in neoliberal societies. Our argument here concerns what we call "neoliberal feeling rules" and the role played by media in producing, disseminating and policing them through ideas that are becoming so familiar and taken for granted that they constitute the background noise or wallpaper of neoliberalism—always there but rarely engaged or critiqued.

The primary aim of the chapter is to develop an understanding of neoliberalism as an everyday sensibility whose reach is extending ever wider, intensifying and increasingly operating through psychological modes. We seek to contribute to a literature about how media are implicated in this psychological turn. The chapter is divided into three broad parts. The first part develops our argument through a theoretical discussion that situates neoliberalism as a quotidian set of ideas, practices and feelings, but also as a technology that increasingly operates through forms of intimate psychological governance such as the promotion of self-esteem, happiness, positive mental attitude, etc. We argue for the need for greater attention to the affective and psychic life of neoliberalism, including its feeling rules (Hochschild, 1983). In the second part of the chapter, we consider how neoliberalism operates within and reinforces a context that is marked by multiple and intersecting power relations, but obscures them through abstract calls to inclusion and shared feelings of affirmation, and aspiration. In particular, we discuss the relationship between neoliberalism, gender and race. The third part of the chapter examines a media case study to illustrate our argument. We look at "body positive" or "love your body" advertising, which is notable for its representation of "diversity" as well as for its emphasis on confidence and self-esteem. Using an intersectional analysis (Collins & Bilge, 2016) we raise questions about the complicated visibilities in an advertisement for L'Oréal's current "All worth it" program, arguing it is organized around postfeminist and post-race optics in which visible differences are displayed only to be emptied of their significance. Finally, we conclude with a discussion of the need to extend theorizations of neoliberalism to attend to its psychic and affective operations in view of the re-articulation of multiple, overlapping forms of inequality into a set of decontextualized, individualized feelings.

Everyday Neoliberalism

Neoliberalism is conventionally understood as a macro-political and economic rationality characterized by privatization, deregulation, and a rolling back of the state from areas of social and welfare provision while instituting intensified surveillance and control of populations through other means. Although it is a "mobile technology" (Ong, 2006) that operates differently in different places across the world, and has also had different phases (Peck & Tickell, 2002), it enrolls whole populations into a world order in which "some lives, if not whole groups, are seen as disposable and redundant" (Giroux, 2008, p. 594). "Neoliberal rationality disseminates the model of the market to all domains and activities—even where money is not at issue—and configures human beings exhaustively as market actors, always, only, and everywhere as *homo oeconomicus*" (Brown, 2015, p. 31). The notion is highly contested both empirically and analytically, with some arguing that it is so broad as to be meaningless, and others, by contrast, perplexed by its ability to endure—to withstand war, global financial crisis and widespread opposition (Crouch, 2011; Mirowski, 2014). "Post-neoliberalism" is already becoming much debated (Davies & Gane, forthcoming).

For our purposes in this chapter, however, what is most significant is the way that neoliberal ideas have moved *beyond* the sphere of economic discourse and have come to saturate *everyday life*, constituting a kind of common sense that shapes the way we live, think and feel about ourselves and each other. Underpinned by ideas of choice, entrepreneurialism, competition and meritocracy, neoliberalism has insinuated itself into "the nooks and crannies of everyday life" (Littler, 2017, p. 9) to become a hegemonic, quotidian sensibility: the "new normal," we might say. The durability of neoliberalism, we suggest, owes much to this everydayness, the extent to which it has taken hold, become part of "us" rather than "them," as Stuart Hall (1988) has argued in another context. Neoliberalism's reach is extending ever deeper and wider, calling into being subjects who are rational, calculating and self-motivating, subjects who will make sense of their lives through discourses of freedom, responsibility and choice—no matter how constrained they may be (e.g., by poverty or racism). Neoliberalism's fantasy is that we are authors of our own destiny. It works on a kind of compulsory individualism (Cronin, 2000) in which languages of structural inequality are rendered unintelligible.

The media have been central to this in multiple ways: constructing the individual as an entrepreneurial and responsibilized subject invested in making over their life (see, e.g., Ouellette & Hay, 2008). A rich and flourishing body of research looking at self-help, reality game shows, makeover television and many other genres facilitates our understanding of the media's role in promoting and disseminating neoliberalism. Laurie Ouellette (2016) argues that lifestyle television has become central to neoliberal governmentality, constructing people "as the agents of their destinies" to achieve "goals of health, happiness, productivity and wellbeing through their individual choices and self-care practices" (p. 77). In turn, Nikolas Rose (2006) contends that lifestyle media shapes neoliberal citizens "who do not need to be governed by others, but will govern themselves, master themselves, care for themselves" (p. 150).

We suggest that neoliberalism increasingly works through a psychological register in which it seeks to makeover subjectivity itself, calling on us—often through media—to transform ourselves and remodel our interior lives. Lifestyle media call forth a self marked by vigilance and self-scrutiny, asking us to reflect upon what kind of friend/mother/boss we are, if we communicate well, whether the way we dress reflects the person we truly are, how confident we feel. Kim Allen and Anna Bull (2018) understand this in terms of a "turn to character" in contemporary neoliberal capitalism, which seeks to locate the source of problems—and their solutions—in individual subjectivity rather than in wider social structures or power relations. A growing body of work examines the way that neoliberalism calls into existence enterprising or entrepreneurial subjectivity (Littler, 2017)—in other words, what has elsewhere been dubbed the "psychic life" and "affective life" of neoliberalism (Gill, 2016; Scharff, 2016). In this way, questions of social injustice become systematically reformulated as psychological issues, as we are enjoined to become "resilient" or to "practice gratitude," and so on.

In producing entrepreneurial and responsible subjects, neoliberal individualization requires the working on and mobilizing of feelings in transparent and communicative ways that Eva Illouz (2007) notes is fundamental to emotional capitalism. It is for this reason that the affective and psychic life of neoliberalism does not necessarily translate into a cold self-absorption or a calculated indifference to others. A focus upon "positive psychology" and "positive mental attitude," and displaying and disseminating such attitudes among others, is increasingly central to neoliberal culture. Akane Kanai's (2017) research on the circulation of "relatable" femininities on Tumblr shows how women in this social media setting produce shareable feelings of endurance and mutuality, negotiating "intensified requirements to demonstrate resilient individuality whilst also enacting a pleasing, approachable femininity." Drawing on Arlie Hochschild's (1983) work, she argues that neoliberal "feeling rules" shape how young women ought to feel and communicate such feelings to others, inciting them to deal with difficulties through "humorous, upbeat quips" in which pain and struggle must be rendered into "safe, funny, 'girl-friendly' anecdotes" (p. 1). Relatability in this context is produced via the projection of a plausible, and pleasing notion of common experience to an unknown audience; it facilitates a sense of intimate togetherness through ironing out complex differences. In these kinds of "girlfriend" cultures (Winch, 2013), a utopia of sameness is offered that promises a collective proximity to the neoliberal, gendered benchmarking that measures the value of lives in unequal ways (Kanai, 2019). Analyzed in this way, the affective and psychic life of neoliberalism can be observed to mine practices of affirmation and validation to enable further investment in ongoing processes of self-actualization that are differentially available. Despite, or perhaps because of, the ongoing existence of embedded inequalities, neoliberal culture favors the production of felt *affinities* and *equivalences*, and a shared optimism in the meeting of one's future aspirations.

The Affective Production of Gender and Race in Neoliberalism

Thus far we have depicted neoliberalism as an everyday ideology that is centered on making individuals into self-optimizing subjects who will work hard, remain positive and take full responsibility for all aspects of their lives and well-being. Formally, the subject of neoliberalism is not "marked" by any distinguishing features. In its purest form neoliberalism applies to us all. Indeed, it systematically renders us all as *individuals* rather than as people who are gendered, raced, classed, (dis)abled, or connected to particular communities of identity or affiliation. In practice, however, neoliberalism is deeply implicated in asymmetrical power relations, and in particular in discursive formations relating to gender, race and class. Christina Scharff (2016) points out that the resources necessary to become an entrepreneurial subject are unevenly distributed. As Ringrose and Walkerdine (2008) have argued, the subject of self-invention is predominantly middle class. Moreover, while discourses of entrepreneurial self-help have appealed to members of minoritized groups such as black and migrant communities (Gilroy, 2013), the celebration of entrepreneurial subjectivities tends to reinforce inequality through the production of its "others" (Scharff, 2011; Williams, 2014). In relation to gender, some authors have argued that entrepreneurship is implicitly equated with the masculine (Bruni et al., 2004). Recent feminist research has, however, made the opposite argument and argued that women, and young women in particular, have become positioned as entrepreneurial subjects par excellence (McRobbie, 2009; Scharff, 2011; Walkerdine, 2003).

A growing body of work also discusses neoliberalism in relation to the ascendance of postfeminist, post-race and diversity discourses and their affective articulation of new subjectivities. It is worth looking briefly at each in turn.

Postfeminism is a term for capturing patterns and regularities in constructions of gender in contemporary culture, highlighting a number of relatively stable contours or features across multiple contexts. First, there is the pre-eminent emphasis upon *the body* as both the locus of womanhood and the key site of women's value (Winch, 2015). While the body has been said to represent a "project" for everyone in late modernity (Featherstone, 1990), for women the requirement to work on and perfect the body has reached such an intensity that it has been suggested that patriarchy has "reterritorialized" in the fashion and beauty complex (McRobbie, 2009). A key aspect of this is the implication that body work or "aesthetic labour" (Elias et al., 2017) must be regarded as freely chosen rather than culturally demanded: women are simply "pleasing themselves" rather than acting according to intense external pressures. This is in turn part of a wider thorough-going commitment to ideas of self-transformation, constituting a profoundly gendered—as well as racialized and classed—"makeover paradigm" that increasingly extends beyond the body to require the remodeling of all aspects of life. Hailed by discourses about self-determination, taking control and empowerment, the postfeminist subject is called upon to self-monitor, self-discipline and transform herself in a manner that is ever more intensive, extensive and psychologized (Gill, 2016). Indeed, it is the body's privileged place in the attainment of normative femininity today that, as we come to later, explains much of the significance and visibility of "love your body" discourses.

More broadly, postfeminism is implicated in the emergence of a set of distinctive *"new femininities"* (Gill & Scharff, 2011), as constructions of gender subjectivities and relations undergo a shift. A large body of work points to the synergies between postfeminism and neoliberalism. Indeed, it has been suggested that postfeminism may be—quite simply—gendered neoliberalism (Gill, 2016).

As women increasingly become responsible for both productive and reproductive labor, the figure of the aspirational entrepreneur has, arguably, become feminized. Concurrent with women's work historically traversing public and private spheres, an entrepreneurial orientation is demanded in all parts of life, personal and professional. Accordingly, the "entrepreneurialism" demanded is not limited to "sexiness," or to work that adds value to or capitalizes the body. In fact, these examples are instances of a much wider trend towards *entrepreneurial selfhood* that is intimately related to neoliberalism. This trend is marked by injunctions to work on, discipline, improve and maximize the self. In cultures marked by a postfeminist sensibility, notions of individual choice and agency are prominent and invoked repeatedly. One of the most profound consequences of this is the implication that women are no longer constrained by any social inequalities or power relations that might hold them back. In both the postfeminist sensibility and in cultures marked by neoliberalism more generally, languages for talking about structures and culture have been eviscerated. Any remaining power differences between women and men are understood as the outcome of individual choices, not of cultural forces or unfair socio-political systems.

Neoliberalism is also profoundly connected to discourses of race, and particularly to the prevalence of ideas of "post-race"—among them the idea that race is no longer a live and active political force in contemporary culture, along with the systematic erasure of connections between race and material inequality. Post-race discourses perform crucial work in "neoliberalizing race" (Goldberg, 2009), cutting off some subjects from entitlement to subjecthood and authorizing others to wealth and power. In turn, neoliberalism underwrites post-racial ideologies

> [m]oving racialization beyond, and away from, the logics of power and phenotype ... Recognizing some racial differences while disavowing others, it confers privilege on some racial subjects (the white liberal, the multicultural American, the fully assimilable black, the racial entrepreneur) while stigmatizing others (the "born again" racist, the overly race conscious, the racial grievant, the terrorist, the illegal).
>
> *(Mukherjee, 2016, p. 51)*

In this sense, as Sivamohan Valluvan (2016) argues, post-race "both incorporates as well as exceeds the explanatory terrain already serviced by the concepts of 'cultural racism' and/or 'new racism'" (p. 2241).

For these scholars, a post-race sensibility selectively draws on the significance of race and remakes it in a highly specific fashion. Race is flexibly dissociated from the continuing power of historical structures in order to hint at "inclusion" within squarely neoliberal paradigms. Such paradigms rearticulate race as a simplistic formula of visibility/invisibility and inclusion/exclusion within narrow terms of consumer citizenship (Banet-Weiser, 2007) that tend to reinstate whiteness and middle-class status as neutral norms and wealth as a universal, doable aspiration (Sullivan, 2014). When race is conceived in this flattened, ahistorical way, it becomes a feature like any other that can be freely interacted (Nakamura, 2008), transacted, alienated. Such framings couch difference in terms of brandable variation, or diverse markets with ultimately similar consumer needs (Banet-Weiser, 2012).

For Kafer (2013), similar deeply depoliticizing dynamics operate in the realm of disability in what she terms "billboard liberation." In the representation of disabled bodies as superhuman in achieving a "better life," again, strategically deploying "feel good" affects tethered to the possibility of individually overcoming barriers, disability becomes a character issue. Personal accountability and traits like determination and strength are foregrounded as the primary means of belonging, while disablist attitudes and material structures that shape people's experience of disability are rendered invisible. In a highly decontextualized fashion, the mediated figure of the "supercrip" (Kafer, 2013, p. 90)—the disabled person who is either the product of extremely low expectations (and thus, the object of benevolence) or extremely high expectations (and thus, inspirational)—is used to underpin a narrative of individualism and compliance with neoliberal values and a (usually heteronormative) vision of the "better life."

Mediating Neoliberalism: "Love Your Body" Advertising

Having set out some general arguments about the way that neoliberalism is at once a profoundly individualizing sensibility as well as one that is structured by gender and race (and also class, disability, sexuality and age), we now want to turn to explore how this materializes in everyday communication through an analysis of what has become known as "Love Your Body" advertising (Gill & Elias, 2014), which has also been understood through notions of the selling and commodification of empowerment (Heath & Potter, 2005), the marketing of self-esteem (Banet-Weiser, 2015), as "femvertising" or as part of a wider cult(ure) of confidence (Favaro, 2017; Gill & Orgad, 2015).

Love Your Body (LYB) advertising emerged in the 2000s, led by brands such as Dove, Always and Nike. In part a response to feminist critiques of the unattainable perfection of advertising images of women, and the role of brands in promoting unhealthily thin body types, the trend can be understood as one example of what Robert Goldman (1992) calls "commodity feminism"—a way of taking on feminist anger and offering it back in depoliticised and consumer-capitalism-friendly ways. Its development as a discursive and visual regime was also related to wider demands for advertising images that were more "authentic" or at least relatable, offering more accessible forms of "cool." The shift can be seen not only in advertising but across feminized media culture, with women's magazines increasingly highlighting "real" or "natural" bodies, and makeover shows promoting a new emphasis upon *feeling* good as well as looking good. The "nastiness" (McRobbie, 2004) of earlier shows such as *What Not to Wear* or *Ten Years Younger* has been replaced by the kinder and gentler tone of *How To Look Good Naked* or *Queer Eye*, with their focus less on losing weight or undergoing cosmetic surgery, than on building confidence and making the most of one's "assets," physical or otherwise.

In advertising, LYB is marked by several distinctive features. Interrupting the longstanding history of forms of address to women that focus on what is *wrong* (dry skin, lips not plump enough, hair lacking volume or shine) and how they can *improve*, LYB deploys a different strategy. Women are enjoined to build self-esteem, to "remember your incredible" (Weight Watchers) and to believe "you are more beautiful than you think" (Dove) through a series of messages that highlight female capacity ("this girl can"—Sport England), individually designed beauty standards ("my beauty, my say"—Dove) and defiance ("you're worth it"—L'Oréal; "let's shut down fat talk"—Special K). LYB advertising is characterized by its intention to produce positive affects, self-belief and gratitude. Formally, the genre is marked by a pared down aesthetic using large, minimally furnished open spaces, simple white or black clothing, frequent use of written as well as spoken text, and by a distinctive, powerful musical score. Indeed, music is used to mark emotional shifts within the advertisements, literally scoring the transition from self-doubt to self-confidence, from insecurity to empowerment. LYB texts are made to be shared virally, and this has been a significant driver of their success, with the most well-known advertisements—for example, Dove's Real Beauty Sketches, in which a police forensic artist draws two different pictures of women, one based on their self-descriptions and the other on what strangers say about them —attracting tens of millions of shares and views on YouTube, as we do the brands work for them, liking and passing on their commercial messages, often with our own powerful commentaries (e.g. "this made me cry").

These texts generate considerable ambivalence (Lynch, 2011; Murphy, 2013). They are both loved and hated, sometimes at the same time (see Gill & Orgad, 2017). They may be welcomed for the way they seem to interrupt the stream of hostile messages targeted at women, as well as for their emphasis upon individual self-worth and the idea that everyone has value. However, the trend has also been repeatedly criticized for espousing the very "fakeness" it ostensibly rejects—for example, recruiting models when it claims to use "ordinary people" or for using filters, make-up or photo retouching while claiming to be entirely natural (Murray, 2012). The ads have also been interrogated for relying upon the cultural pathologization of women's bodies and "re-citing" the hate speech they putatively challenge. This can be seen vividly in an ad for Special K cereal that repeatedly foregrounds hostile comments about women's bodies (with references to cellulite, fat thighs, etc.) while putting the case that we should "shut down fat talk." The fact that many of the same companies who have long been invested in getting women to hate their bodies—or at least to want to change them—are at the forefront of this trend also gives serious pause for concern (Johnson & Taylor, 2008; Murphy & Jackson, 2011). Indeed, the Special K ad campaigning against "fat talk" is accompanied by a link that takes one directly to a Body Mass Index (BMI) counter.

Perhaps more significant than all these criticisms is the way in which LYB messages underscore neoliberal sensibilities around individualism, personal responsibility and blame. LYB advertising at once suggests that low self-esteem or negative body image are trivial issues which can be easily resolved through an injection of positive thinking or self-belief, while also blaming women themselves for having "negative" feelings in the first place. The wider society and culture is exculpated as women are incited to take responsibility for their own self-worth and to see any doubts or insecurities as their own problem—nothing to do with a cultural context that constantly tells women they can never be pretty enough, thin enough, perfect enough. This is illustrated chillingly by Dove's "Patches" ad in which women are recruited to a "study" to see whether a "revolutionary new beauty patch" can make a difference to their self-esteem. Women are told to wear the patch—which resembles a hormone or nicotine patch—and to keep a video diary of whether they feel it is making a difference. After an allotted number of days, the women are brought back to the lab and asked about their progress. Most appear to have experienced a real shift and are shown talking about how the patch has made them feel more confident, show parts of their bodies they would usually hide, and attract compliments from others. The psychologist then asks if each woman would buy the beauty patch—nods of assent all round—and if they would have any interest in knowing what its transformative ingredients are. A patch is handed to each woman and she is asked to turn it over. On the other side is one word: "NOTHING."

Various reactions greet this revelation, but we are shown barely any expressions of anger about this humiliation enacted upon the women. Most women instead seem to express the desired messages that "it's all in my head," and "I have the power to change the way I feel about myself"—a move that presents pressures to conform to particular templates of normative femininity as entirely an individual and personal matter, even as it draws its participants and viewers into a moment of potential resistance or transgression by offering up a potential future self who can feel better if they recognize that change must result from their own individual and psychological work on themselves. We suggest that this type of advertising works on top of—rather than displacing—traditional exhortations to beauty. It is no longer enough to work on the body, disciplining, adorning, moisturizing, depilating and so on. LYB advertising also calls on women to work on their *subjectivity* (Murray, 2012; Rodrigues, 2012), to makeover their psychic life in order to become confident and happy subjects.

This, rather than offering a break from the relentlessness of feminine appearance norms, adds an additional punitive layer of regulation: you must now *feel good* as well as look good. As Dove puts it, "Beauty is a state of mind."

"I'm Worth It, You're Worth It, We're All Worth It": Advertising and Hollow Diversity

In this final section we will explore these dynamics in relation to one particular commercial message, a video for L'Oréal and The Prince's Trust, a charity founded in the United Kingdom in 1976 by Prince Charles to help young people struggling with employment, education and other forms of disadvantage. The video features the self-esteem and confidence messages discussed above. We look in particular at how "diversity" is mobilized in this video and what it is doing and undoing. One potent criticism levelled at LYB advertising has been that its pretensions to diversity are fake, that it offers a kind of "diversity paradox" (Rodrigues, 2012). Very often, we are cued to read an ad as representing a diverse range of people, but in reality the images vary only slightly from more conventional advertising. Dove ads, for example, claim to show a range of different body sizes, yet when looked at alongside images from the fat acceptance movement, the degree of variation from the advertising norm appears miniscule (Johnson & Taylor, 2008). Similarly, the hyperbolic claims about age, ethnic and (dis)ability variations are also often not matched by the reality of these ads. However, this is changing rapidly at the time of writing, with campaigns by H&M and Axe, in particular, self-consciously celebrating "differences" of race, religion, sexual orientation, (dis)ability and even gender—with greater use of trans and non-binary gender.

The #AllWorthIt campaign sponsored by L'Oréal and The Prince's Trust fits into this new shift, and this complicates the representation of diversity, displaying not so much a fake diversity as a *hollowing out of diversity*, in such a way that differences are shown only to be emptied of their significance and severed from histories that make them meaningful.

In #AllWorthit, (www.youtube.com/watch?v=iyHPD8dM3o4) a diverse range of young, attractive speakers who vary in age, body shape, race, gender, sexuality and ability is paired with inspirational affects, music and messages. Characterized by the simple mise en scène and style discussed above—stripped back space, monochrome clothing—the advertisement opens with its celebrity participants speaking to the camera in turn: "I'm worth it, you're worth it, we're all worth it." We then cut to the biggest celebrity of them all, Helen Mirren, striding onto the set, who says: "Famous words I know. But L'Oréal Paris has always believed that *everyone* is worth it." The others take up the script: L'Oréal is:

championing inclusivity and diversity because what makes us different is what makes us beautiful. And when we feel our most beautiful, it gives us the confidence to strive to be the best so that we can accomplish almost *anything*.

In the short, two-minute video, a range of bodies are arrayed—mainly women's—that speak of the importance of erasing self-doubt, building confidence and being "visible." There is little doubt that the advertisement is intended to "feel good," and as such, our critique is not related to authenticity as such, but to the ways in which affects associated with inclusiveness are mobilized in deeply depoliticizing ways that are harnessed to the production of value. The #AllWorthIt ad positions *invisibility*, being forgotten or excluded by brands, as one of the primary wrongs of consumer citizenship in a move that exemplifies Banet-Weiser's (2012) insight that culture and branding can no longer be neatly separated. As brands are now conceptualized as leaders of culture, L'Oréal's advertisement attests to the way in which certain discourses of "acceptance," "inclusion" and "self-worth" have become normatively attached to particular neoliberal projects.

Even in this "diverse" video, we suggest that the diversity bodies are not evenly represented. Despite the variation of the featured bodies, the video implicitly re-centers an immaculate, white, able-bodied femininity. This is enacted, first, through a focus on actress Helen Mirren and her authoritative voiceover of the major part of the ad copy. While we note Mirren is visibly older than the usual models L'Oréal employs in its branded imagery, she is still recognizably polished and glamorous in her role as ambassador for the Prince's Trust, and associated with significant levels of cultural capital more generally. Second, #AllWorthIt arranges the other actors in the video, all beautifully groomed and physically attractive, so as to primarily articulate *one* form of variation from a white, middle-class, able-bodied femininity as the implicit ideal, postfeminist subject of advertising. As such, each person in L'Oréal's vision is positioned as primarily having one difference: having a disability *or* being black *or* being "plus size" *or* being Muslim. Multiple differences are translated into a homogenous plane so that inequality is rearticulated as *one* individual difference from the norm—implicitly presented as a challenge—that can be overcome via self-belief, which is positioned as a simple, doable and uniting means through which we can all be #worthit.

Present in this video, we suggest, is the tendency less to erase difference than to aestheticize it. "Capital has fallen in love with difference," Martin Davidson (1992, p. 199) has argued, but in doing so it empties differences of their cultural, historical and political significance. Henry Giroux (1994, p. 189), discussing race in an earlier trend in advertising for Benetton, characterizes this as a form of "postmodern pedagogy" that renders "racial unity as a purely aesthetic category while eliminating racial conflict completely." A similar argument is made by Roopali Mukherjee (2016) in her brilliant "pre-history" of post-race, arguing that "post-race re-envisions the scriptures of colour blindness by firmly acknowledging a specified range of racial differences that serve to disavow any vestige of their consequence for anyone—of any race—who can fashion themselves as properly neoliberal subjects" (p. 50) One of the moves that post-racial discourses make, then, is in severing identity from history, and in the process erasing any sense of race as a "central organizing principle of American society" (2016, p. 61).

We see this vividly in the #AllWorthIt campaign, a post-race discourse par excellence, but also one that extends this dynamic to multiple differences—class, religion, disability. The ad is striking in making these forms of difference visible—and, in the case of classed regional accents (e.g., north of England), "hearable"—but the specificity of any particular identity is not addressed. Instead, paradoxically, the very differences that are foregrounded are also hollowed and homogenized through a combination of aesthetic means (make-up, clothes, stylization) and affective means (an upbeat emphasis upon self-worth and confidence) that renders everyone the same and that suggests that the interventions needed are uniform psychological programs (e.g., confidence training) rather than material, political, cultural or economic changes. In this way, the response to racism or classism or Islamophobia becomes to work on the self not work to change an unfair world. Yet, interestingly, this individual work is framed as a kind of defiance—a defiant self-belief that buys into ideas of commodified rebellion (Heath & Potter, 2005) and borrows from the tropes of political activism as when the people in the ad paint over the word "self-doubt," rewriting it as "self-worth" in a graffiti-style intervention.

What we see within this advertisement, then, is something more complicated than fake or pseudo diversity. Rather, we see an attempt to use and strategically deploy images of minoritized groups (people of color, disabled people, Muslims, queer people) in commercial culture to "take diversity into account" only to empty any particular differences of their meaning and social significance. As Anandi Ramamurthy and Kalpana Wilson (2013) have argued in relation to other advertisements, this is demonstrably both a way of responding to activisms and social justice movements around race (and also class, sexuality and disability) while at the same time representing an upgrading of global capitalism in neoliberal forms.

This chapter has shown the way in which neoliberalism is also tied into a powerful affective technology mobilized around individual self-worth. In a neoliberal consumer culture that is blind to historical and structural difference, an affective mix of optimism, inspiration and hope is deployed to produce subjects that, despite their differences, are positioned in a formation of homogenous individuality, all made intelligible via their attachment to the same aspirations and dreams. In such a context, the language of politicized differences is increasingly difficult to invoke. Yet the fact that subjects who have previously been systematically erased by advertising are represented here pushes us to move our critiques beyond simple notions of visibility/invisibility or positive versus negative images, and to ask instead about the *kinds of visibilities* facilitated by this kind of discourse. It seems to us that in this moment, "within the logic of restructured global capital markets, cultural differences have to be both acknowledged and depoliticized in order to be contained" (Giroux, 1994, p. 195). They must be "stripped of all social and political antagonisms," and we must all *feel* "we're worth it" while leaving an unjust social system intact and unquestioned. This new advertising trend mobilizes ideas about the "benign nature of contemporary capitalism" and "its potential as a force for the advancement of global equity" (Ramamurthy & Wilson, 2013, p. 2) and it does so, we have suggested, through a neoliberal, individualistic and psychologized form of address that requires urgent challenge.

Conclusion

In this chapter, we have examined the role that the media play in winning consent for neoliberalism as an ongoing political, economic, cultural, and psychological project, with a particular focus on a recent genre of "body positive" and apparently "diverse" advertising. The chapter has made three main contributions. First, it has sought to argue that neoliberalism is productively understood as a quotidian or everyday sensibility, deeply shaped by circulating media, from lifestyle TV to Tumblr posts to smartphone apps or Instagram feeds. Secondly, we have highlighted our contention that neoliberalism increasingly operates not just as an "everyday" sensibility but as a *psychological* technology, seeking to shape the ways we think and feel about ourselves and others. By looking at a genre of advertising ostensibly designed to cultivate self-esteem and feelings of self-belief and body love, we have offered one compelling example of the way a form of mediated neoliberalism seeks to engage our affective and psychic lives. With a particular attentiveness to the way that neoliberalism is connected to discourses of postfeminism and post-race, we have offered a critique of this form of advertising, arguing that it is not only implicated in a novel form of regulating subjects (to be positive, confident, etc.), but that it also hollows out diversity, displaying "difference" only to erase its significance in a field of power relations.

Although we have looked in detail at only one case study, we believe our analysis has wider relevance in understanding the media forms of contemporary neoliberal culture—both in terms of its attempts to shape our feelings and dispositions, and in the way it appropriates and empties diversity. More specifically, we suggest that the L'Oréal campaign we have looked at may be understood as a development or evolution of the genre of advertising that has come to be known as LYB, in which the commodification of difference is at the core, tied to a "defiant" pose of "rule-breaking." These tropes can be seen in a variety of recent and current advertising campaigns for Dove, Apple iPhone X, Axe, H&M and River Island. Since 2016, advertisements for these brands center a self-conscious celebration of people coded as "different" from normative white, cis-gendered, able-bodied culture—whether because they wear hijab or turban, because they are trans or gender-fluid, or because they adopt "alternative" forms of self-styling, such as extensive tattoos or piercings. Alongside this is a parallel emphasis upon "breaking the rules," being true to yourself and speaking back proudly and assertively to a (never-specified) authoritarian culture. "Breaking the rules" advertising, we suggest, may constitute a new mode of engaging (particularly youthful) consumers in media-saturated neoliberal societies, offering novel representations of gender, race, class, sexuality and disability in ways which remain troubling precisely because their affective tenor speaks to a better life that gestures towards, and yet erases, the continuing forms of inequality that underpin this diversity. As Kafer (2013) notes, when a campaign is seen to be "not about politics but hope and community and goodness," "what oppositional stance could one possibly take to the texts?" (p. 98). It is important, we argue, to continue working "against the grain" (Kafer, 2013, p. 99) in attending to the affective and psychic life of neoliberalism and the kinds of inequalities it ignores and reinstates.

References

Allen, K., & Bull, A. (2018). Following policy: A network ethnography of the UK character education policy community. *Sociological Research*. Advance online publication. doi:10.1177/1360780418769678

Banet-Weiser, S. (2007). What's your flava? Race and postfeminism in media culture. In: Yvonne Tasker and Diane Negra (Eds.), *Interrogating postfeminism: Gender and the politics of popular culture* (pp. 201–226). Durham, UK: Duke University Press.

Banet-Weiser, S. (2012). *Authentic TM: The politics of ambivalence in a brand culture*. New York, NY: New York University Press.

Banet-Weiser, S. (2015). "Confidence you can carry!": girls in crisis and the market for girls' empowerment organisations. *Continuum, 29*(2), 182–193.

Brown, W. (2015). *Undoing the demos: Neoliberalism's stealth revolution*. New York, NY: Zone Books.

Bruni, A., Gherardi, S., & Poggio, B. (2004). Doing gender, doing entrepreneurship: An ethnographic account of intertwined practices. *Gender, Work & Organization, 11*(4), 406–429.

Cronin, A. M. (2000). Consumerism and compulsory individuality: Women, will and potential. In S. Ahmed, J. Kilby, C. Lury, & M. McNeil (Eds.), *Transformations: Thinking through feminism* (pp. 273–287). London, UK: Routledge.

Crouch, C. (2011). *The strange non-death of neo-liberalism*. Cambridge, MA: Polity Press.

Davidson, M. P. (1992). *The consumerist manifesto: Advertising in postmodern times*. New York, NY: Routledge.

Davies, W., & Gane, N. (forthcoming). Post-neoliberalism? *Theory, Culture & Society*. [Special Issue].

Elias, A., Gill, R., & Scharff, C. (Eds.). (2017). *Aesthetic labour: Rethinking beauty politics in neoliberalism*. London, UK: Palgrave Macmillan.

Favaro, L. (2017). "Just be confident girls!": Confidence chic as neoliberal governmentality. In A. Elias, R. Gill, & C. Scharff (Eds.), *Aesthetic labour: Rethinking beauty politics in neoliberalism* (pp. 283–299). London: Palgrave Macmillan.
Featherstone, M. (1990). *Consumer culture and postmodernism*. London: Sage.
Gill, R. (2016). Post-postfeminism? New feminist visibilities in postfeminist times. *Feminist Media Studies, 16*(4), 610–630.
Gill, R., & Elias, A. (2014). "Awaken your incredible": Love your body discourses and post-feminist contradictions. *International Journal of Media and Cultural Politics, 10*(2), 179–188.
Gill, R., & Orgad, S. (2015). The confidence culture. *Australian Feminist Studies, 30*(86), 324–344.
Gill, R., & Orgad, S. (2017). Confidence culture and the remaking of feminism. *New Formations, 91*(91), 16–34.
Gill, R., & Scharff, C. (Eds.). (2011). *New femininities: Postfeminism, neoliberalism and subjectivity*. Basingstoke, UK: Palgrave Macmillan.
Gilroy, P. (2013). "… We got to get over before we go under …" Fragments for a history of black vernacular neoliberalism. *New Formations, 80/81*, 23–38.
Giroux, H. A. (1994). *Consuming social change: The United Colors of Benetton*. London: Routledge.
Giroux, H. A. (2008). Beyond the biopolitics of disposability: Rethinking neoliberalism in the new gilded age. *Social Identities, 14*(5), 587–620.
Goldberg, D. T. (2009, May). Neoliberalizing race. *Macalester Civic Forum, 1*(1), 14.
Goldman, R. (1992). *Reading ads socially*. London and New York: Routledge.
Goldman, R. (2005). *Reading ads socially*. New York, NY: Routledge.
Hall, S. (1988). The toad in the garden: Thatcherism among the theorists. In C. Nelson & L. Grossberg (Eds.), *Marxism and the interpretation of culture* (pp. 35–57). Champaign, IL: University of Illinois Press.
Heath, J., & Potter, A. (2005). *The rebel sell: Why the culture can't be jammed*. Chichester, UK: Capstone.
Collins, P. H., & Bilge, S. (2016). *Intersectionality*. Chichester, UK: John Wiley & Sons.
Hochschild, A. (1983). *The managed heart: The commercialisation of human feeling*. Berkeley, CA: University of California Press.
Illouz, E. (2007). *Cold intimacies: The making of emotional capitalism*. Cambridge, MA: Polity Press.
Johnson, J., & Taylor, J. (2008). Feminist consumerism and fat activists: A comparative study of grassroots activism and the dove real beauty campaign. *Signs: Journal of Women in Culture and Society, 33*(4), 941–966.
Kafer, A. (2013). *Feminist, queer, crip*. Bloomington, IN: Indiana University Press.
Kanai, A. (2017). On not taking the self seriously: Resilience, relatability and humour in young women's Tumblr blogs. *European Journal of Cultural Studies*. Advance online publication. doi:10.1177/1367549417722092
Kanai, A. (2019). *Gender and relatability in digital culture: Managing affect, intimacy and value*. Basingstoke, UK: Palgrave Macmillan.
Littler, J. (2017). *Against meritocracy: Culture, power and myths of mobility*. London, UK: Routledge.
Lynch, M. (2011). Blogging for beauty? A critical analysis of operation beautiful. *Women's Studies International Forum, 34*(6), 582–592.
McRobbie, A. (2004). Notes on "What Not to Wear" and post-feminist symbolic violence. *The Sociological Review, 52*(s2), 97–109.

McRobbie, A. (2009). *The aftermath of feminism: Gender, culture and social change*. London: Sage.

Mirowski, P. (2014). *Never let a serious crisis go to waste: How neoliberalism survived the financial meltdown*. London, UK: Verso.

Mukherjee, R. (2016). Antiracism limited: A pre-history of post-race. *Cultural Studies, 30*(1), 47–77.

Murphy, R. (2013). *(De)Constructing "Body Love" discourses in young women's magazines*. Unpublished doctoral thesis, Victoria University of Wellington.

Murphy, R., & Jackson, S. (2011). Bodies-as-image? The body made visible in magazine love your body content. *Women's Studies Journal, 25*(1), 17–30.

Murray, D. P. (2012). Branding "real" social change in Dove's campaign for real beauty. *Feminist Media Studies, 13*(1), 83–101.

Nakamura, L. (2008). *Digitizing race: Visual cultures of the internet*. Minneapolis, MN: University of Minnesota Press.

Ong, A. (2006). *Neoliberalism as exception: Mutations in citizenship and sovereignty*. Durham, NC: Duke University Press.

Ouellette, L. (2016). *Lifestyle TV*. New York, NY: Routledge.

Ouellette, L., & Hay, J. (2008). Makeover television, governmentality and the good citizen. *Continuum, 22*(4), 471–484.

Peck, J., & Tickell, A. (2002). Neoliberalizing space. *Antipode, 34*(3), 380–404.

Ramamurthy, A., & Wilson, K. (2013). Racism, appropriation and resistance in advertising. *Colonial Advertising & Commodity Racism, 4*, 69.

Ringrose, J., & Walkerdine, V. (2008). Regulating the abject: The TV make-over as site of neo-liberal reinvention toward bourgeois femininity. *Feminist Media Studies, 8*(3), 227–246.

Rodrigues, S. (2012). Undressing homogeneity: Prescribing femininity and the transformation of self-esteem in how to look good naked. *Journal of Popular Film and Television, 40*(1), 42–51.

Rose, N. (2006). Governing "advanced" liberal democracies. In A. Sharma & A. Gupta (Eds.), *The anthropology of the state: A reader* (pp. 144–162). Malden, MA: Blackwell.

Scharff, C. (2011). Disarticulating feminism: Individualization, neoliberalism and the othering of "Muslim women." *European Journal of Women's Studies, 18*(2), 119–134.

Scharff, C. (2016). The psychic life of neoliberalism: Mapping the contours of entrepreneurial subjectivity. *Theory, Culture & Society, 33*(6), 107–122. doi: 10.1177/0263276415590164

Sullivan, S. (2014). *Good white people: The problem with middle class white anti-racism*. Albany, NY: SUNY Press.

The Prince's Trust and L'Oréal Paris (2017). #AllWorthIt. Accessible from www.youtube.com/watch?v=iyHPD8dM3o4 (accessed December 4, 2018).

Valluvan, S. (2016). What is "post-race" and what does it reveal about contemporary racisms? *Ethnic and Racial Studies, 39*(13), 2241–2251.

Walkerdine, V. (2003). Reclassifying upward mobility: Femininity and the neo-liberal subject. *Gender and Education, 15*(3), 237–248.

Williams, R. (2014). Eat, pray, love: Producing the female neoliberal spiritual subject. *The Journal of Popular Culture, 47*(3), 613–633.

Winch, A. (2013). *Girlfriends and postfeminist sisterhood*. Basingstoke, UK: Palgrave Macmillan.

Winch, A. (2015). Brand intimacy, female friendship and digital surveillance networks. *New Formations, 84*, 228–245.

9

KITCHEN PORN

Of Consumerist Fantasies and Desires

C. Wesley Buerkle

In 1973, The *New York Times* coined the expression "porno chic" to describe a broadened cultural acceptance of pornography in the United States, marked by open discussion of pornography and attendance at adult theaters (Blumenthal, 1973). Interestingly, some years later, "porn" has been casually attached to any media consumption rooted in gazing desirously: stunning pictures of far-flung destinations (travel porn); transfixing scenes of ornamental flora and landscapes (garden porn); evocative images of literature begging to be read (book porn). In fact, you could say it has become quite *chic* to openly fantasize about that which one does not (yet?) have. This pornographic gazing and fantasizing, I argue, is endemic of a neoliberal sensibility that presents to individuals the possibility that personal happiness and fulfillment comes from choosing to participate in the marketplace. Given most people's lack of the tangible resources of time and money required to achieve or purchase these objects of desire—travelling the globe or cultivating the ideal garden—gazing allows citizens to participate in the marketplace by fantasizing about consumption. Such fantasies are, in fact, much like sexual pornography in that they focus on consuming images of pleasure as part of the pursuit of an idealized self.

Pornography presents a unique rhetorical form different from most texts: it lacks a strong narrative arc and engages desires that the text stimulates but never sates. As such, it follows a rhetorical form of consumption, a genre that fails to satisfy its audience, requiring its members to satisfy themselves. Using Burke's (1968) work on form, I illustrate how the rhetoric of consumption is unique in that it violates the expectation that a text will provide resolution to the conflict it has created, thereby engaging the audience to release its own tension. I then explore the overlapping aspects of traditional pornography and neoliberalism—both focus on desires and utopias of abundance—and connect these to consumer porn by focusing on Food52, a cooking blog and retailer whose motto, "Eating thoughtfully, living joyfully," signals relationships between its advice/merchandise and the lifestyle it promotes. This lifestyle is founded on classist and postcolonial sensibilities of whiteness that define the consumer as a feminine, white sophisticate interested in notions of history, tradition, and refined tastes that can be experienced through the purchase or fantasies of the right products. As such, consumer porn meets the needs of industry by defining consumer desires for them.

Pornography and the Neoliberal Citizen

The casual complaint that the proliferation of pornography in the U.S. signals the loss of a previous morality is true insofar as it suggests a cultural change from public discourses of sexuality emphasizing social contribution to discourses emphasizing recreation (Buerkle, 2011). With a shift from industrial, production-oriented, Fordist ideals of socio-economic values and citizen responsibility to the marketplace, consumer-oriented, neoliberal principles, now dominant, U.S. culture has embraced a key attitude of pornography—pleasure yourself. The profusion of available sexual pornographic materials speaks to an emphasis upon individuals satisfying their own desires, often in the marketplace. Tuck (2009) puts it succinctly: "We are a profoundly self-pleasuring society at both a metaphorical and material level" (p. 78).

The economics of pleasure is closely linked with neoliberalism, in which an economy is left largely unregulated, allowing the marketplace to sort out the best, most efficient means of everyone getting ahead (Dean, 2008). An outgrowth of this thinking for the individual has been an emphasis on one's need to improve the self to be successful. In this way, success and happiness become rooted in following *de rigueur* tastes that regularly involve expending money in the marketplace (Sender, 2006). Effective participation in society also means knowing how to sculpt one's public identity through consumptive choices (Ouellette, 1999) that reflect back on one's character (Winslow, 2010). Schor (2011) adds that success stems not from mere participation as consumers but "competitive consumption" in which individuals emulate those they see above them in an attempt to further their own status (p. 207). Neoliberalism also encourages us to give ourselves over to hopeful fantasies and illusions of idealized identities, seducing us with the hope that if we will just do our consumerist part, all will be well (Dean, 2008). For example, reality and other improve-your-life television claim that social, romantic, and financial success are possible through proper market performances, as seen in personal (Marwick, 2010; Sender, 2006) and home-makeover programming (Dixon, 2007; Winslow, 2010).

Buying goods not only brings success and legitimacy but also fulfillment so long as one possesses the necessary capital to self-actualize. When Selfridge's department store opened in London in 1909, it heralded the store as a site of entertainment and spectacle, as much as commerce: "The pleasures of shopping as well as those of sightseeing begin from the opening hour" (Rappaport, 2001, p. 163). Some hundred years later, Pinterest launched its website for users to personally collect for public display images of goods and places they desire, simultaneously emphasizing and homogenizing consumers' aspirations and ideals (Lui, 2015). In much the same way, representations of weddings in the U.S. emphasize the bride as a celebrity-for-a-day through careful, conspicuous consumption that produces bride and ceremony as a celebration of capital bliss (Engstrom, 2008).

Just as media crafts consumers' desires for what they could buy to be happy, so, too, pornography suggests performances of sex that will lead to a more satisfied self. In connecting sex and visual food pleasures (i.e., gastro or food-porn), Cruz (2013), like Chan (2003), parallels luscious images of food from television, in cookbooks, and on Instagram with those of pornography, finding both offer "irreproducible fantasy" that audiences derive pleasure from without the intention or ability to replicate at home or consume/perform themselves. Writing from the perspective of Christian fundamentalism, Jones (2012) sermonizes in her article, "Pinterest and Porn," that the "diabolical temptation of Pinterest is in the part of it that is trite, banal, and predictable" for celebrating what is "possible only if you have mountains of money" (p. 43). Moralizing aside, pornography and consumerist gazing both celebrate what is inaccessible to most, and in the case of the latter, leaves consumers disappointed when faced with their financial inadequacies to realize these images for themselves (Engstrom, 2008). Landay (2008) recounts her experience in Second Life (a virtual community where people own all manner of capital), finding that the ability to virtually consume with considerable freedom roused her to imagine her potential to consume in "real" life and question her satisfaction with what she had. Landay's post-fantasizing letdown is not unlike the effect of viewing hardcore pornography that induces feelings of inadequacy (Aubrey, 2007; Morrison et al., 2007).

The link between pornography and neoliberal-inspired consumerism, however, is not merely metaphoric. Beggan and Allison (2001) document how, early on, *Playboy* emphasized bourgeois tastes for fashion and cultural performance. Hugh Hefner categorizes *Playboy* in its first issue as a publication for the non-outdoorsman who prefers cocktails, jazz, and conversation about art to "thorny thickets": "If we are able to give the American male a few extra laughs and a little diversion from the anxieties of the Atomic Age, we'll feel we've justified our existence" (qtd. in Beggan & Allison, 2001 p. 353). Hefner's characterization of his publication as, first, for the aesthete and, second, as a valuable diversion—one robed in upper-middle class style and sentiments about leisure—without much reference to the naked women ensconced within the magazines' pages, puts sexual and upper-middle class pleasures in parity. In the case of *Playboy*, pornography was for the *flaneur*—a bourgeois dilettante keyed into the tastes and fashions of the moment—who consumes women's bodies as simply as the trendiest cocktail. *Playboy* rode a cultural mood that embraced engaging in fantasies of desire as an upper-middle class pastime.

Beyond *Playboy*, pornography is about pleasure, but more than the mundane sense of sexual stimulus. Williams (1999) and Fejes (2002) argue that pornography for male audiences creates utopias of abundance in response to insecurities about sexual fulfillment and social acceptance.[1] These abundancies respond to feelings of scarcity (Dyer, 1992), emphasizing imagined pleasure over realistic expectations and experiences. As Tuck (2009) argues, masturbation to pornography is empty because the stimulus promises a more meaningful experience than participants can have: "Sexual consumers see an image not a body, hear an electrical transmission not a voice, and whether they touch themselves directly or through a mass-produced sex toy, the flesh of the other remains absent" (Tuck, 2009, p. 78).

Rather than a puritanical response to masturbation, Tuck (2009) warns that pornography offers image in place of substance, making promises it cannot fulfill. Likewise, consumerist rhetoric offers images of utopia to distract from scarcity—promising self-actualization through consumption—without ever actually bringing meaning and importance to the individuals' lives.

Form and Desire

Much as genre refers to established style and themes, Burke's (1968) notions of form pertains to the expected elements and structure of a text, such as the expectation that in a romantic comedy a chance meeting between two characters will lead to a romantic connection thwarted by an obstacle until the lovers are united at last. Ironic in a discussion of pornography, Burke (1968) describes form as the "arousing and fulfillment of desires" (p. 124); thus form functions to stimulate audience expectations (Heath, 1979). He shifts the focus of the text from the characters within them to the characters reading them, and in so doing suggests that the concept's "form" and "psychology" are interchangeable with their emphasis placed on the needs and desires of the reader and not the protagonist:

> That is, the psychology here is not the psychology of the *hero*, but the psychology of the *audience*. And by that distinction form would be the psychology of the audience. Or, seen from another angle, form is the creation of an appetite in the mind of the auditor, and the adequate satisfying of that appetite.
>
> *(p. 31)*

Thus, form is about the content of the text only inasmuch as the narrative effectively piques and sates the audience's desires. Burke (1968) notes that delays in a story's resolution, which he evocatively calls "frustrations," create their own pleasure as these delays in completion "prove to be simply a more involved kind of satisfaction, and furthermore serve to make the satisfaction of fulfillment more intense" (p. 31).

Given that pleasure comes from the fulfillment of form, Burke (1968) notes that the type of form a text follows dictates the means by which the audience derives its pleasure. Some forms follow a logical narrative arc reaching a satisfyingly rational conclusion; others repeat a valued theme in a series of variations; and still others adhere to an anticipated storyline satisfying the audience by giving it exactly what it came for. Whatever the pattern assumed, Burke (1968) asserts that a form "is 'correct' insofar as it gratifies the needs which it creates. … [F]orm is the appeal" (p. 138). Texts, then, serve to satisfy their own narratively induced wants. The argument is not that form alone provides pleasure, rather that form provides pleasure when we return to it again and again (Burke, 1968). As an example of this, Burke (1968) notes that unlike with other types of texts, the reason "music can stand repetition so much more sturdily than correspondingly good prose is because music, of all the arts, is by its nature least suited to the psychology of information, and has remained closer to the psychology of form" (p. 34). Accordingly, people rewatch a movie because they appreciate the text's form rather than the narrative resolution itself: we already know who the murderer is, but we enjoy the journey of discovery.

At first blush, the link between pornography and Burke's notions of form seems rather neat: pornography follows a form of sex acts in a generally anticipated sequence until the predictable fulfillment of the money shot. I argue, rather, that instead of a form that both creates and satisfies an appetite, pornography, as a rhetoric of consumption, may attempt a narrative resolution (a money shot), but it leaves the audience wanting gratification in their own lives, not merely in the text. The inability of the text to actually sate the desires it creates precisely demonstrates the form of consumption, which includes pornography. Arguably, a romantic text such as a book or movie may provide satisfaction in terms of its narrative structure while still generating a desire for romantic intrigue in one's own life. Yet, by its nature, the rhetoric of consumption leaves the consumer feeling incomplete and desiring without benefit of a textual satisfaction. Just as Burke found music to be heavy with form and light on narrative conducive to frequent or repetitive listening, the rhetoric of consumption is a form with minimal narrative that allows the reader to continually revisit the text in an attempt to find pleasure in a fantasy of abundance.

Kitchen Fantasies

Food52 (named so because people cook all 52 weeks of the year) is a food blog and kitchen and dining wares retailer (Hesser & Stubbs, n.d., "About

Us"). Founded in 2009 "to bring cooks together," Food52 opened a shop in 2013, explaining the decision not as an attempt to improve profits but to equip cooks:

> Because great food isn't just about ingredients, it's about everything that makes a meal—it's the platter you serve tacos on; the composter in your kitchen; the knife you take on picnics; the beeswax candles that burn on your table; and the honey from the same apiary that you stir into your tea ... We look forward to cooking with you! Amanda & Merrill
> *(Hesser & Stubbs, n.d., "About Us")*

The description of a properly appointed kitchen tells the consumer fantasy of meals as a public performance ("the platter you serve tacos on") with proper food ethics ("the composter in your kitchen") done as an act of leisure ("the knife you take on picnics"). Additionally, written in the first person ("We look forward to cooking with you") and signed with images of their handwritten first names, Food52 establishes itself as a voice of two white women, presumably to women like themselves. Though nothing about Food52 precludes men from enjoying its goods, the site does little to break the long tradition of domestic concerns linked to women's labor (Bentley, 2001; Nathanson, 2009), with the stray inclusion of a man using a product against the regular use of what reads as women's bodies, such as hands grating cheese or holding barware (e-mail, October 1, 2016). The shop has become an integral part of Food 52's outreach. For example, of the 52 e-mails sent in one month to those on its e-mail list, 31 directly addressed a product or service (e.g., coffee bean subscription) for purchase or the virtues of the shop. The sales-oriented e-mail count suggests the significance of merchandising to Food52's brand and mission, as well as demonstrating a rhetoric of consumption that offers a neoliberal fantasy of self-actualization from acts of conspicuous consumption.

To discuss the use of pornographic form as a consumerist rhetoric, I examined Food52's marketing e-mails and content in their online store. The e-mails came from the 52 e-mails sent in October 2016. Analysis included the 31 marketing e-mails (excluding 21 e-mails addressing cooking advice or recipes) and 40 product descriptions from the online store, using the first eight products listed under each of the shop's five main categories, Kitchen, Table, Home, Outdoors, and Pantry. Using directed content analysis (Hsieh & Shannon, 2005), I coded each of the 71 texts for how they potentially represented neoliberal sensibilities, identifying recurrent and emergent themes that were then sorted by larger concepts. These coalesced into three categories: objects of affection, performance anxieties, and authentic gaze. The images used to sell the products were also incorporated into this analysis to examine the ways the visual compositions contributed to readers' understanding of the themes.

Objects of Affection

An e-mail from October 9, 2016, with the subject, "Today, *anything* can happen," invites the reader to browse the online store: "A Chance Meeting is in Your Future: Take a spin through our Shop and see if there's a pretty little something that catches your eye." The suggestive use of "*anything*" implies a sexual, emotional connection between products and customers, who are encouraged to gaze across goods for "a pretty little something." The playful, sexual tone speaks to the pleasures and promise of gazing that creates personal satisfaction as befits a pornographic form. Much like one of Benjamin's (1999) *flâneurs* strolling through a Parisian arcade, browsers are encouraged to be charmed by the products, these objects of desire. One e-mail introducing a line of cooking ware turns shopping into cruising: "Staub dressed up their pro pots in a deep blue with a flirty brass handle—just for us. All your enameled cast iron crushes are here (hi French oven! hi rice cooker!), looking extra fine" (October 3, 2016). Here, both sides of the "crush" are explained: pots are "dressed up" and "flirty" while the cruising shopper calls them out as "looking extra fine." Like pornographic performers playing to the camera to create desire in viewers gazing back, the pots want us and we are to want them back. As a later e-mail explains, "we've got a Shop find you'll want to take home with you ASAP. We think you two will be very happy together" (October 23, 2016). Part matchmaker, part brothel madam, Food52 states bluntly that the products within—like the fantasies of pornography—will create meaningful bonds of affection, although these connections, also like pornography, are themselves money shots that depict an abundance to meet an audience's insecurities.

Many product descriptions emphasize the beauty of an otherwise utilitarian object (e.g., a biscuit cutter) in ways that make function secondary to aesthetics. For instance, Food52 describes a stovetop rice cooker as "cute-as-can-be" with a color combination "that makes us swoon!" (Food52 x Staub petite French oven stovetop rice cooker, 1.5QT). The pot's purpose seems at least as much about something to adore as to cook grains. Pictured on the webpage sitting atop a subtly scuffed table, surrounded by lightly tarnished silver flatware in mismatched patterns, the scene epitomizes Food52's aesthetic of patina. Where shabby chic (a style featuring heavily worn and faded items) wards off economic anxiety by experiencing poverty in a controlled, upper-middle class setting (Halnon, 2002), patina would seem to respond to an insecurity about social standing by suggesting a heritage of social position. Pairing shiny cookware with signs of gentry repeats pornographic notions of abundance of wealth and erotic potential against economic instabilities that supposedly threaten white, middle-class ascendance.

This regular emphasis on an object's beauty throughout Food52's Shop also implies the right kind of aesthetic for consumers in much the same way pornography normalizes sexual desires and performances. For instance, copper mugs that "[are] a dose of sheen," or a flask characterized as "quirky" emphasize the charms of the products while assigning them human qualities (Hammered copper Moscow mule mugs; ZYX black matte flask). Food52's emphasis on character over use models white, upper-middle class taste for the consumer (Arsel & Bean, 2013). Other times product descriptions mention instructions with "beautiful illustrations" (DIY felted animal kits) or an item "beautifully packaged" arriving in "a handmade pine gift crate" (Essential garden tools gift set) celebrate meticulous performances of wealth as a utopia (Golec, 2006). An apron advertised as "a truly special piece for the most special room in your home" (Handwoven stripes apron) interpolates the presumed woman browsing the webpage as much as pornography might: the webpage situates her as domestically obsessed and literally modeled as young, slender, and white (conveniently cropped at the neck) with *four* seasoned wooden spoons at the ready, telegraphing a discerning taste for proper wooden spoons over déclassé nylon and an ample readiness to work culinary magic and please others' appetites.

Much like pornographic performances of abundant pleasures, Food52 insists the pleasure found through their objects brings an otherwise unobtainable social fulfillment. The loveliness and connection found in bowls described as "melamine beauties" or "beloved" cocktail shakers (e-mail, October 1, 2016; Hammered copper Boston shaker) conveys for the consumer the right sort of tastes to be loved. The aesthetic of white, upper-middle class femininity conveyed begets both admiration and aspiration, projecting neoliberal promises of fulfillment from market participation.

Performance Anxieties

In addition to the fantasy of connection through commerce/pornography, Food52 regularly invokes the importance of fulfilling white, upper-middle class performance expectations epitomized by the post-feminist notion of "having it all," of being professionally successful at work while domestically successful at home. Thus, the products represent the potential to garner respect and admiration from peers as a stylish consumer and exemplary homemaker, marking the consumer rather than the product as the ultimate object of admiration.

This is illustrated by a description for a $185 dustpan and brush:

> Is it an ordinary dustpan, or a shiny new piece of wall art for your home? This handsome, tarnished brass and horsehair set is such a stunner that you'll want to accidentally-on-purpose leave it out around the house, just for the compliments. Good thing it comes with a magnetic peg that easily mounts to the wall, so you can hang it up proudly.
>
> *(Brass & horsehair brush and dustpan)*

The description makes plain the purpose of conspicuous consumption while the accompanying photo repeats themes of white, upper-middle class style with paperclips strewn from a patinaed silver cup. The suggestion of a dustpan as wall art, itself, speaks to an economically privileged domesticity in which tools of domestic labor become art and cleaning suggests leisure.

Performing style for an audience appears as a central theme at Food52. Like the dustpan, other products promise compliments for effective class performance as when textured glass vases displayed in variety make for "a casually elegant centerpiece that says, 'Oh, this? I just threw it together'" (e-mail, October 7, 2016). Some products are part of a literal performance, as when using an unusual oil decanter becomes "performing [a] little magic trick" or a cheese box with a lid/cheese board is a "good party trick" (Brass oil decanter; Cheesebox). As a "trick," it inspires images of awe and surprise by a clever hand in a fantasy of pleasure from the item's use, rather than what it does. The performance here also visually represents style, like a cheese box to transport cheeses "safely and in style" (Cheesebox) shown as part of a picnic with white wine, fruit, and soft cheeses cut with patinaed silverware spread over a linen sheet—a scene of classed bliss.

Food52 products may even become necessary to a fantasy of class-privileged, white taste. It may "set the mood at home," "make a striking piece on a shelf," or "[strike] the perfect balance between modern and traditional, which means they're right at home in any room" (Mini beacon lantern; Vintage French stoneware bottle with stopper; Brass pin candleholder). An especially telling description for a planter presupposes the class performance readers and consumers enjoy: "this planter's geometric shape is a modern home for succulents in your modern home" (Hickory planter). Similarly, an e-mail marketing sheepskins suggests the reader "Use one as a throw or a rug to add instant warmth to any room (or is that the crackling fire?)" (October 21, 2016). At once the advertisement presumes the luxury of a wood-burning fireplace while also suggesting that sheep hides conjure up classed coziness for those without a hearth.

Food52 sometimes invokes the very anxieties it offers to resolve, specifically the sin of lacking sophistication in the eyes of others. A double candleholder promises to "[lend] unusual intrigue to even the simplest tablescape" just as a bowl is "a no-brainer for classing up your table setting" (Brass eleven candleholder; Dearborn glass bowl). Both products focus on one's "tablescape," understood here as a stage on which we perform the right sort of taste before those we invite into our homes. In so doing, the Shop shames a "simple" table setting for lacking sophistication, needing to be "classed up" with "intrigue," which is "a no-brainer." The codes of class performance run deep in these narratives as when the website pictures the glass bowl holding sugar cubes next to a bottle of champagne, which nods to those versed in champagne cocktails and intimidates the uninitiated who may not know why the cubes are present.[2]

Other times, the items complete a larger class performance of leisure. Champagne coupes "make every night worth celebrating" and "[give] your happy hour a beautifully eclectic feel" (Vintage French champagne coupes). The fantasy here includes a hip social scene with weekly(?) happy hours, accentuated by chic, "eclectic" barware. Many times the products are represented within the social scene it is said to be made for. Thus, mini lanterns for "a weekend getaway into the woods" or a cheese box for when "you've been assigned the cheese plate at the next get-together" signify a fantasy of upper-middle class leisure with camping trips and cocktail parties replete with cheese plates (Mini beacon lantern; Cheesebox).

These fantasies depict a pornographic abundance of wealth and time. Not only does Food52 present for potential customers fantasies about the good taste to select their products and the money to buy them, but also about having the time to perform with them, to perform having it all. The phenomenon of "money-rich and time poor" (Rosen, 2015) creates unique pressures for women to perform a domestic femininity crafted from the white middle and upper classes while excelling in the workplace (Nathanson, 2009). In the utopia of Food52, the pressures from professional and domestic demands (e.g., housework and childcare) dissolve, leaving behind dreams of smart tablescapes and admired dustpans. The fantasies told about performing for others offer indulgent images of admiration and the possibility of a life more interesting and "classed up," thus creating the idealized neoliberal, consuming citizen (Brooks & Wee, 2016).

Authentic Gaze

Key in the fantasy of the self-actualized subject engaged in upper-middle class performance is the notion of authenticity. For Zimmerman (2015), the impulse for the "authentic" speaks to a "historically masculinized, whitened and upper-middle classed performance of taste preference" (p. 46). Situated within the home, any masculine association with artifacts from exploration and conquest become mere status of those who know to find the best, borrowing and then domesticating images of far-flung adventures. Likewise, the authentic are not necessarily "exotic" locales, but places, experiences, and skills consumers may claim for themselves in much the same way that tourists moving through "foreign" spaces claim a familiarity with and ownership of those cultures.

Some authenticity comes from the pedigree of the product. For instance, glass bowls that are "handcrafted by a master glassblower" certify the goods are not produced for the unselect masses, and the fact that "their designer is the recipient of several awards" (Dearborn glass bowl) confirms the consumer's borrowed savviness and sophistication. A product's value may also come from its scarcity. Copy for truffles regularly emphasizes the difficulty in obtaining them:

We're stocking our Shop shelves with some of the best white truffles in the world. Shave a bit on top of everyday staples like pasta and eggs and you'll immediately know why they're one of the most sought-after ingredients ever.

(e-mail, October 31, 2016)

How to use the food item is mentioned between references to its quality ("best ... in the world") and popularity ("most sought-after ingredients"). Within the Shop, the theme of exclusivity continues, with a supplier of white truffles described as one of the "leading purveyors" and the truffles themselves as "snapped up quickly by chefs and food lovers alike," with black truffles "sought after by epicureans" (White Italian truffle; Black Perigord truffle). The competition the consumer wins by snatching up truffles from those who know quality mimics the boast of the traveler who takes pride in reaching a remote destination as a status statement.

The source of the goods also becomes a point of pride, with the product becoming a pseudo-souvenir of travel as well as a sign of refined taste: "The mountains and meadows of the infamous Alba region of Italy are home to the most superior white truffles in the world" (White Italian truffle). Here, the consumer engages in a narrative of exploration with hints of colonialism as a fantasy of class actualization. Food52 also prides itself on others' labor: "Handwoven in North Carolina [and] naturally dyed with extra care," "hand picked and sourced from farms all over Greece," or "from all organic produce from farms in Washington. ... [with] Jacobsen Sea Salt, harvested from the coast of Oregon" (Handwoven striped apron; Greek herb gift set; Eastern European-style sauerkraut). Imagery of weaving, farming, and sea scavenging emphasize non-industrialized production, distancing producers and sites of production from the consumer as a type of tourism for shoppers (Gray, 2013; Powell & Engelhardt, 2015). This distance accentuates the class position of the reader/buyer who consumes the product or its image, while fetishizing the labor of the producers, a case of "otherness parlayed as the repository of the authentic, the real, and the true" (Shugart, 2008, p. 86).

Product descriptions at Food52 provide readers with a fantasy in which products stand in for history and culture. A blanket using "a vintage plaid from the brand's archives" or seafood from a "third generation of family-run business" create a story of history-as-authenticity in which the consumer becomes a part of that story through purchasing (Pak-a-robe travel blanket with case; Ramón Peña Spanish seafood). Likewise, tortillas—a synecdoche to Mexican/Latin-American culture—allow any home kitchen to claim authenticity since "The best fresh flour tortillas aren't made with a tortilla press" (Flour tortilla kit). The corn tortilla kit offers food as a cultural visit with "taco night" and includes a handwoven tortilla basket, evoking the feel of visiting an imagined peasant culture. These consumptions of others' culture or food acts as the consumers' display of privilege (Shugart, 2008).

Conclusion

Food52 presents goods as manifestations of idealized lifestyles of the white upper-middle class into which readers can interject themselves through narratives and images of the texts as well as the purchase of the products. The fantasies promise affective relations, proficient class performance, and a sense of privilege through authenticity. While never overt, Food52's reader/consumer is inescapably coded as feminine, reminiscent of Martha Stewart's approach to domestic advice (Bentley, 2001). Likewise, race appears invisible, yet appeals to traditional aesthetics of the white middle class through seemingly race-free conventions—such as the obsession with mundane tasks/domestic labor or appropriation of non-domestic labor as status [e.g., harvested sea salt]—and the tendency to call out anything that differs from that aesthetic (Dyer, 1997; Powell & Engelhardt, 2015). Through complex associations of taste, gentility, and values, Food52 crafts a marketplace of and for white, upper-middle class women. As fantasies of abundance, Food52 promises an ideal, fulfilling life that its products can only promise but not deliver. Thus, these consumer advertisements function like pornography by piquing desires without ever meeting them, requiring the viewer to attempt to satisfy wants the text only excites.

Beyond mere pleasure, Burke (1966) argues that form also supports the goals of the text, a "generating principle" that creates an internal coherence motivated by a core value or idea, encouraging the audience's acceptance of the text's purpose (Leroux, 1992). All performances of abundance hinge upon an audience's lack thereof (Dyer, 1992). In the case of pornography, the text responds to feelings of sexual anxiety by offering an abundance of desires (Fejes, 2002; Williams, 1999). Kitchen porn similarly rests upon an anxiety of meeting gendered class expectations that can be met by an abundant performance of a white, upper-middle class style.

That the fantasies of consumption follow a form similar to pornography implies the parallel between masturbation and capitalist consumption. Tuck (2009), in a discussion of consumerist and sexual impulses, suggests that capitalism needs the public to focus on satisfying its own desires for the market to thrive: "As a moment of pure consumption, masturbation seems to generate exactly the type of individual consuming subject required by capitalism" (p. 86). Former Vogue editor Lucinda Chambers admits the sabotaging effect of aspirational literature: "Most [fashion magazines] leave you totally anxiety-ridden, for not having the right kind of dinner party, setting the table in the right kind of way or meeting the right kind of people" (qtd. in Cronberg, n.d.). Both Tuck and Chambers highlight how consumerist and literal pornography create feelings of inadequacy that they attempt to meet through fantasies of abundance that only deepen the sense of insufficiency in a cycle of permanent deficiency.

Just as pornography consumption often occurs in the absence of actual erotic contact with another, the consumption of kitchen porn likewise occurs with few going beyond mere dreaming. Fantasizing, however, has an important role in a neoliberal economy and in cementing the value of marketplace participation. The dreaming that occurs celebrates what is out of reach, with market aspirations appearing to emanate from the consumer rather than the producers who create the fantasies for consumers to inhabit (Brooks & Wee, 2016). These consumerist fantasies pertain to personal choices, providing "lifestyle instruction" that "offers individuals tools for cultivating various competencies, preferences and ways of thinking that can be stitched into the details of daily life and, in turn, reproduce a liberal professional middle class *habitus*" (Zimmerman, 2015, p. 38). Consumerist rhetoric ascribes the characteristics and importance of an upper-middle class lifestyle that embodies white, post-colonial values upon a citizenry that ignores inherent structural barriers as it suggests that success is an individual matter of desire and acquisition.

By shifting the burden of success to individuals and their desires, neoliberalism promises to be a democratizing force by empowering individuals singularly and en masse through market participation. Responding to the notion that citizens have power because the customer is king/queen, Schwarzkopf (2011) warns that "this emperor is without clothes: consumer sovereignty is a fiction, and a dangerous one at that since it delegitimizes more democratic and human alternatives to current regimes of market capitalism" (p. 124). The danger, as with pornography, lies in the relations people form with images of desire rather than the humans around them, leading to a consumer-oriented identity rather than one rooted in community (Schor, 2011).

All this is not to say that citizens are necessarily dupes. Drew Magary provides a "Hater's guide to the Williams-Sonoma catalog" in which he mocks the rhetoric of consumption for the values and insecurities it seeks to sell to consumers. For instance, in response to an $80 glass aerator that promises it "instantly multiplies oxygenation" of wine poured through it, Magary (2016) first calls out the copy for shaming consumers and then proceeds to shame the producer:

> Oh, I bet it does. Here I am, drinking non-oxygenated Two-Buck Chuck like a goddamn SUCKER. I bet Jeffrey (Garten)'s[3] wine has multiplied air in it. Anyway, the only reason to own a fancy decanter that looks like a test beaker from Dr. Jekyll's laboratory is so that you can decant wine in front of other people and impress them. "Holy shit, he poured that wine from one container into another! He must be some sort of chemist."

Magary's critique and others, like Liz Galvao's (2012) "Let's make fun of: Anthropologie furniture," see the rhetoric of consumption for what it is—a lure into a life and aesthetic focused entirely on class performance and image.

Much as the appeal of sexual pornography lies in its abundance of sex, pleasure, and idealized bodies, the rhetoric of consumption revels in the profusion of wealth and classed and raced notions of taste. Pornography of bodies and merchandise both appeal to audiences' needs and desires by rousing those wants through performing excess before audiences and projecting ideals onto those that watch. Part of the appeal of this form for audiences, then, comes from the imaginary interjection of themselves into scenes of eroticized flesh or tasteful tablescapes. In both cases, the image will always be better than what can be realized and the promise of feeling connected, confident, and masterful—as a talented lover or supreme hostess—will likely never come to pass. Disappointed in their deficiency, though, many will return to the image trying again to find the sense of satisfaction that has eluded them.

Notes

1 Williams (1999) argues this abundance is evident in the "money shot," a term in television production now referring to the reveal of fulfilled desires, such as the dish fresh from the oven or the newly redone living room.
2 They are often dashed with bitters and dropped in the glass before pouring: I looked it up.
3 Professionally a respected economist, Jeffrey Garten is the husband of Ina Garten, a Food Network celebrity whose show, *The Barefoot Contessa*, celebrates home cooking as part of an upper-middle class life of leisure.

References

Arsel, Z., & Bean, J. (2013). Taste regimes and market-mediated practice. *Journal of Consumer Research, 39*(5), 899–917.
Aubrey, J. S. (2007). The impact of sexually objectifying media exposure on negative body emotions and sexual self-perceptions: Investigating the mediating role of body self-consciousness. *Mass Communication & Society, 10*(1), 1–23.
Beggan, J. K., & Allison, S. T. (2001). The *Playboy* rabbit is soft, furry, and cute: Is this really the symbol of masculine dominance of women? *The Journal of Men's Studies, 9*(3), 341–370.
Benjamin, W. (1999). *The arcades project* (H. Eiland & K. McLaughlin, trans.). Cambridge, MA: Belknap.
Bentley, A. (2001). Martha's food: Whiteness of a certain kind. *American Studies, 42*(2), 89–100.
Blumenthal, R. (1973). Porno chic. *New York Times Magazine, 21*, 30–33.
Brooks, A., & Wee, L. (2016). The cultural production of consumption as achievement. *Cultural Politics, 12*(2), 217–232.
Buerkle, C. W. (2011). Masters of their domain: *Seinfeld* and the discipline of mediated men's sexual economy. In E. Watson and M. E. Shaw (Eds.), *Performing American*

masculinities: The 21st-century man in popular culture (pp. 9–36). Bloomington, IN: Indiana University Press.
Burke, K. (1966). Dramatic form—and: "Tracking down implications". *The Tulane Drama Review, 10*(4), 54–63.
Burke, K. (1968). *Counter-statement*. Berkeley, CA: University of California Press.
Chan, A. (2003). La grande bouffe. *Gastronomica, 3*(4), 46–53
Cronberg, A. A. (n.d.). Will I get a ticket? A conversation about life after *Vogue* with Lucinda Chambers. *Vestoj*. Retrieved from http://vestoj.com/will-i-get-a-ticket/
Cruz, A. (2013). Gettin' *Down Home with the Neelys*: Gastro-porn and televisual performances of gender, race, and sexuality. *Women & Performance: A Journal of Feminist Theory, 23*(3), 323–349.
Dean, J. (2008). Enjoying neoliberalism. *Cultural Politics, 4*(1), 47–72.
Dixon, W. W. (2007). Hyperconsumption in reality television: The transformation of the self through televisual consumerism. *Quarterly Review of Film and Video, 25*(1), 52–63.
Dyer, R. (1992). *Only entertainment*. New York: Routledge.
Dyer, R. (1997). *White*. New York: Routledge.
Engstrom, E. (2008). Unraveling the knot: Political economy and cultural hegemony in wedding media. *Journal of Communication Inquiry, 32*(1), 60–82.
Fejes, F. (2002). Bent passions: Heterosexual masculinity, pornography, and gay male identity. *Sexuality & Culture, 6*(3), 95–113.
Galvao, L. (2012, August 29). Let's make fun of: Anthropologie furniture. [Web log comment] Retrieved from http://lizgalvao.tumblr.com/post/30461401480/lets-make-fun-of-anthropologie-furniture
Golec, M. J. (2006). *Martha Stewart Living* and the marketing of Emersonian perfectionism. *Home Cultures, 3*(1), 5–20.
Gray, J. (2013). *The Amazing Race*: Global othering. In E. Thompson & J. Mittell (Eds.), *How to watch television* (pp. 94–101). New York: New York University Press.
Halnon, K. B. (2002). Poor chic: The rational consumption of poverty. *Current Sociology, 50*, 501–516.
Heath, R. L. (1979). Kenneth Burke on form. *Quarterly Journal of Speech, 65*, 392–404.
Hesser, A., & Stubbs, M. (n.d.). About us. Retrieved from https://food52.com/about
Hsieh, H. F., & Shannon, S. E. (2005). Three approaches to qualitative content analysis. *Qualitative Health Research, 15*, 1277–1288.
Jones, B. F. (2012, October 31). Pinterest and porn. *Christian Century*, pp. 42–43.
Landay, L. (2008). Having but not holding: Consumerism and commodification in Second Life.". *Journal of Virtual Worlds Research, 1*(2), n.p.
Leroux, N. R. (1992). Perceiving rhetorical style: Toward a framework for criticism. *Rhetoric Society Quarterly, 22*(4), 29–44.
Lui, D. (2015). Public curation and private collection: The production of knowledge on Pinterest. com. *Critical Studies in Media Communication, 32*, 128–142.
Magary, D. (2016). The 2016 hater's guide to the Williams-Sonoma catalog. *Deadspin*. Retrieved from http://adequateman.deadspin.com/the-2016-hater-s-guide-to-the-williams-sonoma-catalog-1789529261
Marwick, A. (2010). There's a beautiful girl under all of this: Performing hegemonic femininity in reality television. *Critical Studies in Media Communication, 27*, 251–266.
Morrison, T. G., Ellis, S. R., Morrison, M. A., Bearden, A., & Harriman, R. L. (2007). Exposure to sexually explicit material and variations in body esteem, genital

attitudes, and sexual esteem among a sample of Canadian men. *The Journal of Men's Studies, 14*(2), 209–222.

Nathanson, E. (2009). As easy as pie: Cooking shows, domestic efficiency, and postfeminist temporality. *Television & New Media, 10*(4), 311–330.

Ouellette, L. (1999). Inventing the Cosmo girl: Class identity and girl-style American dreams. *Media, Culture & Society, 21*(3), 359–383.

Powell, L. J., & Engelhardt, E. S. (2015). The perilous whiteness of pumpkins. *GeoHumanities, 1*(2), 414–432.

Rappaport, E. D. (2001). *Shopping for pleasure: Women in the making of London's West End*. Princeton, NJ: Princeton University Press.

Rosen, R. J. (2015, November 4). Money-rich and time-poor: Life in two-income households. *Atlantic*. Retrieved from www.theatlantic.com/business/archive/2015/11/work-life-balance-pew-report/414028/

Schor, J. (2011). The new politics of consumption: Why Americans want so much more than they need. In G. Dines & J. M. Humez (Eds.), *Gender, race, and class in media: A text-reader* (pp. 205–211). Los Angeles, CA: Sage.

Schwarzkopf, S. (2011). The political theology of consumer sovereignty towards an ontology of consumer society. *Theory, Culture & Society, 28*(3), 106–129.

Sender, K. (2006). Queens for a day: *Queer eye for the straight guy* and the neoliberal project. *Critical Studies in Media Communication, 23*, 131–151.

Shugart, H. A. (2008). Sumptuous texts: Consuming "otherness" in the food film genre. *Critical Studies in Media Communication, 25*, 68–90.

Tuck, G. (2009). The mainstreaming of masturbation: Autoeroticism and consumer capitalism. In F. Attwood (Ed.), *Mainstreaming sex: The sexualization of western culture* (pp. 77–92). New York: I.B. Taurus.

Williams, L. (1999). *Hard core: Power, pleasure, and the "frenzy of the visible"*. Berkeley, CA: University of California Press.

Winslow, L. (2010). Comforting the comfortable: *Extreme Makeover Home Edition*'s ideological conquest. *Critical Studies in Media Communication, 27*(3), 267–290.

Zimmerman, H. (2015). Caring for the middle class soul: Ambivalence, ethical eating and the Michael Pollan phenomenon. *Food, Culture & Society, 18*(1), 31–50.

PART V
Identity and Representation

10

"I DESERVED TO GET KNOCKED UP"

Sex, Class and Latinidad in *Jane the Virgin*

John S. Quinn-Puerta

Jane the Virgin, a soap opera that airs on the CW network, was loosely adapted from a Venezuelan telenovela entitled *Juana La Virgen*. It centers on Jane, a Latina in her 20s. In the flashback sequence that opens the series, Jane makes a vow to God and her grandmother that she will "save herself" for marriage. This is a promise that becomes complicated by the fact that, during what is supposed to be a routine pap smear, Jane's emotionally distraught gynecologist accidentally artificially inseminates her with another man's sperm.

Cut to two weeks later, and Jane collapses on a bus, leading to a trip to the ER where it is confirmed that she is, in fact, a pregnant virgin. The matter is further complicated by the fact that the donor of this sperm is Rafael, the owner of the Miami Beach hotel where Jane works as a waitress – a man she had kissed five years prior. And this is just the beginning of the story; the web of relationships and characters impacted by this accident extends beyond just Jane and Rafael. An entire world of coincidences and deception lies ahead, with plots and problems ranging from the capacity of an ultrasound room to the murder of a man with connections to a face-changing drug lord – and that's only in the first two episodes.

But what is perhaps most notable about *Jane the Virgin* is not its intricate plot or its high-concept pedigree, but rather its focus on a diverse array of Latinx-coded[1] characters, and its choice to be a staunchly bilingual and bicultural show. One of the main characters, Jane's grandmother, Alba, speaks entirely in Spanish, with her dialogue translated through English subtitles. No explanation is provided or asked for by any of the characters. In addition to functioning in two languages, the show also emphasizes the cultural experiences of Latinx families and their upbringing, with Jane, her mother, and her grandmother gathering almost daily to watch their favorite telenovela, *The Passions of Santos*, and sharing in cultural food like arepas or croquettas. *Jane the Virgin* lives in Latinx culture, a fact acknowledged by Gina Rodriguez in her acceptance speech for the Golden Globe Awards for Best Actress for her role as Jane: "This award is so much more than myself; it represents a culture that wants to see themselves as heroes" (Aguilera, 2015). The television program operates in a space targeted at Latinxs and young people (Miller, 2016), and it is important to note what political messaging might be embedded in the show's narrative choices. Some might be obvious, and some might not. But an analysis of *Jane the Virgin*'s first five episodes can shed light on some of the ways that a neoliberal political message may be coded within the broadcast. After all, the CW, which owns the show, is itself owned by both CBS and Time Warner, two major media corporations that benefit from the neoliberal deregulation of media industries. I posit that despite its occasional forays into progressivism and its calls for immigration reform and activism, *Jane the Virgin* still participates in a construction of the false neoliberal American dream, with an emphasis on labor, rational choice, personal responsibility, and aspirational success stories as a response to economic issues faced by all U.S. citizens. Additionally, it engages in a falsely homogeneous representation of the Latinx experience. To do this, I will rely heavily on the work of Duggan (2003) and De Fina (2013).

Literature Review

Duggan (2003) defines neoliberalism as a political movement based upon the dominance of free market solutions and freedom of choice, and, most importantly for our purposes, an ethic of "personal responsibility" surrounding those choices and the circumstances people might find themselves in. She identifies the rise of neoliberalism as beginning in the early 1970s when U.S. corporate interests launched "a counter-movement" to combat their falling profit rates (pp. ix–x). Duggan explains that "the architects of contemporary neoliberalism drew upon classical liberalism's utopianism of benevolent 'free' markets and minimal governments," (p. x) and she argues that the very crux of neoliberalism is an embrace of free market solutions as "pro-corporate capitalist guarantors of private property relations" (p. xii). In other words, neoliberal officials, like Ronald Reagan or Bill Clinton, worked to dismantle institutions like welfare and other social supports in an effort to redistribute resources upward (Duggan, 2003). For the purposes of my analysis however, we don't focus on the upper echelons of neoliberal power but, instead, on those whose resources are distributed away. In the words of Duggan (2003):

> Neoliberalism's avatars have presented its doctrines as universally inevitable and its operations as ultimately beneficial in the long term – even for those who must suffer through poverty and chaos in the short term.
>
> *(p. xiii)*

For our purposes, we analyze "the shapeshifting array of alliances and issues through which a neoliberal policy agenda has been promoted in the United States and abroad" (Duggan, 2003, p. xiii) as it is portrayed within *Jane the Virgin*. Duggan (2003) argues that there has been a loss of efficacy in progressive-left activism due to the schism between those activists who prioritized identity politics and those who prioritized political economy (pp. xvi–xvii). Because of this split, the neoliberal establishment "included civil rights/equality politics within a framework that minimized any downwardly redistributing impulses" in its political platform, thus continuing to shrink the economic power specifically of already underprivileged populations, like Latinos and African-Americans, through catering to a more neoliberal friendly identity politics (pp. xix–xx). However:

> The actual policies of the legislation ... expose its underlying assumption: The sexual practices and household structures of poor women, especially black women, are the central causes of poverty and of associated social disorder and criminality.
>
> *(Duggan, 2003, p. 16)*

This emphasis on the responsibility of poor women of color for their sexual choices goes hand-in-hand with the very premise of *Jane the Virgin*. Chmielewski, Tolman, and Kincaid (2017), in discussing the moral panics surrounding adolescent sexuality in a neoliberal, post-feminist society, found that neoliberal discourses attempt to be depoliticized and emphasize free choice but "attribute blame and responsibility only to girls, concealing the gender, race, and class systems of oppression that impinge upon girls' access to their own desires and sexual choices" (p. 412). They found that girls were "expected to negotiate boys' ... sexual appetites and advances ... [but] were held accountable for 'making choices' in a neoliberal context of assumed sexual agency" (p. 416). In other words, the sexual double standard places the burden of responsibility for consequences and actions that can result in victimization or harm on girls, who are expected to express an agency not placed on boys.

Chmielewski et al.'s (2017), examination of news articles found that "Black and Latina girls were discussed as always already hypersexual and 'at-risk' teens by virtue of their inherently 'excessive' bodies" (p. 416). They conclude that "even when regarded with pity as victims ... [girls] are nevertheless judged as poor gatekeepers, serving as examples of personal weakness and the downfalls of losing control" (p. 423). This overall idea of victimhood not as something placed upon girls by a traumatic event or an accident, or a systemic disadvantage, but rather as a result of poor choices and inherently excessive hypersexuality plays directly into the neoliberal policy pursuits that Duggan (2003) describes. These ideas reaffirm and support the continued distribution of resources, be they economic or otherwise, away from the poorer, more marginalized populations of women and people of color. Considering that the focus of *Jane the Virgin* is on a woman of color who is abstinent from sex for religious and cultural reasons, these neoliberal assumptions play a large role in the show's portrayal of sexuality, among women of color, in particular.

As for the portrayal of Latinx culture on the show, De Fina's (2013) work on the construction of ethnic identities in regional Spanish-language radio defines two competing strategies of Latinx identity construction in the U.S. by examining the practices of advertisers, owners, and hosts in Washington–Baltimore area Spanish-language radio station Radio El Zol. The first method, favored by advertisers, is top-down, which defines all Latinxs as a unified community through the emphasis of shared cultural practices, like soccer or dancing, and the emphasis of Spanish as the dominant language, as well as support for undocumented immigrants and migration reform (De Fina, 2013).

The second method is bottom-up and emphasizes the individual ethnic backgrounds of different Latinxs and their varied levels of proficiency in Spanish and English. De Fina specifically emphasizes the choices of radio hosts to, both identify with Spanish over English and to ridicule or poke fun at their colleagues who might be more comfortable with English, reinforcing the use of accented English and Spanish as an identifier for Latinxs in the U.S. Even though Spanish proficiency is here seen as a point of division within the relationships of Latinxs, it still emphasizes the use of Spanish as a unifying factor for the Latinx diaspora.

It becomes clear through reading De Fina (2013) that the dominant forces of cultural production favor top-down constructions, as her examples of bottom-up identity construction seem submissive to the messages of pan-Latinx unity conveyed by the radio station's branding and advertising. The station defines the Latinx diaspora as "us" and non-Latinxs as "them," even through its choice of dominant language:

> The choice of Spanish as the privileged language of the radio is therefore functional to its identity as a voice for the community of Latin@s (*sic*) and to the construction of the audience as constituting a transmigrant minority that is still not fully integrated.
>
> (De Fina, 2013, p. 563)

Even bottom-up strategies that emphasize the heterogeneity of the Latinx community, such as the "performance rituals" in which Latinx callers are asked to reveal their diasporic nationality, are still met with universal applause, regardless of the nationality mentioned. Seemingly more telling is the fact that individual callers can be treated as "the voice of the entire group just based on Latin American origin" (De Fina, 2013, p. 562). Overall, both strategies contribute to a homogenized Latinx identity defined by shared cultural markers (e.g., Spanish as the dominant language, migrant experiences, etc.) rather than national boundaries. An examination of production and plot choices on *Jane the Virgin* similarly reveals the ways in which Latinx culture has been homogenized for consumption in primetime.

Much of the literature agrees that Latinx women specifically are subject to multiple stereotypes within the programming landscape, the most common being the spitfire and the maid (Valdivia, 2016), which still persist on ABC. It's important to note that ABC, which is owned by Disney was home to another telenovela remake targeted largely at English-speaking Latinxs: *Ugly Betty*. Avila-Saavedra (2010) finds that *Ugly Betty* relied on two strategies of Latinx identity construction. First, the show emphasized Latinx otherness as a source for conflict. At the same time, the show also tended towards an aspiration of assimilation into the dominant neoliberal culture (Avila-Saavedra, 2010). *Jane the Virgin* is not the first network show to embrace these characterizations while wrapped in the guise of positive Latinx representation.

Methodology

For the sake of introduction to the premise of the show, my analysis will focus on plot points, characters, and dialogue in the first five episodes of the first season of *Jane the Virgin*, which started airing in the autumn of 2014. Using Lisa Duggan's (2003) definition of neoliberalism and examples of co-option of progressive movements by the neoliberal establishment, I will examine the way that the narrative either subverts or promotes neoliberal ideals and agendas. I will also draw on Chmielewski et al.'s (2017) work on sexuality and responsibility in neoliberal America, especially with regard to adolescent and young adult women of color, to discuss the way that sexuality and pregnancy are discussed among the characters of the program.

Jane the Virgin

The first episode of *Jane the Virgin* opens with a Latinx-accented, male voiceover introducing the three women of the Villanueva family in a flashback. We meet a ten-year old Jane, her young mother, Xiomara, who gave birth to Jane as a single teenager, and her grandmother, Alba, who hands Jane a white flower and instructs her to crumple it, explaining that it is impossible for the flower to be made new after it has been destroyed. "That's what happens when you lose your virginity," Alba preaches, in subtitled Spanish. "You can never go back. Never forget that, Jane." Thus, the show's discussion of sexual agency begins. Jane's attitude towards sexuality is framed as mixed; she is depicted as a fan of romance novels and telenovelas, but she is very committed to a planned version of a romantic and sexual life. Our first glimpse of Jane as an adult is during a heavy makeout session with her boyfriend, Michael, which she stops when she perceives it as getting too close to infringing upon the promise she has made to her grandmother.

Jane is depicted as rational and responsible when it comes to her emotional and physical urges: she is an ideal neoliberal sexual citizen, delaying sex not only out of an obligation to her grandmother, but in an effort to not repeat her mother's mistakes. Jane works her way through college as a waitress in a hotel, planning to be a teacher rather than a writer, because she knows it's more practical and attainable. Her life is depicted as a series of choices leading her on a carefully laid-out path. She seems to epitomize the good girl described by Chmielewski et al. (2017), able to engage in safe sexual contact while ever mindful of the consequences of crossing the line into sexual intercourse. Before her accidental insemination, she is almost the poster-child for moral neoliberal sexuality. This is starkly contrasted with her mother, who, like the women of color seen in Chmielewski et al.'s (2017) study, became a victim of her own sexuality, with Jane as her seemingly accidental baby.

The accidental insemination is presented as the stumbling block in Jane's pursuit of a practical, upwardly mobile life. She is a victim of her gynecologist, Dr. Luisa's, mistake. But, regardless of the circumstances, Jane still feels a level of responsibility for the situation. The next four episodes of *Jane the Virgin* center on Jane's attempts to maintain a semblance of normalcy in pursuit of her personal goals, which include marriage, work, and her teaching degree, while attempting to determine the fate of her eventual baby. The decisions Jane must make regarding whether to terminate her pregnancy, raise the baby, or give the baby to the father, Rafael Solano, who also happens to be her employer and her gynecologist's brother (the show does not stray far from its telenovela roots), are the main throughline for the first five episodes. Essentially, Jane's decision comes down to one factor: she wants the baby to be in a loving home with both parents, rather than a single parent, as was her experience. Abortion is briefly considered, but dismissed after a conversation with her devout Catholic grandmother.

Jane's focus on ensuring the baby grows up with a stable nuclear family, rather than being raised by her, supposedly stems from her desire not to repeat the mistakes of her mother. The focus on the idea of a two-parent family plays into Duggan's (2003) identification of the family as one of the primary private sites of neoliberal socialization, while also engaging with Chmielewski et al.'s (2017) ideas regarding neoliberal sexual discourse. The two-parent family is revered under neoliberalism as a source of support and responsibility. The legislative efforts and policies over the past several decades cutting back social programs were disproportionately targeted at single mothers of color (Duggan, 2003). So, accepting the neoliberal ideal of a two-parent family and the presumed stability and advantages for her future child in that situation, *Jane the Virgin* seems to acknowledge the dominance of that particular familial consideration. But rather than pointing out the success of the lead character, herself the daughter of a single mother, the show emphasizes the benefits of achieving that neoliberal ideal, and Jane's reluctance to allow her baby to be raised outside of it. By the fifth episode of the series, Rafael, the father, has begun the process of divorcing his wife, Petra. Rather than continue with the plan to give up her child to Rafael, Jane instead opts to raise the baby herself with her fiancé, an option that she had deemed out of the question just three episodes prior.

The show also attempts to emphasize that Jane desires her independence in spite of her circumstances. While contemplating whether to sue her doctor for malpractice, Jane balks at the idea of accepting a handout in the form of a settlement or money from Rafael. She is committed to working her way through her problems, rather than accepting help from outside sources that are, generally speaking, in a more stable economic situation than she is, as a waitress in college. Jane emphasizes the idea that she is responsible for her baby's well-being, even though the plot points to the responsibility of almost anyone else involved in the insemination. Jane seemingly holds herself responsible for this accident based on the way that she approaches the situation.

This is the ultimate conclusion of Chmielewski et al.'s (2017) thinking regarding the sexual double standard. Under neoliberalism, women are always held to a higher standard regarding sexual conduct, regardless of the circumstances surrounding potential victimhood. Even the dialogue attempting to dissuade Jane from accepting her responsibility re-emphasizes this double standard. As her mother, Xiomara, explains in "Chapter Two," Jane conducted herself responsibly: "Not like me. I deserved to get knocked up." Pregnancy is here seen as a punishment for misconduct. Jane, even though she has never had sex, continues to treat it as such, as she shoulders the burden herself. Thus, *Jane The Virgin* promotes this neoliberal idea of the sexual double standard, emphasizing personal responsibility.

Moving away from the sexual politics of the program, there is another way that *Jane the Virgin* promotes neoliberal ideology: through Jane's choices concerning self-determination, individual responsibility and self-improvement, as well as her aspirations for a middle-class lifestyle for herself and her child. In addition, Jane's father, Rogelio de la Vega, provides a rags-to-riches narrative steeped in the individualism and pull-yourself-up-by-your bootstraps motivation of neoliberalism. In a flashback scene that opens "Chapter Four," we find out that Xiomara has never told Jane anything about her father other than a lie that he was a soldier who she never saw again. In reality, Jane's father was one of Xiomara's classmates in high school – like her, a working-class Latinx. In "Chapter One," it is revealed that Jane's father has actually become an international telenovela star, and that Xiomara has hidden the truth from Jane. When the truth eventually comes out, Jane visits her father on the set of his telenovela, and he regales her with a tale of visiting the Mayan ruins of Chichen Itza as a child, climbing to the top of its temple/pyramid, and wishing for fame. It is clear that he has achieved it – he wears the finest clothes, drinks the finest wines, and sends expensive gift baskets to the women he sleeps with. Rogelio is an exemplar of the Latinx nouveau riche, and though the show pokes fun at some of his mannerisms, he is still presented as a model for Latinxs to strive for.

But the reality that Duggan (2003) describes is not one of upward mobility for people of color and people in poverty, but further downward mobility. Rogelio may present a success story, but it is still fictional. He emphasizes that he was able to ascend the ranks of telenovela stardom not through luck or charm, but hard work. He represents the classic neoliberal bootstrap narrative that is still sold to people of color: your problems are not systemic, but, rather, personal. The show presents economic and social success as inherently open to people of all ethnicities, while failing to depict the real struggles of the poor and working class and people of color under neoliberalism. In doing so, it serves to reinforce the neoliberal myth that all that is necessary for success is hard work and responsibility, all supported by the freedom of choice. Even though the show – occasionally and in small ways – acknowledges the restraints placed on lower-income people, such as Jane's unwillingness to leave her job in "Chapter Two" for fear of losing her health insurance, it only addresses those issues superficially and tangentially.

The class divide is, of course, not a problem when it comes to her pre-natal care, due to the wealth of Rafael, the father of the unborn child. As the son of a wealthy hotel owner, and a hotel owner himself, money is never an object for Rafael, and it will thus never be a question for Jane or their unborn child. Through the influence of wealthy men who either inherited or earned their money through hard work and responsibility, *Jane the Virgin* is able to sidestep issues of class struggle, outside of its use for a few jokes about shopping preferences.[2]

But this is simply not the reality for most Latinx. According to the Pew Research Center (2016), Latinx people complete college at less than half the rate of White people (p. 19). Sixty-seven percent of Latinxs complete high school, as compared to 93 percent of Whites (Pew Research Center, 2016, p. 20). This deficit in education is reflected by deficits in home ownership, median income, and employment. The unemployment rate for Latinxs in 2016 was double that of Whites: 7.2 percent versus 3.6 percent (Pew Research Center, 2016, p. 26).

Beyond class, there's a problem of culture. First, consider the casting choices for the main characters. Jane is written as the granddaughter of Venezuelan immigrants. She is played by Gina Rodriguez, who is not of Venezuelan, but of Puerto Rican descent. Similarly, her mother is played by Andrea Navedo, also of Puerto Rican descent, and her grandmother is played by Ivonne Coll, who was born in Puerto Rico.

Puerto Rico is not Venezuela geographically, culturally, or politically. Though the two countries share a language and a background of Spanish colonialism, that is where the similarity ends, as Venezuela gained its independence from Spanish control in the nineteenth century during the revolutions led by Simon Bolivar, whereas Puerto Rico has been dominated by a colonial power since 1493, be it Spain or the U.S. In spite of this, the Villanueva women still participate in activities that can be coded as generically Latinx, rather than specific to Venezuela or Puerto Rico, whether it's viewing telenovelas, cooking dishes associated with all Latin countries, like arepas, or dancing to salsa and reggaeton (styles of music originating in Puerto Rico and Mexico, respectively). These cultural activities are not explained or associated with any specific country, but rather coded as simply Latinx. They also are coded as female. As Avila-Saavedra (2010) pointed out, telenovelas and cooking are traditionally associated with women in the Latinx family structure. The consumption of so-called low-brow entertainment like telenovelas, which largely depict wealthy families with servants, can be viewed as aspirational. These activities reflect the intersectionality of the show's main characters as women from a Latin culture who are also working class.

This homogenization of Latinx culture extends beyond the Villanueva women. Jane's best friend, Lina, is portrayed by noted Colombian-American actress Diane Guerrero. However, her ethnicity is incidental to her character at best, as she is written as the standard romantic comedy best friend. We have no idea about her background. Outside of her relationship to Jane, she is one-dimensional. Jane's father, Rogelio, is played by Mexican actor Jaime Camil, famous for his work on telenovelas like *Betty la Fea*. However, Rogelio's ethnicity is never expanded upon beyond his thick accent and Miami childhood. We know his English is accented, but not the origin of the accent within Latin America, although a childhood visit to Chichen Itza seems to imply that he's Mexican.

This is not only lazy storytelling but negligence on the part of *Jane*'s writers. Latinidad is not one size fits all. This becomes especially apparent when non-Latinx actors are coded as Latinx in the writing. For example, Rafael, the father of Jane's immaculate conception, is played by Justin Baldoni, an actor of Jewish and Italian descent. But with a last name like Solano, and a father who speaks on-screen with a subtle, but present, Spanish accent, the character is clearly coded as Latino. The writers and directors rely on his dark hair and skin tone to make him appear ethnic, especially when compared with Jane's fiancé Michael, who is clearly White. Rafael is written as the unattainable playboy with a hedonistic past, in a move bordering on exoticization. Much like the rest of the characters, his ethnicity is never explicitly stated in the text of the show, but he is clearly comfortable with dancing salsa, eating arepas, and, eventually, speaking Spanish. These seem to be the go-to markers of Latinidad for the show. We are left to decide for ourselves if this is another case of whitewashing.[3] If the character was written as a Latino, why is he not played by a Latino?

De Fina's (2013) work suggests that we consider how the show has taken advantage of the top-down strategies used by advertisers in media targeted at the Latinx diaspora as a whole. Rather than getting caught in the weeds of distinct national cultures that vary throughout Latin America, *Jane the Virgin* seeks to portray an approachable Latinidad that can be generalized beyond Venezuelan immigrants to the U.S. as a whole. Later storylines map issues that face the Latinx diaspora as a whole onto Jane's family, such as Alba's quest for a green card, something that might be more likely for a Mexican or Guatemalan family. This is a top-down homogenization of convenience for storytelling purposes. It's missing the true subtlety of Latinx culture, but attempts to make up for it by the abundance of Latinx characters and stories.

This is not to say that *Jane the Virgin* is a universally harmful representation of Latinidad. It functions almost like a primer, a counterpoint to other network television programming that might not feature Latinx representation of any kind or perpetuate negative stereotypes when Latinxs are present. The choice of adapting a telenovela additionally shows an understanding of the value of Latin American media and stories. But the Latinidad it portrays, much like its portrayals of sexuality and class, is toned down to fit with the classic narrative of the U.S. as a melting pot. It seems almost too convenient a coincidence that the showrunner of *Jane the Virgin*, Jennie Snyder Urman, is White.

We must additionally consider the placement of *Jane the Virgin* on the CW's primetime lineup – a network that primarily targets a young, multicultural audience – and that this show purports to present the Latinx experience to a wider audience. Rodriguez, in her Golden Globes acceptance speech, emphasized the importance of representation, for Latinxs to be able to see themselves as heroes. But what of those who are viewing this show from an outsider's perspective? The show essentially presents a sanitized, easily palatable Latinidad for wider audiences, yet still manages to include the previously mentioned sexual stereotypes of Latinxs as playboys enveloped in machismo or irresponsible young seductresses subject to teen pregnancy – all the while affirming Jane as a type of Latinx neoliberal model who through self-determination, individual responsibility and making the right choices demonstrates a commitment to improving her life and not making the same mistakes as her mother.

In her audience study of Latinxs in the U.S., Diana Rios (2003) found that watching telenovelas is often seen as a cultural and familial activity. They watch telenovelas like *Jane the Virgin* in an effort to relate to their own cultural experiences and the shared experiences of their family. It becomes a social activity that is a bonding experience for families and communities in a multicultural diaspora. Thus, as we consider *Jane the Virgin*, we must consider that its target audience watches it for cultural experiences and education. Through its acceptance and promotion of neoliberal ideas and situations about sexuality, class, and personal responsibility, *Jane the Virgin* paints with a broad brush over the systemic inequality faced by Latinxs. Though in its later seasons and episodes it addresses issues related to immigration policy and racism, it does not strike at the core economic inequalities that continue to plague Latinxs. In addition, its homogenization of Latinxs as nearly assimilated citizens comfortable working within the neoliberal hegemony does not reflect the realities of life in diaspora. In doing this, *Jane the Virgin* continues the work of the neoliberal establishment by separating the politics of identity from the politics of the economy.

Notes

1 Latinx is a gender-neutral term used here to indicate a person of Latin American origin or descent and as an alternative to Latina and Latino.
2 Xiomara emphasizes Jane's preference for shopping at Target as compared to Rafael's preference for high-end merchandise to demonstrate their inherent differences.
3 Whitewashing is the term associated with the casting of white actors for roles originally written as being for people of color.

References

Aguilera, L. (2015, January 11). 2015 Golden Globes: Gina Rodriguez made us all cry with her incredible acceptance speech. Retrieved from www.etonline.com/news/156131_2015_golden_globes_gina_rodriguez_made_us_all_cry_with_her_incredible_acceptance_speech/
Avila-Saavedra, G. (2010). A fish out of water: New articulations of U.S.–Latino identity on *Ugly Betty*. *Communication Quarterly*, *58*(2), 133–147.
Chmielewski, J. F., Tolman, D. L., & Kincaid, H. (2017). Constructing risk and responsibility: A gender, race, and class analysis of news representations of adolescent sexuality. *Feminist Media Studies*, *17*(3), 412–425.
De Fina, A. (2013). Top-down and bottom-up strategies of identity construction in ethnic media. *Applied Linguistics*, *34*(5), 554–573.
Duggan, L. (2003). *The twilight of equality? Neoliberalism, cultural politics, and the attack on democracy*. Boston, MA: Beacon Press.
Miller, L. S. (2016, May 27). Why the CW deserves your attention. Retrieved from www.indiewire.com/2014/11/why-the-cw-deserves-your-attention-68139/
Pew Research Center. (2016, June 16). *On views of race and inequality, Blacks and Whites are worlds apart*. Washington, DC: Pew Research Center.
Reims, J. (Writer). (2014, November 10). Chapter five [Television series episode]. In *Jane the Virgin*. The CW.
Rios, D. I. (2003). U.S. Latino audiences of "Telenovelas". *Journal of Latinos and Education*, *2*(1), 59–65.
Urman, J. S. (Producer). (2014). *Jane the Virgin* [Television series]. Los Angeles, CA: The CW.
Valdivia, A. N. (2016). Contemporary mainstream Latindad: Disney tales and spitfire endurance. *Limite*, *11*(37), 66–78.

11
AN INTERSECTIONAL ANALYSIS OF CONTROLLING IMAGES AND NEOLIBERAL MERITOCRACY ON *SCANDAL* AND *EMPIRE*

Cheryl Thompson

Scandal, the third television series created by Shonda Rhimes – the first African American writer/producer of a prime-time network drama (*Grey's Anatomy*, 2005–) – premiered on April 5, 2012. The show, which ended after seven seasons in 2018, centers on an African American woman in a leading role, Olivia Pope (played by Kerry Washington), who is head of a crisis management firm dedicated to protecting and defending the public images of the nation's elite by ensuring that their secrets remain hidden. Olivia is a freely choosing sexual woman who is a high-powered D.C. mover and shaker. She attended private school and went to law school with one of her "gladiators," Abby Whelan (Darby Stanchfield). Her other three "gladiators," who are her employees and will fight to the death to protect her, are Huck (Diego Muñoz), Quinn Perkins (Katie Lowes), and Harrison Wright (Columbus Short). Harrison, the show's only African American male gladiator, was killed off in season 3. Although Olivia has never been imprisoned, she sends people there, even her parents, "Eli" Rowan Pope (Joe Morton) and Maya Lewis (Khandi Alexander), for sophisticated acts of treason.

The never-been-married Olivia also has an on-again, off-again interracial love affair/relationship with President Fitzgerald "Fitz" Grant (Tony Goldwyn), as well as Jake Ballard (Scott Foley), the former head of B613, a covert government agency that was once controlled by her father. While the narrative changed season to season, the plotline of Olivia, her gladiators, Fitz/Jake, and her parent's entanglement in some sort of drama remained a constant.

Empire, co-written and co-created by Lee Daniels (director) and Danny Strong, debuted on the Fox network on January 7, 2015. Unlike *Scandal*, it uses hip-hop culture and Black working-class spaces as a backdrop to advance its storylines. Its narrative centers on the life and times of a fictional music family led by Lucious Lyon (Terrance Howard), a former drug dealer turned rapper who is CEO of Empire Entertainment. His three sons are Andre (Trai Byers), who serves as CFO, Jamal (Jussie Smollett) an openly gay R&B singer, and Hakeem (Bryshere Y. Gray), the rebellious rapper poised to follow in his father's footstep in terms of the family's hip-hop production but also with respect to his sexuality. In the show's first season, both Hakeem and Lucious engage in a sexual relationship with the same woman, Anika Calhoun (Grace Gealey). After serving a 17-year sentence for drug dealing, Lucious' ex-wife Cookie Lyon (Taraji P. Henson) joins the Lyon family in season 1, and, from then on, the plotline centers on Lucious, Cookie, and their children vying for control of Empire.

Patricia Hill Collins (1991) coined the term *controlling images* to explain how representations of Black subjects become powerful ideological justifications for intersecting oppressions of race, class, gender, and sexuality. For Black women, the most common controlling images have been the "Mammy," the "Sapphire," and the "Jezebel." For Black men, historical representations have centered on Black male bodies, with controlling images of Black men as inherently violent, hypersexual, and in need of discipline (Hill Collins, 2005). This chapter explores the representation of these controlling images on *Scandal* and *Empire*, and the ways in which contemporary Black representation intersects with neoliberal modes of behavior such as being self-maximizing, self-regulating, and exercising personal responsibility in the pursuit of entrepreneurial success (Ouellette & Hay, 2008). In the sections that follow, I first explain how controlling images of Black femininity and Black masculinity have appeared on television. Second, I outline the theoretical concepts of "post-racial," "postfeminist," and neoliberalism that are explored in the chapter, followed by a brief overview of today's convergent media landscape. And third, I explain why I use critical discourse analysis as a methodological approach to explore how neoliberal notions of hard work, success, and individual achievement intersect with controlling images of Blackness to obscure the interlocking oppressions of racism, sexism and homophobia.

Controlling Images of Blackness on Television

Mammy, according to Hill Collins (2005), is the loyal servant created under chattel slavery who has dedicated her life to serving whites. Distinguished by her fierce independence, asexuality, fat body, and aggressive attitude, the advertising trademark Aunt Jemima best symbolizes the mass-consumed image of Mammy. The Jezebel controlling image, also born under slavery, is a characterization of Black women as sexually depraved, immoral, and lascivious. As Willis and Williams (2002) state, the sexualized Black female body in the form of the Jezebel is the "bad-black-girl" character, a Black woman who also possesses features that are considered European, especially straightened hair. The Sapphire, unlike Mammy and Jezebel, was born on radio, first on the *Amos "n" Andy* show in the 1940s, and then on the sitcom when it transitioned to television in 1951. The stereotype of Sapphire is the "Black Bitch," an emasculating figure who is "a super-tough, super-strong woman" (Hill Collins, 2005, p. 124). Dunn (2008) argues that the Jezebel image that circulates in media culture today intersects with the Sapphire image to create the "bitchy deceptive Black female" (p. 115). Reality television (RTV) has helped to create the controlling image of the "Angry Black Woman," a hyper-depiction of the Sapphire/Jezebel. As Allison (2016) observes, the "angry gold-digger," the so-called Angry Black Woman depicted over and over again on RTV today, "is loud, aggressive, intimidating and sassy" (p. xxiii). Both Rhimes and the Black woman TV characters she has created – *Grey's Anatomy's* Dr. Miranda Bailey (Chandra Wilson), *Scandal's* Olivia, and *How to Get Away with Murder's* Annalise Keating (Viola Davis) – have been called Angry Black Women by critics and social commentators. A *New York Times* contributor even penned an article suggesting that Rhimes should rename her shows, "*Being* an Angry Black Woman" (Fisher, 2014).

I contend that *Scandal's* Olivia and *Empire's* Cookie are a combination of the Sapphire/Jezebel – the Angry Black Woman and the Modern Mammy, described by Hill Collins (2005) as requiring a delicate balance between being appropriately subordinate to white and/or male authority (like the Mammy) yet "maintaining a level of ambition and aggressiveness needed for achievement in middle-class occupations" (p. 140). As professional Black women, both must negotiate the slippery terrain of distancing themselves from the assumptions of being too aggressive (i.e., Sapphire-like) and sexual (i.e., Jezebel-like). On the other hand, these Black women characters often appear as Angry Black Women, who serve as a foil to Black male figures (*Scandal's* Eli and *Empire's* Lucious) with whom they frequently engaged in conflict, as evidenced by "an ongoing verbal dual" between the two (Briceño & Estwick, 2016, p. 70).

Cookie, for example, wears outlandish outfits that scream for attention – from leopard to leather, shoes, and hats to match – and her constant "finger-pointing, neck-rolling, and name-calling" attitude, often directed at Lucious or her youngest, Hakeem, is every bit the Sapphire (Allison, 2016, p. 239). At times, however, Cookie gives over her power to Lucious and even Hakeem when it comes to making business decisions about the company to "please them," as befits the image of the Mammy. Olivia often performs the role of "a political Mammy mixed with a hint of Sapphire" when she faithfully bears the burden of the oh-so-fragile U.S. political system on her shoulders, including the successes and/or failures of the president (Maxwell, 2013, para. 14). She also performs the role of Jezebel, most notably in the show's second season when Olivia tells Fitz in reference to their sexual relationship, "I'm feeling a little, I don't know, Sally Hemings/Thomas Jefferson about all this."[1] Both Olivia and Cookie ultimately reflect the historical complexities of creating racial portrayals in a fictitious world where the creators cannot escape the sensibilities of the real world in which they live (Filoteo, 2014).

Unlike *Scandal*, *Empire* provides multiple controlling images of Black male characters with which to analyze "the discourse used to frame and maintain Black masculinity" (Rodriguez, 2017, p. 2). While characters like Lucious and Hakeem reflect the image of Black men as not only perpetrators of violence but also as hypersexual (Hill Collins, 2005), Jamal, as a gay Black man, does not fit historical controlling images of Black gay characters on television, which were typically "peripheral characters, often in comedic roles that border on ridicule" (Hill Collins, 2005, p. 171). The most common portrayals depict Black gay men as "effeminate, cute, comic homosexuals" who are reduced to a caricature stripped of both culture and masculinity (Riggs, 1991). With the exception of Omar (Michael K. Williams) of HBO's *The Wire* (2002–2008), who was a street-smart, criminally inclined, masculine depiction of a Black gay male, the majority of Black gay characters in television dramas have typically appeared as "out" and juxtaposed against other characters, primarily white males, in middle-class environments (Rodriguez, 2017). Despite this distinction, all Black male characters on *Empire* "express themselves in a heterosexual manner and perform in traditional patriarchal gender roles to be perceived as masculine, including Jamal" (Rodriguez, 2017, p. 8). These performances of masculinity include, sexual encounters with women, using violence when necessary to get what they want, and in the case of Jamal, avoiding displays of "feminine" qualities like crying, showing emotion, and complaining when things do not go his way.

The merger between hip-hop culture and television first appeared via RTV shows like *The Ultimate Hustler* (2005), *Making the Band* (2000–2002), *DMX: Soul of a Man* (2006), *Welcome to Hollyhood* (2007), *Run's House* (2005–2009), and *Flavor of Love* (2006–2008). Unlike traditional television, RTV has added new layers of signification to controlling images of Black masculinity. MTV's *From G's to Gents* (FGTG) (2008–2009), for example, took the notion of an *authentic* Blackness a step further when it aligned Black masculinity with the prison system and criminalization. Through the show's emphasis on changing one's appearance, speech, and mannerisms to get ahead – each week, troubled young Black men were offered the opportunity to change their lives and become "gentlemen" – FGTG drew on neoliberal discourse about how to succeed within an entrepreneurial culture (Page, 2015). Similarly, both parental figures on *Empire* have been to prison and are normatively entangled within the criminal justice system. But their appearance, speech, and mannerism once "out" of that system reflects the same neoliberal impulse to transform one's appearance to achieve success.

Theoretical Concepts

The concepts of post-raciality and post-feminism intersect with neoliberalism. Post-raciality argues that race no longer matters. It is also grounded in a normalizing narrative that seeks to neutralize racial difference. Teasley and Ikard (2010) assert that Barack Obama's 2008 presidency "engendered a new and indeed intoxicating feeling of optimism across race, class, and gender lines and pressed many of us to reassess, if not overhaul, our basic assumptions about the ways that 'race matters' in the 21st century" (p. 412). The discourse of a post-racial America overlaps with the individualistic impulse under neoliberalism which, as Warner (2014) explains, is central to post-race ideology:

> separating an individual from his or her group status also disconnects the person from a historical trajectory of disenfranchisement. The individual alone becomes responsible for her lot in life and cannot claim racism as an injustice or an issue.
>
> *(p. 7)*

Postfeminism, as Gill (2007) argues, "is understood best neither as an epistemological perspective nor as an historical shift, nor (simply) as a backlash in which its meanings are pre-specified. Rather, postfeminism should be conceived as a sensibility" (p. 148). Postfeminism depoliticizes gendered subjects and replaces the static notion of women as being acted upon by media (and by men) with an "empowered" subject whose choices are self-determined. These choices, however, are constrained within an individualizing discourse that assumes universal access to citizenship and consumer culture and that constructs access as a simple matter of individual consumer choice (Thoma, 2009). The active, freely choosing, self-reinventing subject of postfeminism thus shares a strong resemblance to the autonomous, calculating, self-regulating subject of neoliberalism (Gill, 2007).

The term neoliberalism is,

> in the first instance, a theory of political economic practices that proposes that human well-being can best be advanced by liberating individual entrepreneurial freedoms and skills within an institutional framework characterized by strong private property rights, free markets, and free trade.
>
> *(Harvey, 2005, p. 2)*

Importantly, neoliberalism is not simply a set of economic policies; it is not only about facilitating free trade or maximizing corporate profits. When deployed as a form of governmentality, neoliberalism reaches "the soul of the citizen-subject" (Brown, 2005, p. 39). Governmentality, as conceived by

Foucault (1991), refers to the processes through which individuals shape and guide their own conduct – and that of others – with certain aims and objectives in mind.

Scholars of governmentality aim to look beyond formal institutions of official government to emphasize the proliferation and diffusion of the everyday techniques through which individuals and populations are expected to reflect upon, work on, and organize their lives and themselves as an implicit condition of their citizenship. Scholars of televisual governmentality have focused on RTV and the technologies that govern the conduct of "ordinary" people while simultaneously reconfiguring the parameters of "good" and "bad" citizenship (Ouellette & Hay, 2008). Other scholars have explored how racialized bodies are "made over" and managed through the discursive deployment of hegemonic modes of behavior, which acts as a form of governmentality (Orbe, 2008). This chapter argues that there is an intersecting relationship between post-racial, postfeminist narratives on *Scandal* and *Empire*, and neoliberalism, which act as a form of televisual governmentality over viewers/consumers.

Black feminist scholar Crenshaw (1991) coined the term *intersectionality* in her article "Mapping the Margins: Intersectionality, Identity Politics, and Violence against Women of Color" to

> illustrate that many of the experiences Black women face are not subsumed within the traditional boundaries of race or gender discrimination as these boundaries are currently understood, and that the intersection of racism and sexism factors into Black women's lives in ways that cannot be captured wholly by looking at the race or gender dimensions of those experiences separately.
>
> *(p. 1244)*

Since then, one of the core tenets of intersectionality includes the notion that critical inquiry must emanate within and from multiple theoretical frameworks. As Hill Collins and Bilge (2016) observe, an intersectional framework attempts to grapple with social inequality and provides an understanding of the interlocking nature of mutually constructed and intersecting systems of power. Intersectionality embraces a *both/and* framework rather than an *either/or* binary. Analyses of race must not only consider the intersections of class, but – as it relates to television – gender and sexuality alongside the question of how media convergence has reframed the relationship between television content, advertising, and the viewer/consumer.

Since the 1970s, the media market has steadily become dominated by five conglomerates (Comcast, Twentieth Century Fox, Disney, Time Warner, and National Amusements) that control over 90 percent of the market. This shift in ownership occurred when content providers began acquiring content creators through what is known as "media convergence." This vertically integrated media market has led to hyper-fragmentation of media outlets, with hundreds of cable channels, and millions of websites – all of which make it difficult for marketers to reach potential customers with traditional advertising (Turow, 2005). Adding to this is the fact that U.S. consumers are increasingly able to escape advertisements via digital technologies such as TiVo, a digital video recorder (DVR). These technologies allow viewers to "keep the content and zap the commercials without even looking at them" (Turow, 2005, p. 108). This media landscape has led to "meta-integration," a form of product placement that involves incorporating televisual narratives to integrate branded products directly into the text itself.

Scandal and *Empire* as Neoliberal, Meritocratic Representations

The concept of meritocracy is at the center of neoliberalism. Michael Young's 1958 book, *The Rise of the Meritocracy*, describes a society where those at the top of the system ruled autocratically with a sense of righteous entitlement while those at the bottom were incapable of protecting themselves against the abuses leveled by the merit elite above (Lui, 2011). Meritocracy is based on the belief that everyone has an "equal opportunity" to compete for rewards (Lui, 2011, p. 389) and that economic opportunity is available to all those with a desire for personal improvement, a good idea, and a commitment to hard work. As McNamee and Miller (2004) state:

> you get out of the system what you put into it. Getting ahead is ostensibly based on individual merit, which is generally viewed as a combination of factors including innate abilities, working hard, having the right attitude, and having high moral character and integrity.
>
> *(para 1)*

This belief in the self-made, "rags-to-riches" individual, is linked to the nineteenth-century writings of Horatio Alger, whose folktales celebrated the rise from poverty to wealth of the self-made businessman. Alger's dime novels helped to affirm a belief that "rags to riches" stories could, indeed, become *true*. Self-employment is at the cornerstone of this myth. It is seen as the most viable path of economic advancement for those who are outside the mainstream of economic opportunity, and for those who see self-invention as the pathway to achieving *true* financial success (Hundley, 2008).

Whereas *Empire* is a "rags to riches" tale of African American uplift out of poverty through meritocratic hard work via a family-owned business, *Scandal* is about the individual choices and self-employed success of a freely choosing woman. Power in the worlds of *Scandal* and *Empire* do not reflect a world where Black people take action in connection with others or where power is shared. Instead, in line with neoliberal ideology, "There is little emphasis on solidarity, cooperation, harmony, mutual enablement ... the emphasis falls on rugged individualism, on meeting self-centered needs, on the self-sufficient neoliberal subject who is untethered and who embodies a do-your-own-thing, mind-your-own-business culture" (Stoffel, 2016, para. 9). For instance, Olivia has no Black friends or extended family, she does not speak Black Vernacular (BV) English, and her home décor is engulfed in whiteness – for example, white sheets and a white sofa. There are no visual cues that link her to Black culture and/or the wider Black community in Washington. On the other hand, Lucious and Cookie grew up in poverty on "the streets" of Philadelphia. They both have family who speak BV and, when needed, they evoke "the streets" as the *authentic* site of their identities. The narrative of a Black drug dealer-turned CEO is just as much a discursive trope for "doing it on one's own" as a self-made Black woman entrepreneur.

For example, we know little of the *Empire* family's sociocultural struggles as African Americans and yet, even though they came from "the streets," both Lucious and Cookie excel at running a company, speak Standard English impeccably, and maneuver in the business world with ease and comfort. On *Scandal*, significant attention is paid to the decisions Olivia makes, how she takes personal responsibility for her problems, and her continual quest for self-improvement. In addition to reflecting an *ethos* of individualism, consumption, and colorblindness that have become the measures of success in contemporary media culture (Marira & Mitra, 2013), both shows ignore the realities of African Americans in a society and culture in which the basic economic, social, and political divisions and inequalities are linked to race, gender, and class. For example, in some cases, the Black unemployment rate is more than two times that of white Americans, and Black families earn significantly less than white families (Strayhorn, 2008). Yet, in both *Scandal* and *Empire*, the shows take self-employed success, educational attainment, and socioeconomic mobility as *always already* part of the African American experience when this is not and has not been the case. Thus, where Andre is the only presumed-to-be college graduate on *Empire*, there is no mention of his college alma mater, his academic area(s) of expertise, or his struggles with racism. Similarly, Olivia has no college memorabilia in her house; she never reminisces about her college days or shares her experiences and/or challenges with racism and sexism that would have impeded her career achievements.

Methodological Approach

This chapter seeks to probe how *Scandal* and *Empire* use make-over techniques from RTV shows and convergent media techniques to link narratives involving controlling images, post-racial, and postfeminist notions with neoliberal, meritocratic success myths. Using critical discourse analysis (CDA), I examine two episode arcs in each show. Where an episode is a singular narrative unit within a larger television series, an episode arc typically covers three or four related, consecutive episodes that aim to move or change a character from one state to another. In *Scandal*'s season 4, a four-episode arc focused on Olivia's personal transformation when she is kidnapped, auctioned for sale, and ultimately returned to Fitz. On season 2 of *Empire*, in partnership with Pepsi, Daniels and writers crafted a three-episode arc in which Jamal, through hard work and merit, won an endorsement deal from the beverage corporation, and the real-life Jussie Smollett, as Jamal, appeared in an extra-textual Pepsi commercial that aired during the arc's last episode in a combined promotion of Jamal, *Empire*, and Pepsi.

CDA is a useful method of analysis for television because it allows for the identification and probing of economic, class, political, cultural and other social practices while positioning discourse not singularly as language but as inclusive of visual images involving social actors (Chouliaraki & Fairclough, 1999). By using CDA to examine both shows, my aim is to add new layers of complexity to theories of Black femininity and Black masculinity on television.

The Neoliberal, Reinvented Self on Season 4 of *Scandal*

In season 4, episode 10, titled "Run," Olivia is kidnapped from her apartment by masked men and is taken to an unknown location where she is held hostage. Throughout her ordeal, she struggles with the thought of never seeing Fitz and Jake again, and through a dream sequence she envisions both rescuing her. Abby also appears in her dream to warn her: "Jake and Fitz can't help you. There is no man to rescue you .... You are the only gladiator in the place. You are all you've got. You have to rescue yourself." By the episode's end, Olivia discovers that she is not simply being kidnapped for ransom but is instead being held as a pawn to force Fitz to declare war against the West African nation of Angola. In the following episode, "Where's the Black Lady," Fitz is sent a video of a kidnapped Olivia, which he gives to Jake for him to assist in her safe return. Eventually, Fitz declares war on Angola, believing it to be the only possible way to see Olivia again. Olivia subsequently convinces the kidnappers to sell her at auction as the woman who controls the President of the United States. "You're sitting on one of the most valuable assets in the world and not using it," Olivia tells her kidnappers, adding, "Imagine the price I'd fetch on the open market."

In the arc's third episode, "Gladiators Don't Run," Olivia goes up for auction on the Dark Net. Fitz, Jake, and her gladiators – Huck and Quinn – attempt to get access to the auction to foil her kidnapper's plan. All parties prove unsuccessful, however, and Olivia is sold to an outside buyer for more than $1 billion. At one point, Fitz pleads to his Chief of Staff, Cyrus Beene (Jeff Perry), "We have to get Olivia back. Not just because I love her, not just because having her out there is a threat to national security. There are soldiers who are never coming home because I tried to get her back – someone's father, someone's husband."

In the concluding episode, "No More Blood," Olivia is about to be handed over to her Iranian buyers but her ability to speak both English and Farsi spoils the plot and she is once again placed on the auction block, allowing Huck and Quinn to bid on her once more. In the end, she is sold to a group in Russia, but then, Stephen Finch (Henry Ian Cusick), a former gladiator, saves Olivia, bringing her back to the U.S. Upon her return, fearing that she had been abused and/or raped, Fitz goes to her apartment to explain why he went to war for her:

OLIVIA: Everything I've sacrificed to get you here, to keep you here, so you could be the best, so you could make history, so you could be the president you were meant to be. And you were. You were the president you were meant to be and then, when the true test came along, when I was taken because of you, you go to war? You sent thousands of innocent soldiers into harm's way, some of them to their deaths, for one person.
FITZ: I had to save you.
OLIVIA: You didn't save me. I'm on my own.

The very premise of this episode arc – a Black woman being sold at auction to white male bidders – along with the invocation of Africa as a "natural" target of Western aggression, has roots in U.S. imperialism, colonialism, and slavery. In the antebellum South, where Black women were bid on and sold to white slave owners, white men became voyeurs of Black women's bodies on the auction block (Hill Collins, 1991). When Fitz asks Olivia if she had been raped while kidnapped, it speaks to the sexual relations between Black women and the white men who bought and raped them. Throughout four episodes, Olivia is in physical distress, her hair is wild, untamed. The refined Olivia of D.C. politics is replaced by a raw, "animalistic" Olivia whose very survival depends on her "natural" ability to adapt to her surroundings. The reference to Angola also links the relationship between Olivia and Fitz to a period of slavery when Black women from the West African coast were shipped and traded across the Americas. The idea that *Scandal* would avoid any reference to the history of Black women being sold at auction during slavery speaks to the post-racial tenets of the show. As Warner (2014) observes, such narratives are smart because

> it guarantees the network that she has no secret revolutionary agendas and will serve their primary demographic … in ways that will cause the least amount of discomfort to white audiences while providing an

illusion that under liberal individualism, the marketplace will do right by historically marginalized individuals.

(p. 15)

The postfeminist tenets of *Scandal* were realized just before the fourth season aired, when the audience was given a first peek at The Scandal Collection, based on Olivia Pope's wardrobe, which hit retail stores in the spring of 2015. This act further positioned Olivia Pope within an individualistic neoliberal entrepreneurship where, as Tasker and Negra (2007) observe, consumption becomes a strategy "for the production of the self" and a strategy that glosses over social differences (as cited in Thoma, 2009, p. 411). In anticipation of the launch, *InStyle* proclaimed, "Attention Gladiators: Your relentless fangirling over Olivia Pope's fashion has paid off! *Scandal*'s lead, played by the gracious and gorgeous Kerry Washington, and costume designer Lyn Paolo have taken their killer style to The Limited" (Kanter, 2014, para. 1). "Dressing as a gladiator means not being afraid to have it all – to be glamorous, smart, powerful, and sexy," Washington said in her interview with *InStyle* (para. 1).

Olivia's representation as a fashion icon to be emulated occurs simultaneously with her portrayal within the confines of the controlling images of Black women. She is unrestrained sexually and is verbally aggressive with the men in her life (the Jezebel/Sapphire), but she paradoxically performs the role of traditional (white) womanhood in need of saving and/or protection. She is appropriately aggressive in order to achieve entrepreneurial success yet unwavering in support of white men in positions of authority (Modern Mammy). Finally, she performs the role of a freely choosing postfeminist, neoliberal subject who is also the Angry Black Woman with an attitude when she needs to be. At the same time, the post-racial, postfeminist space created by *Scandal* appears devoid of racism or sexism.

Hard Work and Neoliberal Meritocracy on Season 2 of *Empire*

The Pepsi brand-integration arc begins in season 2, episode 8, "My Bad Parts," when Jamal is one of ten candidates approached by the soft drink brand to win a chance to appear in a new television commercial, which would also feature the winner's song. A white Pepsi spokeswoman tells Jamal that he needs to compose a song within the week to submit it for consideration. If he wins, he will become the new face of Pepsi. Lucious tells the Pepsi spokeswoman that the song will be finished within the week, adding that he will personally help Jamal produce the song. Later, while working on it with Cookie, Jamal tells her, "I think it's perfect, Mom. I love working with you." "Yeah, I know you do,'cause you can feel when it's real," Cookie responds. When Jamal performs the Cookie/Lucious-produced song

"Ready to Go" for the Pepsi executives, he wins the competition, becoming the new face of Pepsi.

In the next episode, "Sinned Against," Alicia Keys guest stars as Skye Summers (alongside her real-life, white mother), an R&B singer who is looking to collaborate with Jamal on a new "edgier" song to take her sound in a different (i.e., more "street") direction. While Lucious advises Skye to stay with what she knows – being a pop star, a singer/writer of "breakup songs" – Jamal encourages her to "live her truth" and, in collaboration, they co-write the song, "Powerful," which they perform together during the episode. After singing the song together, Skye and Jamal kiss. This suggests both that he could be attracted to a woman and that homosexuality is a choice, "something an individual selects to be, a fluid nature that can be changed if one so chooses" (Rodriguez, 2017, p. 7). The subtext to this episode is also that because Jamal has two Black parents, unlike Skye, he is better able to cultivate an *authentic* Blackness that she lacks.

In the arc's final episode and mid-season finale, "Et Tu, Brute?," the American Sound Award (ASA) nominations are announced, and Jamal is nominated for several. Both he and Skye speculate about his chances of winning an ASA for Song of the Year, and during a moment of intimacy between the two, Lucious walks in, interrupting them. Later he quips, "Are you hitting that?" to which Jamal reminds him, "I'm still gay, alright. So, don't get weird." During the final round of ASA nominations, both Jamal and Lucious are up for Song of the Year, but Jamal's excitement is dampened by a look of resentment from Lucious who reacts with, "Ain't that a bitch." As the episode ends, Lucious is once again in a struggle with his sons' (and Cookie's) individual ambitions in competition with his and those of Empire.

The episode's brand-integrated narrative takes place when Jamal introduces the Pepsi commercial during the ASA nomination ceremony. Immediately thereafter, the real 60-second Pepsi commercial aired during an ad break. In it, Jamal exits a car with his personal driver (an older white man) and enters a New York City subway. Once on the train, he is immediately recognized by an older Black man who shouts while throwing a Pepsi into Jamal's hands, "Hey, you're Jamal, right? Take a Pepsi." After drinking the Pepsi, the song "Ready to Go" starts playing and Jamal joins in on a spontaneous dance on a train filled with multicultural, multigenerational passengers. As Jamal exits the train and walks up the stairs of the subway, the lyrics, "I grew up, stood up, and now I'm ready to go" match his ascension. When he reaches the last step, over a loudspeaker we hear an announcer proclaim, "Ladies and gentlemen, please welcome to the stage, Jamal Lyon," to which an unseen crowd roars.

While the terms of the deal between Pepsi and Fox were not disclosed, according to the *Wall Street Journal*, the cost of brand integration was believed to be in the range of $20 million (Spargo, 2015, para. 5). The song, "Ready to Go," written by Swizz Beatz, Alicia Keys' real-life husband, was also made available on iTunes immediately following the show, along with the song "Powerful." If you consider that the first season finale of *Empire* drew 23.1 million viewers, making it the highest rated freshman show in ten years (Fox's "Empire," 2017), and the fact that the portrayals of Black gay men on television have worked to "renormalize heteronormativity" (Shugart, 2003, p. 80), it may not be a coincidence that Jamal engages in sexual relations with a woman for the first time during the Pepsi storyline. This episode arc reveals the power of neoliberal ideology to reduce homosexuality to a matter of individual choice.

Further, Blackness, as represented in a post-racial context in which it "must be *seen* as evidence for the alleged color blindness that seemingly characterizes contemporary economic opportunity. A meritocracy requires evidence that racial discrimination has been eliminated" (Hill Collins, 2005, p. 178). Jamal won that contest based on his talent, hard work, and determination, embodying the ideal of colorblindness which seeks to "transcend stereotypes in favor of treating people as individuals free from racial group identification" (Peller, 1990, as cited in Warner, 2014, p. 7). Neither his race, sexuality, nor lack of "real" street cred seemed to matter in Jamal's climb to the top. Rodriguez (2017) states that, even though hip-hop has become a "bedrock of Black identity" it also reifies a Black masculinity "that is homophobic, effemiphobic, and misogynistic" (p. 5). Cookie and Lucious speak to Jamal using BV slang and sexual terms that aim to render him heteronormative but also to authenticate his Blackness. Examples of Cookie's discourse throughout the show include "you bitched out on me after you told me you's was gonna come out in public"; "I know how you divas like to decorate"; "Oh honey, you didn't tell me you were dating a little Mexican! Look at her, she's adorable … you need to get la cucaracha to clean up around here baby"; and "I wanna show you a faggot really can run this company" (Rodriguez, 2017, p. 9). As a Black gay man not born in poverty but of meritocratic privilege, he must be shown what *real* Blackness and maleness looks like by *authentic* Black parents who have been to prison, and who are ultimately the arbiters of *real* Black identity. While the audience is asked to celebrate Jamal's triumph in the Pepsi competition, homophobia and racism are rendered invisible and inconsequential to his success as a Black gay man in America.

Conclusion

Foucault's (1978) notion of "a regime of truth" is an important reminder that attempts to reconfigure controlling images of Black femininity and Black masculinity can never remove them from the history from which they were created. Because the media provide a space where individuals are able to become familiar and potentially identify with representations of racialized characters (Fiske, 1987), it is imperative that we begin to probe how these representations are changing in a convergent media landscape where marketers are finding new ways to get their brand names in front of viewers. And in turn, as more television viewing takes place on ad-free platforms and marketers, television executives and audiences alike are now forced to rethink what is possible in a traditionally non-interruptive commercial experience (Poggi, 2016).

As texts are deeply wedded to post-racial, postfeminist ideologies, more questions need to be asked about shows like *Empire* and *Scandal* and the ways in which they obfuscate the realities of African American progress while overhyping the neoliberal myth of self-employed meritocratic success. The problem with post-racial thinking under neoliberalism is that it makes it nearly impossible to understand the ways racial and class inequality reduce the capacity of citizens to engage in modes of self-determination removed from the capitalist marketplace (Teasley & Ikard, 2010). Where Ouellette and Hay (2008) asked how we might evaluate RTV's efforts to insert itself into diffuse, privatized networks of self-fashioning and care, it is my contention that the same question must be asked of scripted television, along with the question of what new roles do television, consumer brands and advertising agencies now play in reconfiguring the audience into neoliberal citizen/consumers?

Note

1 Sally Hemings was an enslaved woman of mixed race many believe was the long-term mistress of President Thomas Jefferson (Thompson, 2017).

References

Allison, D. C. (2016). Introduction: A historical overview & conclusion: Discussion with implications. In D. C. Allison (Ed.), *Black women's portrayals on reality television: The new sapphire* (pp. ix–xxix & 233–242). Lanham, MD: Lexington Books.

Briceño, M. E., & Estwick, E. (2016). Are black women loud? Neoliberal and postfeminist protagonists in OWN televisual sphere. In D. C. Allison (Ed.), *Black women's portrayals on reality television: The new sapphire* (pp. 63–82). Lanham, MD: Lexington Books.

Brown, W. (2005). *Edgework: Critical essays on knowledge and politics*. Princeton, NJ & Oxford: Princeton University Press.

Chouliaraki, L., & Fairclough, N. (1999). *Discourse in late modernity: Rethinking critical discourse analysis*. Edinburgh: Edinburgh University Press.

Crenshaw, K. (1991). Mapping the margins: Intersectionality, identity politics, and violence against women of color. *Stanford Law Review*, *43*(6), 1241–1299. doi:10.2307/1229039

Dunn, S. (2008). *"Baad bitches" and sassy supermamas: Black power action films*. Champaign, IL: University of Illinois Press.

Filoteo, J. (2014). ABC's Scandal. *Media Review*, *38*(2), 212–215. doi:10.1177/0160597614532191

Fisher, L. (2014, October 9). Shonda Rhimes speaks her mind on "Angry Black Woman" flap. *ABC.com*. Retrieved from http://abcnews.go.com/blogs/entertainment/2014/10/shonda-rhimes-speaks-her-mind-on-angry-black-woman-flap/

Fiske, J. (1987). *Television culture*. London: Routledge.

Fogel, M. (2005, May 8). "Grey's Anatomy" goes colorblind. *The New York Times*. Retrieved from www.nytimes.com/2005/05/08/arts/television/greys-anatomy-goes-colorblind.html

Foucault, M. (1978). *The history of sexuality, volume I*. New York, NY: Random House.

Foucault, M. (1991). Governmentality. In G. Burchell, C. Gordon, and P. Miller (Eds.), *The Foucault effect: Studies in governmentality* (pp. 87–104). Chicago, IL: University of Chicago Press.

Gill, R. (2007). Postfeminist media culture: Elements of a sensibility. *European Journal of Cultural Studies*, *10*(2), 147–166. doi:10.1177/1367549407075898

Harvey, D. (2005). *A brief history of neoliberalism*. New York, NY: Oxford University Press.

Hill Collins, P. (1991). *Black feminist thought: Knowledge, consciousness and the politics of empowerment*. New York, NY: Routledge.

Hill Collins, P. (2005). *Black sexual politics: African Americans, gender, and the new racism*. New York, NY: Routledge.

Hill Collins, P., & Bilge, S. (2016). *Intersectionality*. Malden, MA: Polity Press.

Hundley, G. (2008). Assessing the Horatio Alger myth: Is self-employment especially beneficial for those from less-advantaged family backgrounds? *Research in Social Stratification and Mobility*, *26*, 307–322.

Kanter, S. C. (2014, September 21). Exclusive first look: The Scandal collection for The Limited. *InStyle*. Retrieved from www.instyle.com/celebrity/scandal-collection-limited-exclusive-first-look

Lui, A. (2011). Unraveling the myth of meritocracy within the context of US higher education. *Higher Education*, *62*, 383–397. doi:10.1007/s10734-010-9394-7

Marira, T. D., & Mitra, P. (2013). Colorism: Ubiquitous yet understudied. *Industrial and Organizational Psychology*, *6*(1), 103–107. doi:10.1111/iops.12018

Maxwell, B. (2013, February 7). Olivia Pope and the scandal of representation. *The Feminist Wire*. Retrieved from www.thefeministwire.com/2013/02/olivia-pope-and-the-scandal-of-representation/

McNamee, S. J., & Miller, Jr., R. K. (2004). The meritocracy myth. *Sociation Today*, *2*, 1. Retrieved from www.ncsociology.org/sociationtoday/v21/merit.htm

Orbe, M. P. (2008). Representations of race in reality TV: Watch and discuss. *Critical Studies in Mass Communication*, *25*(4), 345–352.

Ouellette, L., & Hay, J. (2008). Makeover television, governmentality and the good citizen. *Continuum: Journal of Media & Cultural Studies*, *22*(4), 471–484.

Page, A. (2015). Advance your freedom: Race, enterprise, and neoliberal governmentality on *From G's to Gents*. *Television & New Media*, *16*(5), 439–453. doi:10.1177/1527476414533833

Poggi, J. (2016, April 18). Dear TV: We love you. You're perfect. Now change. (But not too much.). *Advertising Age*. Retrieved from http://adage.com/article/media/future-tv-advertising/303565/

Riggs, M. T. (1991). Black macho revisited: Reflections of a snap! Queen. *Black American Literature Forum*, *25*(2), 389–394. doi:10.2307/3041695

Rodriguez, N. S. (2017). Hip-hop's authentic masculinity: A quare reading of Fox's *Empire*. *Television & New Media*, 1–16. doi:10.1177/1527476417704704

Shugart, H. A. (2003). Reinventing privilege. The new (gay) man in contemporary popular media. *Critical Studies in Media Communication, 20,* 67–91.

Spargo, C. (2015, November 19). Pepsi paid $20M for Empire storyline about fictional making soda ad. *Daily Mail Online.* Retrieved from www.dailymail.co.uk/news/article-3325642/How-Pepsi-scored-three-episode-storyline-hit-Empire-real-TV-commercial-brand-featuring-breakout-star-Jussie-Smollett.html

Stoffel, A. (2016, March 14). Emerging feminisms, is Shonda Rhimes a feminist? *The Feminist Wire.* Retrieved from www.thefeministwire.com/2016/03/emerging-feminisms-is-shonda-rhimes-a-feminist/

Strayhorn, T. L. (2008). Influences on labor market outcomes of African American college graduates: A national study. *The Journal of Higher Education, 79*(1), 28–57. doi:10.1080/00221546.2008.11772085

Tasker, Y., & Negra, D. (Eds.) (2007). *Interrogating postfeminism: Gender and the politics of popular culture.* Durham, NC: Duke University Press.

Teasley, M., & Ikard, D. (2010). Barack Obama and the politics of race: The myth of postracism in America. *Journal of Black Studies, 40*(3), 411–425. doi:10.1177/0021934709352991

Thoma, P. (2009). Buying up baby: Modern feminine subjectivity, assertions of "choice," and the repudiation of reproductive justice in postfeminist unwanted pregnancy films. *Feminist Media Studies, 9*(4), 409–425. doi:10.1080/14680770903233001

Thompson, K. (2017, Februay 19). For decades they hid Jefferson's relationship with her. Now Monticello is making room for Sally Hemings. *The Washington Post.* Retrieved from www.washingtonpost.com/lifestyle/style/for-decades-they-hid-jeffersons-mistress-now-monticello-is-making-room-for-sally-hemings/2017/02/18/d410d660-f222-11e6-8d72-263470bf0401_story.html?noredirect=on&utm_term=.73f7352857ed

Turow, J. (2005). Audience construction and culture production: Marketing surveillance in the digital age. *The Annals of the American Academy, 597,* 103–121. doi:10.1177/0002716204270469

TV Week. (2017, April 7). Fox's "Empire" notches TV's highest-rated freshman season finale in almost 10 years – And that's just one of the show's impressive achievements. Retrieved October 10, 2017, from www.tvweek.com/tvbizwire/2015/04/foxs-empire-notches-tvs-highest-rated-freshman-season-finale-in-almost-10-years-and-thats-just-one-of-the-shows-impressive-achievements/

Warner, K. (2014). The racial logic of *Grey's Anatomy*: Shonda Rhimes and her "post-civil rights, post-feminist" series. *Television & New Media,* 1–17. doi:10.117/152746414550529

Willis, D., & Williams, C. (2002). *The black female body: A photographic history.* Philadelphia, PA: Temple University Press.

12

DOING WHITENESS "RIGHT"

Playing by the Rules of Neoliberalism for Television's Working Class

Holly Willson Holladay

As fictional representations of working-class families have all but disappeared from the situation comedy format, reality television has experienced a "blue collar boom" (James, 2013) with series like *Ice Road Truckers*, *Swamp People*, *Hillbilly Handfishin'*, *Duck Dynasty*, *Here Comes Honey Boo Boo*, and *Moonshiners* offering often comedic insight into the lives of workers with precarious, manual labor jobs and families on the economic margins. As such, the current reality television landscape is a fruitful space through which to explore the representation of class in America. This analysis derives from the assumption that televisual representations of identity are "inherently political" and "help shape national norms tied to the power of one group of people to rule over the majority" (Mittell, 2010, p. 305). That is, the representation of working-class characters sheds light on the expectations and assumptions we have about them as a group. As Mittell argues:

> Representations of identity help define what a culture thinks is normal for a particular group, how behaviors and traits fit into a society's shared common sense. Such representations also directly impact how we think about ourselves: when television constructs norms for a group we belong to, we might compare our own behavior to that representation; when it represents a group different from ourselves, television can shape how we view other people.
>
> *(p. 306)*

In turn, representations of what it means to be working class have the potential to justify stereotypes and policy decisions that affect the upward mobility of working-class Americans.

To provide a theoretical guide for understanding how class is manifest in modern culture, and in reality televisual representations specifically, I explore class and its intersection with gender, Whiteness, and rural belonging through the lens of neoliberalism within the reality TV shows *Duck Dynasty* and *Here Comes Honey Boo Boo*. Because it is explicitly framed through economics, neoliberalism has clear implications for studying class in contemporary culture. Both in the United States and abroad, neoliberal policies are discussed in conjunction with a persistent culture of poverty (e.g., Houtart, 2005). Thus, neoliberalism provides the theoretical framework through which to place representations of class into a broader cultural framework. Like all television series, reality programs are specifically engineered to garner ratings and subsequently court advertisers. While it is impossible to determine the "authenticity" of identity in reality performance, reality series do offer one way to explore the representations of dominant ideological meanings about class, Whiteness, gender, and place in the "redneck" subgenre, and how those meanings are structured by a culture of neoliberalism.

Neoliberalism in Contemporary Culture

As a political and economic philosophy, neoliberalism has shaped cultural beliefs about class in the United States. Bockman (2013) refers to neoliberalism as both an approach to governance and a contemporary political movement that began to gain traction in the early 1970s as an attempt to mitigate capitalist crises (e.g., the oil crisis, debt crisis, the widespread popularity of socialism in Latin America). She argues that neoliberal philosophy posits that it is not the government's responsibility to create economic growth; by even trying, the government makes the world worse for everyone, including those it purports to help. Instead, neoliberalism encourages a reliance on private companies, private individuals, and free markets to generate economic growth and promote social welfare. In his *The Birth of Biopolitics* (2008), Michel Foucault notes that neoliberal states are truly marked by the use of the market logic of efficiency, competitiveness, and profitability to govern. With these privatized technologies of governance in place, citizens are consigned control of their own lives without government interference. Simply, neoliberalism can be understood as the idea that "the 'free' market [is] the best way to organize every dimension of social life" (Ouellette, 2008, p. 140).

Duggan (2003) maintains that neoliberalism's overarching dominance can be attributed to the fact that it discursively constructs economic policy as "primarily a matter of neutral, technical expertise" (p. x), which is separate from politics and culture. This rhetorical separation, she points out, makes neoliberalism immune from political accountability and cultural critique. The result is the concentration of power and resources in the hands of only a few with "neoliberal policies" framed as "due to performance rather than design, reflecting the greater merit of those reaping larger rewards" (p. x). In other words, neoliberalism justifies class stratification by emphasizing a merit-based distribution of resources, and it obfuscates the role racial- and gender-based marginalization play in economic inequality.

Neoliberalism, Gender, and Racial Identity

In addition to neoliberalism's clear implications in the understanding of class, neoliberal ideology also bears significant connections to contemporary discourses surrounding gender and race. Despite neoliberalism's rhetorical separation between economics and political and cultural life, Duggan (2003) indicates it is impossible to disentangle these areas in practice. She concludes:

> In the real world, class and racial hierarchies, gender and sexual institutions, religious and ethnic boundaries are the channels through which money, political power, cultural resources, and social organizations flow. The *economy* cannot be transparently abstracted from the *state* or the *family*, from practices of racial apartheid, gender discrimination, or sexual regulation.
>
> *(p. x)*

Any attempt, then, to conceptualize neoliberalism in purely economic terms is reductionist, given that economic conditions are so intimately tied to every other dimension of social life.

For example, concerning gender in particular, neoliberal philosophies are inherent in postfeminist discourse. Gill and Scharff (2011) maintain that the "powerful resonance" between neoliberalism and postfeminism operates on three levels. First, they contend that both philosophies are structured within a context of individualism which rejects "notions of the social or political, or any idea of individuals as subject to pressures, constraints or influence from outside themselves" (p. 7). They further argue that the "autonomous, calculating, self-regulating subject of neoliberalism" is in many ways similar to the "active, freely choosing, self-inventing subject of postfeminism" (p. 7), indicating that postfeminism is not simply a response to feminism, but also partly structured through the pervasiveness of neoliberal ideologies. Finally, Gill and Scharff conclude that the most important parallel between neoliberalism and postfeminism exists in their third connection, or the ways that women in particular are called on to be self-regulating, self-disciplining subjects. The authors explain:

> To a much greater extent than men, women are required to work on and transform the self, to regulate every aspect of their conduct, and to

present all their actions as freely chosen. Could it be that neoliberalism *is always already gendered*, and that women are constructed as its ideal subjects?

(p. 7)

Thus, as Gill and Scharff point out, exploring neoliberalism's connection to gender in a postfeminist culture allows scholars to interrogate how women and men experience the expectations of neoliberalism differently.

Barclay (2014) points out another important difference in neoliberal enactment for men and women as she traces the historical trajectory of the household division of labor, pointing out that social reproductive labor (e.g., caring for the young, preparing meals, etc.) has become industrialized in the neoliberal economy of the last four decades. Although the service sectors have created new jobs, women occupy most of these low-paying "pink collar" occupational roles. Now that so-called "women's work" has become monetized, many women who work in these jobs are paid for their daytime labor, but not for the exact same labor they perform in their own homes in what Hochschild (1989) calls their "second shift." Moreover, neoliberal ideology dovetails neatly with traditionally hegemonic notions of masculinity, particularly as it relates to a man's ability to be a familial "provider" within the capitalist system, and to how that economic success is predicated on notions of rugged masculinity. As Fleras and Dixon (2011) note, mediated representations of working-class men have sought to recoup masculine economic, political, and cultural authority in the feminized post-industrial service economy.

Scholars have also observed a relationship between neoliberalism and race. Duggan (2003) argues that both overt and covert racial politics have been central to the neoliberal project from its inception. In particular, neoliberalism's focus on personalized achievement has implications for racial inequality, as racism can be obfuscated under the guise of identity-blind meritocracy. As Davis (2007) suggests, neoliberal societies purport that "individuals are supposedly freed from identity and operate under the limiting assumptions that hard work will be rewarded if the game is played according to the rules" (p. 350). In line with Rose's (1996) notion that neoliberal citizens are personally to blame for their shortcomings, Davis (2007) argues that "any impediments to success are attributed to personal flaws," which "affirms notions of neutrality and silences claims of racializing and racism" (p. 350). Ultimately, neoliberalism acts as an erasure of difference, crafting a society in which all individuals ostensibly enjoy the same chance of success. As Roberts and Mahtani (2010) maintain, "neoliberalism effectively masks racism through its value-laden moral project: camouflaging practices anchored in an apparent meritocracy, making possible a utopic vision of society that is non-racialized" (p. 253).

The two primary tenets of neoliberal thought—meritocracy and individualism—are narratives of success that inevitably blame the working class for "fluctuating economic and political conditions that affect working-class whites" (Levine-Rasky, 2013, p. 111). As Levine-Rasky points out, given "the belief that personal merit and innate talent promote economic well-being, the implications of 'downward mobility' are more likely to oppress members of the White working class than the White middle class" (p. 112). Beliefs in meritocracy and individualism position Whites who have not achieved upwardly mobility as uniquely responsible for their own lack of success. Grindstaff (2002) argues that the "White trash" cultural stereotype brings attention to the relationship between Whiteness and poverty, which are usually separated in popular discourse. Moreover, the term "White trash" implies that working-class Whites are not "doing Whiteness" appropriately (Bettie, 1995). Indeed, Grindstaff (2002) notes that the "White middle-class rely on the attributes embodied by White trash to distinguish themselves from the lower orders, in effect saying, *We are not that*," (p. 264, emphasis in original). Working-class Whites have also recouped the term "redneck" to exemplify this differentiation. As Hubbs (2011) suggests, the term "redneck," often used interchangeably with terms like "hillbilly" and "White trash," "is conspicuously classed, but its working-class valence is also marked in terms of race—white; locale—provincial; and sex—the 'redneck' label conventionally attaching to maleness and connoting a rough style of masculinity, often, but not exclusively, Southern" (p. 47).

Contemporary Texts: *Duck Dynasty* and *Here Comes Honey Boo Boo*

To explore how the ideological codes of class, gender and Whiteness are represented in conjunction with neoliberal ideology in working-class, rural domestic reality television, this essay analyzes the first seasons of *Duck Dynasty* (13 episodes) and *Here Comes Honey Boo Boo* (10 episodes). *Duck Dynasty* follows the professional and personal lives of the Louisiana-based Robertson family. Phil Robertson, who became wealthy through his Duck Commander hunting supply business, owns the family-based enterprise, which is now run by his son Willie. The extended Robertson family, including Willie's brother, Jase, his uncle, Si, his mother, Miss Kay, and his wife, Korie, are regularly featured in the series. Since its premiere in March 2012, *Duck Dynasty* has become a ratings powerhouse for cable network A&E. Although it debuted to just 1.81 million viewers in Season 1, the program's fourth season premiere drew 11.8 million viewers, the largest audience ever for any non-fiction cable series (Kissell, 2013). Critics' reception of the program reflects its status as a ratings success. Ryan (2013) suggests that *Duck Dynasty*'s popularity is partly rooted in its similarity to the domestic sitcom genre, calling it an uplifting, zany comedy about a close-knit family that has its share of squabbles but still demonstrates intense loyalty ... a TV recipe that seems to have worked out well for everything from *The Addams Family* to *All in the Family* to *Modern Family*.

(para. 7).

Here Comes Honey Boo Boo follows child beauty contestant Alana "Honey Boo Boo" Thompson, who became an Internet viral sensation after originally appearing on TLC's *Toddlers & Tiaras*. The show additionally features members of the Shannon/Thompson family: Alana's mother, June Shannon, a stay-at-home-mother, her father, Mike Thompson (a.k.a. Sugar Bear), a chalk miner, and her older sisters, Lauryn, Jessica, and Anna Shannon. The show's narrative is structured around the Shannon/Thompson's family life in rural McIntyre, Georgia. The *Here Comes Honey Boo Boo* debut, which aired on TLC in August 2012, drew 2.2 million viewers, making it the number one cable program in its time slot ("TLC's *Honey Boo Boo* Scores," 2012). The third season finale, which aired in September 2013 and featured the wedding of June Shannon and Mike Thompson, netted a series high viewership of 3.2 million (Kondolojy, 2013). Critics have maligned the show for making an "exploitative mess" (Paskin, 2012, para. 3) of the family. Goodman (2012) points out that "The show uses subtitles, because the apparent lack of education and the Georgia accents mesh together like some kind of indecipherable Scottish accent," indicating that the Shannon/Thompsons lack the particular verbal markers of the middle class. Others defend the family's portrayals for the perceived authenticity with which it represents a particular subset of the American population. For example, Yarrow (2013) argues that more than most representations on reality television, the Shannon/Thompson family hold a mirror to the real lives of many in the U.S.: "For many Americans, poverty, obesity, teen pregnancy, and unemployment are facts of life, just as they are for the Thompson/Shannons."

Method

Fiske (2011) argues that television is structured through codes, or "a rule-governed system of signs, whose rules and conventions are shared amongst members of a culture, and which is used to generate and circulate meanings in and for that culture" (p. 4). He notes that viewers are only able to make sense of the "reality" we see on television through the conventional codes of representation, such as the narrative, conflict, character, action, and setting, which are structured through the ideological codes of a given culture. These three codes of television—"reality," representation, and ideology—work together, making what appears on television "a coherent, seemingly natural unity" (p. 6).

Given that the first season of a program introduces us to its characters, establishes the plot, and suggests central themes, examining the first season of each text will provide evidence for understanding how ideology structures the "reality" represented on each program. Thus, this chapter is guided by critical ideological analysis. Specifically, it explores how the codes of class work to form ideological messages about what it means to be working class. To conduct the analysis, I watched each season of each program in its entirety and recorded available information about the family structure, occupations, and education levels. Additionally, I made thorough notes regarding television's representational components, including narrative, mise en scène, and dialogue, that structure meanings about class. I then reviewed these components to explore how gender and race intersect to influence the meaning ascribed to a character's class position. After the notation of the representational components of class, gender, and race, themes emerged from the texts to suggest how these elements of identity work together to represent working-class belonging in *Here Comes Honey Boo Boo* and *Duck Dynasty*.

In examining two "blue collar" reality shows, I argue that the application of neoliberal rules has heavily gendered implications for the working class. In an environment that is postfeminist and neoliberal, women are expected to adhere to rules of disciplined femininity, both in personal care and in the home. For working-class men, notions of rugged masculinity and manual labor jobs underscore the "provider" mandate of traditional masculinity, as men "work hard" to ensure economic stability for their families. Moreover, I argue that Whiteness is fractured along lines of class belonging and regional identity such that an endorsement of neoliberal beliefs about hard work and individualism accounts for the working-classness of Whites and, in particular, "White trash" individuals. I posit that the "White trash" family in *Here Comes Honey Boo Boo* and the upwardly mobile "rednecks" of *Duck Dynasty* serve as exemplars of how working-class Whiteness—and the cultural, working class performance of hard work, individualization, and participation in the competitive free market—are illustrative of a neoliberal success story and serve to reinforce neoliberal ideology. Lastly, I maintain that the Robertsons' simultaneous economic success and working-class cultural performance complicate how working-class Whiteness can be read in a neoliberal environment.

Neoliberal Femininity and Masculinity

A number of scholars have maintained that the culture of self-discipline and consumption central to neoliberal philosophy has different implications for women than it does for men (e.g., Gill & Scharff, 2011; McRobbie, 2008). Gill (2007) relates contemporary postfeminist sensibility to neoliberalism by suggesting that, in popular culture discourses, "*women* are called on to self-manage and self-discipline. To a much greater extent than men, women are required to work on and transform the self, regulate every aspect of their conduct, and present their actions as freely chosen" (p. 164, emphasis in original).

An example of undisciplined femininity exists in the bodily representation of the Shannon-Thompson women of *Here Comes Honey Boo Boo*, all of whom are overweight. Their weight is made central in the family's portrayal. Although Mama June recognizes she's "not the most beautimous out of the box," she additionally points out that, "there are a lot of people fatter than me that have 500 chins. I only have two or three." Yet when daughter Jessica, who weighs 175 pounds at age 15 and is nicknamed "Chubbs," expresses that she would like to lose weight, Mama June agrees to also go on a diet for moral support. They begin a weight-loss competition, with each member recording her starting weight. When Mama steps on the scale, the display shows an error message, and daughter Alana laughs, "It won't weigh Mama because she's too big!"

Mama June's unruly body is continually presented as a visual spectacle of excess. In "A Bunch of Wedgies," her daughters Jessica and Lauryn struggle to remove an inner tube that has become lodged around Mama's too big body. Later, two lifeguards must help Mama sit down in an inner tube to ride down a waterslide, as her large body limits her mobility and makes sitting down gracefully difficult. Mama is unapologetic about her body, however, choosing to label herself as "voluptuous" and repeating a mantra of self-acceptance and loving one's self no matter her size. Even so, the Shannon-Thompson women, and Mama in particular, are framed through a lack of self-control. Their diet challenge fails because of their inability to engage in the self-discipline necessary to lose weight; instead of consuming smarter choices and smaller quantities, they eat cake, cheese balls, and oatmeal pies. As Alana says about her mother, "I hope Mama don't eat Glitzy [her pet pig]. She eats everything else." Although Alana's fears that Mama is so unbridled that she may, in fact, eat Alana's pet pig are certainly hyperbolic, her comment underscores, when coupled with the visual representation of Mama's body, Mama's unwillingness to discipline her body along lines of conventional femininity. Much as Pitcher (2008) contends in her analysis of Anna Nicole Smith's body and the discourse surrounding it,[1] Mama June's corporeality is a transgressive representation of hegemonic expectations for feminine performance; reveling in junk food and general excess means that she "was not the docile, disciplined body, as society demands" (p. 111).

Mama June's large body is not only a rejection of the disciplined female form that has come to be expected in the neoliberal climate, but it is also a marker of how that lack of discipline can translate to class belonging. Bettie (1995) describes a similar correlation between the body and class in the TV sitcom *Roseanne*,[2] pointing out,

> In *Roseanne*, the socially "low" is marked by Roseanne and Don Conner's large bodies, in striking contrast to the thin and normatively beautiful characters of middle-class sitcoms. In the U.S., where weight is inversely correlated with socioeconomic status, fat, itself, becomes associated with "lowbrow" status.
>
> (p. 137)

Although Bettie suggests that fatness, in general, is indicative of the socially low, the added pressure of self-surveillance for women demonstrated by the numerous comments made by Mama June about her body indicate how neoliberalism is intertwined with working-class womanhood.

Despite the necessity for dual-income households for many families (Bianchi, 2013), the matriarchs in both *Here Comes Honey Boo Boo* and *Duck Dynasty* do not work outside the home. As such, the gender divide is also apparent within these series' homes through the reinforcement of "women's work" in the domestic sphere. For example, in *Duck Dynasty*, Miss Kay is consistently framed within the confines of traditional domestic femininity as she spends most of her time on screen cooking for her family. Patriarch Phil seems to perceive this as Miss Kay's greatest asset: "There ain't nothin' I love more than Ms. Kay's cookin'. She ended up cookin' better than my mama. If your woman cooks better than your mama, then you got one. You better hold onto her." Further, he offers this advice to his grandson:

> My first prerequisite for marrying a woman is—can she cook? ... She doesn't have to be a pretty girl. Just'cause she looks a little homely, that's alright. It's hard to get a pretty one to cook and carry a Bible anymore.

This traditional notion of the gendered division of domestic labor presents a generational rift among the members of the Robertson family in *Duck Dynasty*. For the younger generation of Robertsons, labor in the business and in the home at times seems much more egalitarian. In the opening episode of the first season, Willie states in an interview that his wife, Korie, "helps him run the entire business," and Korie's beliefs about relatively equal partnering in her marriage come through as the family shoots Miss Kay's cooking DVD in the episode "Family Funny Business." During the filming, Phil continually refers to the assumed audience of the DVDs as "ladies," which prompts Korie to chastise him: "You keep saying 'ladies,' but men are cooking, too. It's not just gonna be ladies watching the DVD." Phil, reemphasizing his beliefs about domestic gender norms, replies, "Girly men."

The men in *Here Comes Honey Boo Boo* and *Duck Dynasty* primarily engage in manual labor associated with working-class masculinity to provide for their families. For example, in the episode "Shh! It's a Wig," *Here Comes Honey Boo*

Boo's audience learns that Sugar Bear works seven days a week as a chalk miner to provide financial support for their six-member family. The men of *Duck Dynasty*, despite working warehouse positions involving relatively low bodily impact, are constructing devices for hunting, which is typically coded as a masculine endeavor.

Importantly, deviations from rugged masculinity are subject to scorn and ridicule in these televisual representations. While we never see Sugar Bear in his work environment at the chalk mine, he is presented as relatively incompetent at the masculine household tasks he is asked to perform. When Sugar Bear buys an above-ground pool for the family, Mama questions his ability to successfully construct it. She notes that Sugar Bear "don't like puttin' shit together," and he hasn't "put nothin' together in probably ten years." Alana's sister Pumpkin adds, "If he had to build a barn, he'd probably kill hisself." The portrayal of Sugar Bear as incompetent with manual labor generally suggests his failure to adequately provide for his family, further justifying the family's working-class identity within a gendered neoliberal framework.

Similarly, the success of the Robertson family business is predicated on masculine toughness and ruggedness. In the episode "Willie Stay or Willie Go," Willie takes the Duck Commander employees, including his family, to a team-building camp rather than their normal yearly retreat of hunting in the woods. He is ridiculed for the "softness" of the team-building exercises, with Si remarking that they should be "sittin' around a campfire holding hands singing kum-ba-ya." The Duck Commander employees frustrate the counselor when they refuse to take seriously the activities he has had planned, and he chastises them for teasing each other, saying, "Guys, if we could really try to be encouraging." By mocking the self-help nature of the retreat, the family reifies the notion that, in the context of working-class masculinity, the neoliberal rhetoric of mental and emotional self-improvement, when combined with the building of relationships and intimacy, is feminized and should therefore be avoided. Willie expresses his displeasure at his family's reaction to the retreat, and reveals he brought them to the team-building camp because he was offered another job with "workers who actually work." Jase tells him, "Calm down. You're acting all emotional like a woman," further implying that emotional expression is a feminine characteristic.

As evidenced in the analysis of *Here Comes Honey Boo Boo* and *Duck Dynasty*, traditional gender dynamics are reflected in these working-class portrayals. Both series depict working-class men in ways that dovetail with traditionally normative masculinity. Rather than contributing to domestic duties, working-class men engage in manual labor to act as financial providers for their families. Failure to perform this traditional form of masculinity resulted in ridicule. From Sugar Bear's technical incompetence to Willie's feminized desire for team-building, working-class masculinity incorporates the hard work and competitive rules of neoliberalism in a traditional way.

In addition, the women are primarily responsible for domestic duties such as housework and childcare. Although Bettie's (1995) analysis of *Roseanne* revealed a relatively egalitarian arrangement between the central couple in the working-class series, these contemporary working-class portrayals in *Duck Dynasty* and *Honey Boo Boo*, for the most part, revert to a stereotypical gendered division of labor. Moreover, the women's bodies in these series are policed as sites of discipline. Although this is also true for all women in a postfeminist and neoliberal cultural climate, working-class women must contend with the added burden of disciplining their bodies in a consumer culture that places them at an economic disadvantage.

Neoliberalism and the Mandate of "Doing Whiteness Right"

The intersection between rural, Southern Whiteness and working-class belonging is clearly evident in *Here Comes Honey Boo Boo* and *Duck Dynasty*, albeit to differing ends. In *Here Comes Honey Boo Boo*, "redneck" becomes synonymous with "White trash"—the family is represented as not "doing Whiteness" appropriately, and, in turn, their working-class belonging is justified. Conversely, the Robertsons of *Duck Dynasty* use the "redneck" label to situate themselves within the identity of rural, working-class, Southern Whiteness. In essence, the label allows them to remain "authentic and true" to their working-class roots, although their financial circumstances belie the culturally downward mobility often associated with the term.

In the pilot episode, the Shannon-Thompson family debates their status as "rednecks" before attending McIntyre, Georgia's, annual "Redneck Games." Patriarch Sugar Bear asserts that the family should, indeed, be classified as "redneck," which prompts Jessica to ask: "We all have our teeth, don't we?" Sugar Bear responds by addressing their participation in what he deems "redneck" leisure activities, asking, "We ride four-wheelers and play in the mud, don't we?" We see the family engaging in these activities in the episode "What is a Door Nut?" in which Mama mentions, "This is what we do for fun all time," and Alana offers that she "likes to get down and dirty, redneck style."

Later in the episode "This is My Crazy Family," the family does attend and participate in the "Redneck Games," which Mama asserts is "all about Southern pride. It's like the Olympics, but with a lot of missing teeth and a lot of butt cracks showing." Later in the episode, Mama passes judgment on many of the spectators at the games, stating, "There are some broke-down people out there. Please, women who are of voluptuous size. All that vajiggle jaggle is not beautimous." Mama June's judgment is particularly ironic given that Mama's unruly body is portrayed in the show in the same way as the women she criticizes.

Apart from their "Southern pride," the Shannon-Thompsons' exaggerated embodiment of the "redneck" culture of Southern Whites has led the popular press to describe the family as "White trash" (e.g., Lavine, 2013). The program is edited to draw attention to the family's "crass" nature; in the opening credits, Mama June passes gas, and every member of the family routinely belches, blows their noses loudly on camera, and sneezes into the open air. Sugar Bear is often shown spitting tobacco into an old plastic soda bottle. In the episode "Time For Sketti!" Pumpkin patronizes the neighborhood gas station barefoot, which is apparently a normal occurrence. The store manager states, "When I see Pumpkin come in, I call that the Bamm-Bamm[3] look 'cause there's no shoes on." Moreover, despite speaking English, the family is regularly subtitled, as if to indicate their particular vernacular of Southern English is another language entirely imperceptible to the audience who views the show. Following Grindstaff's (2002) assertion, the Shannon-Thompson family exists in a space of "White trash" Otherness given their inability to enact cultural rules of White middle-classness. Importantly, this is a choice they continually make, which places them outside the bounds of neoliberal prudent decision-makers.

The term "redneck" has also been reappropriated by Southern Whites who, like Mama June's description of the "Redneck Games," wear it is a badge of rural Southern pride, as is the case with the Robertsons of *Duck Dynasty*. Dubbing themselves "high-tech rednecks," the second generation of the Robertson clan (i.e., Willie and Jase) mix modernity with the pastoralism of the rural South. The Robertsons run a very successful hunting business that is predicated on a willingness to embrace neoliberal, free-market business sense. They are continually trying to find new ways to expand the company's offerings and increase profits. Phil remarks in the episode "High Tech Redneck," "I'm a low-tech man in a high-tech world. Willie took the whole thing way further than I ever would," suggesting that Willie's use of modern technologies has helped grow the business.

However, Willie is consistently portrayed as at odds with his rural, Southern, working-class roots and his family's desire to "remain true" to the place from which they came. In the episode "Frog in One," Willie must rescue his family when security guards apprehend them trying to catch frogs in the golf course pond at night. After Willie expresses his disapproval of his family's behavior, his uncle Si observes in an interview, "Will is going through an identity crisis. He's done forgot who he is." Jase says about Willie later, "What has happened to my brother? Either be proud of who you are or shave that stuff off your face and buy you a three-piece suit." In response to claims from his family that he's "forgotten what it's like to be a redneck," Willie drives his truck off-road through the mud, which he describes as "going crazy redneck up in here." In this instance, rural, working-class leisure is juxtaposed against responsible, business-like behavior. Willie must prove his "redneck-ness" to recoup that identity and remain an authentic member of the Robertson men.

This tension appears later through the constant struggle Willie faces to get his family to participate in the business when they would rather be in the wilderness. While Phil, Si, and Jase prefer to spend leisure time engaged in masculine activities like hunting, catching frogs, and blowing up beaver dams, Willie maintains that spending time building the business is necessary. Even when Willie does participate in his family's leisure activities, the family derides him for his inability to perform the manual labor associated with blue-collar masculinity. For example, in the episode "Redneck Logic," the family works together to construct a deer stand out of an abandoned recreational vehicle (RV). Willie claims to have an injury that prevents him from participating, which prompts Jase to state, "Willie doesn't like manual labor. He doesn't like to sweat." Phil goes on to say, "It's been my opinion that once you get the title 'CEO,' if you interject manual labor, injuries begin to occur." Again, Willie's masculinity is contrasted against the other men in his family, who represent true "redneck" manhood.

Because the Robertson family has built a successful business and, thus, has amassed economic capital, they must engage in "authentic" performances of working-class, "redneck" identity to maintain and legitimate their position in this culture. In addition to their leisure activities and general preference for "living off the land," they position themselves as "regular" folks who understand the value of money, and, for the most part, do not spend frivolously. Before they build the deer stand from the old RV, Phil points out, "What people need to realize about the South is that everything is usable. One man's junk is another man's treasure." In this way, he appeals to rural Southern culture as well as working-class resourcefulness. In the episode "Too Close for Comfort," Jase observes that, "In the South, road kill is a redneck's paycheck. ... Just because I have money in my pocket doesn't mean I'm too good to stop and pick up a $5 bill that's laying in the middle of the road." Jase's insistence that he is not "too good" to pick up road kill or a mere five dollars reinforces the family's rural, working-class ethos.

Unlike the Shannon-Thompsons of *Here Comes Honey Boo Boo*, the Robertsons are an exemplary "redneck" success story. Couched within the neoliberal rhetoric of hard work, the family repeatedly states that they "came from nothing" and have built a "multi-million dollar empire." The Robertsons are an example that suggests that, if the Shannon-Thompsons wanted it enough, they could, too, transcend their "White trash" label. Further, through the Robertsons' continued willful claiming of the "redneck" label and the lifestyle that goes with it, they are able to embody the working-class ethos of the rural South. Their "redneck" identity is a performance that underscores their continued working-class belonging.

Conclusion

Given television's role in shaping cultural discourses (Mittell, 2010), it is imperative to consider how televisual representations influence our understanding of the intersections between gender, race, and class belonging. In particular, both *Here Comes Honey Boo Boo* and *Duck Dynasty* point to the ways that neoliberal ideology has impacted expectations related to the disciplined body, work, and normative femininity and masculinity. The manual labor jobs occupied by the characters are gendered, and domestic duties in the home are still unevenly the responsibility of women. For the economically affluent but culturally working-class Robertson family in *Duck Dynasty*, women are relegated to supporting roles in the home and the business. In *Here Comes Honey Boo Boo*, Mama June's body serves as an unruly site of excess and tastelessness, serving as neoliberal justification for working-class belonging; that is, her body stands proxy for her unwillingness to abide by the neoliberal mandates of self-discipline and hard work.

Moreover, class, Whiteness, and rural belonging coalesce in these series to obscure the ways that these identity markers are understood in contemporary culture. As Grindstaff (2011) notes, "Race and class distinctions reflect and reinforce one another; their intersection seemingly 'naturalized' by the overrepresentation of people of color among the poor and working classes" (p. 200). That is, the conflation of "racial minority" and "poor or working-class" on television allows these identity categories to stand in for one another, which constructs White middle-classness as normative, and, thus, invisible. Coupled with the cultural expectation that individuals play by the "rules" of neoliberalism to achieve upward mobility, doing Whiteness "right" means consistently and consciously performing a neoliberal subjectivity that will allow poor and working-class Whites to become middle-class Whites.

The families featured in *Here Comes Honey Boo Boo* and *Duck Dynasty* offer a comparative way to examine how neoliberalism structures appropriate performative middle-class Whiteness. By brazenly refusing to adopt the rules of neoliberalism in a quest for upward mobility, much like Mama June rejects neoliberal feminine self-discipline, the Shannon-Thompsons self-identify as "redneck" and seem to revel in their "White trash" status. While "White trash" and "redneck" are not synonymous terms, they both function to "other" the provincial, poor and working-class Whites who refuse to adopt the morality and taste standards of middle-class Whites. However, the Robertsons of *Duck Dynasty* complicate the notion that the economic success afforded by adopting the hard-working, individualistic ethos of neoliberalism necessarily means they have transcended their working-class roots. As evidenced in the series, the Robertson men's "redneck" performance often belies their financial prowess; they have retained many of their working-class tastes, hobbies, and interests, always careful to construct their identities as authentically "redneck." Willie, the most middle-class performing of the Robertson men, is regularly chastised for "forgetting who he is" (i.e., a "redneck"). Despite the fact that Willie is CEO of Duck Commander and has generated significant financial gains for the company, the Robertson men place primacy on the "redneck" identity—one that is masculine, rural, White, and has working-class taste, regardless of financial status. Because the Roberstons have done Whiteness "right" by becoming upwardly mobile through their endorsement of neoliberalism, they are freer to partake in "redneck" culture without the judgement ordinarily reserved for poor and working-class Whites.

Indeed, class identity is a complex construct, especially when considered in conjunction with gender, race, and rural spatiality. Like scripted domestic situation comedies, these comedic reality portrayals are meant to be a source of humor for audiences as they consider, perhaps implicitly, the intersections of these identity categories. While it is unclear without speaking to audiences whether they are laughing *at* or *with* the families in *Here Comes Honey Boo Boo* and *Duck Dynasty*, the series offer important discursive lessons about what it means to perform White, working-class masculinity/femininity in rural America. In a culture that is so deeply entrenched with the tenets of neoliberalism, the programs also construct what it means to be successful in performing these identities "right."

Notes

1 Anna Nicole Smith, *Playboy*'s 1993 Playmate of the Year, married octogenarian billionaire J. Howard Marshall. She starred in her own reality TV show after his death and was roundly condemned by critics for her weight gain and "white trash" behavior (Pitcher, 2008).
2 *Roseanne* originally was broadcast on the ABC network from 1988 to 1997. Its second incarnation premiered on March 30, 2018, and was cancelled two months later when the show's star, Roseanne Barr, tweeted a racist comment about an African American advisor to President Barack Obama. Bettie (1995) is here referring to the original show.
3 Bamm-Bamm Rubble was a child character in the children's animated cartoon, *The Flintstones*. Like others in the Stone Age TV show, he was always barefoot.

References

Barclay, B. (2014, June 14). Fathers' day: Reproduction, production and the gender division of labor. *Chicago Political Economy Group*. Retrieved from www.cpegonline.org/2014/06/14/fathers-day-reproduction-production-and-the-gender-division-of-labor/

Bettie, J. (1995). Class dismissed? *Roseanne* and the changing face of working-class iconography. *Social Text*, *45*, 125–149.

Bianchi, J. (2013, November 4). 4 dual-income households tell all: How we save and spend. *Forbes*. Retrieved from www.forbes.com/sites/learnvest/2013/11/04/4-dual-income-households-tell-all-how-we-save-and-spend/

Bockman, J. (2013). Neoliberalism. *Contexts*, *12*(3), 14–15.

Davis, D. A. (2007). Narrating the mute: Racializing and racism in a neoliberal moment. *Souls: A Critical Journal of Black Politics, Culture, and Society*, *9*(4), 346–360.

Duggan, L. (2003). *The twilight of equality?: Neoliberalism, cultural politics, and the attack on democracy*. Boston, MA: Beacon Press.

Fiske, J. (2011). *Television culture* (2nd ed.). New York, NY: Routledge.
Fleras, A., & Dixon, S. M. (2011). Cutting, driving, digging, and harvesting: Re-masculinizing the working-class heroic. *Canadian Journal of Communication, 36*, 579–597.
Foucault, M. (2008). *The birth of biopolitics: Lectures at the College de France, 1978–1979*. Hampshire, UK: Palgrave MacMillan.
Gill, R. (2007). Postfeminist media culture: Elements of a sensibility. *European Journal of Cultural Studies, 10*(2), 147–166.
Gill, R., & Scharff, C. (2011). Introduction. In R. Gill & C. Scharff (Eds.), *New femininities: Postfeminism, neoliberalism, and subjectivity* (pp. 1–20). London, UK: Palgrave Macmillan.
Goodman, T. (2012, August 22). "Honey Boo Boo": That joke isn't funny anymore. *The Hollywood Reporter*. Retrieved from www.hollywoodreporter.com/bastard-machine/here-comes-honey-boo-boo-alana-mama-364933
Grindstaff, L. (2002). *The money shot: Trash, class, and the making of TV talk shows*. Chicago, IL: University of Chicago Press.
Grindstaff, L. (2011). From *Jerry Springer* to *Jersey Shore*: The cultural politics of class in/on US reality programming. In H. Wood & B. Skeggs (Eds.), *Reality television and class* (pp. 197–209). Hampshire, UK: Palgrave Macmillan.
Hochschild, A. R. (1989). *The second shift: Working parents and the revolution at home*. New York, NY: Penguin Books.
Houtart, F. (2005). Neoliberalism and poverty. In R. Fisk (Ed.), *Inside the crusader fortress* (pp. 52–58). Nottingham, UK: Spokeman Books.
Hubbs, N. (2011). "Redneck woman" and the gendered poetics of class rebellion. *Southern Cultures, 17*(4), 44–70.
James, K. (2013, September 15). Redneck TV: *Honey Boo Boo, Duck Dynasty* and cable's blue collar boom. The Hollywood Reporter. Retrieved from www.hollywoodreporter.com/gallery/redneck-tv-honey-boo-boo-408551#3-america-larry-cable-guy
Kissell, R. (2013, August 15). *Duck Dynasty* premiere shatters cable records with 11.8 million viewers. *Variety*. Retrieved from http://variety.com/2013/tv/news/duck-dynasty-premiere-shatters-cable-records-with-11-8-million-viewers-1200578066/
Kondolojy, A. (2013, September 12). Wednesday cable ratings: *Duck Dynasty* wins night + *Modern Dads, Here Comes Honey Boo Boo, Royal Pains, The Challenge: Rivals II*, and More. *TV by the Numbers*. Retrieved from http://tvbythenumbers.zap2it.com/2013/09/12/wednesday-cable-ratings-duck-dynasty-wins-night-modern-dads-here-comes-honey-boo-boo-royal-pains-the-challenge-rivals-ii-more/202249/
Lavine, R. (2013, May 20). The harsh reality behind *Here Comes Honey Boo Boo. The Guardian*. Retrieved from www.theguardian.com/commentisfree/2013/may/20/here-comes-honey-boo-boo-harsh-reality
Levine-Rasky, C. (2013). *Whiteness fractured*. Farnham, UK: Ashgate Publishing.
McRobbie, A. (2008). Young women and consumer culture: An intervention. *Cultural Studies, 22*(5), 531–550.
Mittell, J. (2010). *Television and American culture*. New York, NY: Oxford University Press.
Ouellette, L. (2008). "Take responsibility for yourself": *Judge Judy* and the neoliberal citizen. In C. Brunsdon & L. Spigel (Eds.), *Feminist television criticism: A reader* (2nd ed., pp. 139–153). Berkshire, England: Open University Press.

Paskin, W. (2012, August 9). "Honey Boo Boo": Loveable racist dysfunction. *Salon*. Retrieved from www.salon.com/2012/08/09/honey_boo_boo_lovable_racist_dysfunction/

Pitcher, K. C. (2008). The multiply transgressive body of Anna Nicole Smith. In M. Meyers (Ed.), *Women in popular culture: Representation and meaning* (pp. 101–119). New York, NY: Hampton Press, Inc.

Roberts, D. J., & Mahtani, M. (2010). Neoliberalizing race, racing neoliberalism: Placing "race" in neoliberal discourses. *Antipode, 42*(2), 248–257.

Rose, N. (1996). Governing "advanced" liberal democracies. In A. Barry, T. Osborne, & N. Rose (Eds.), *Foucault and political reason: Liberalism, neo-liberalism, and rationalities of government* (pp. 37–64). Chicago, IL: University of Chicago Press.

Ryan, M. (2013, March 6). *Duck Dynasty* and the Robertson clan: The formula for their success. *The Huffington Post*. Retrieved from www.huffingtonpost.com/maureen-ryan/duck-dynasty_b_2820874.html

TLC's *Honey Boo Boo* scores winning ratings with series premiere. (2012, August 10). *The Hollywood Reporter*. Retrieved from www.hollywoodreporter.com/live-feed/honey-boo-boo-tlc-ratings-360966

Yarrow, A. (2013, May 22). *Here Comes Honey Boo Boo* is a fabulous cultural ambassador for America. *The Atlantic*. Retrieved from www.theatlantic.com/entertainment/archive/2013/05/-i-here-comes-honey-boo-boo-i-is-a-fabulous-cultural-ambassador-for-america/276102/

13
NEGOTIATING IDENTITY AND WORKING CLASS STRUGGLES IN NBC'S *SUPERSTORE*

Lauren Bratslavsky

The NBC sitcom *Superstore* is set in an icon of neoliberalism: the big box store, known for low wages and cheap products. Justin Spitzer, the show's creator and a writer on NBC's *The Office*, reportedly thought of the show after his father-in-law mentioned that his law firm was representing workers in a class action lawsuit against Walmart (Staff, 2015). Instead of writing about the world of office workers, Spitzer imagined a world of retail workers. Inside the fictional store called Cloud 9, we see store employees gripe about inane corporate policies, trade tips on how to look busy, and only really rally to work when a small monetary reward compels them to sell more products. This satire about consumerism and working conditions is connected to activist rhetoric about the failures of multibillion-dollar corporations to pay living wages. The season finale directly critiques corporate actions such as the lack of health benefits and mandatory seminars about why unions are bad as the employees walk out in solidarity after their manager is fired.

Drawing on contemporary issues for sitcom content is certainly nothing new. Still, *Superstore*, which began airing in 2015, differs from past representations of the workplace and social class in other U.S. sitcoms. The differences stem from both form and content. Whereas the standard form of the sitcom once relied on laugh tracks and problems that required quick resolutions by the end of the episode, the genre now accommodates longer arc storylines and carries a sense of authenticity by drawing on documentary codes of production (Thompson, 2007). Shifts in the sitcom form have enabled narratives that are not easily resolved in a half hour slot, or what Mittell (2006) calls narrative complexity, when writers "use television's episodic form to undercut conventional assumptions of returning to equilibrium and situational continuity while embracing conditional seriality" (p. 34). For a sitcom, the narrative arc within a single episode does not necessarily have an easy resolution that returns the sitcom universe to equilibrium; thus, stories and characters may develop with more nuance and depth. In this sense, *Superstore* not only depicts working in a low-wage job at a big box retail store *as the premise*, the show also foregrounds a sustained critical commentary about structural inequalities and employees' tensions with the corporation. A problem such as access to health care is not a single-episode special issue; it's a sustained narrative throughout the season without an easy resolution. Before analyzing these depictions, the following section briefly explores television as a discursive site about social class.

Class on Television

As a representational system, the depictions we see on television matter. Stuart Hall (2011) explains media produce and construct "images, descriptions, explanations and frames for understanding how the world is and why it works as it is said and shown to work" (p. 82). The media discursively construct and limit representations, thus fostering images, narratives, and frameworks for how we think about something such as social class. Representations of social class are symbolically and rhetorically powerful: narratives, aesthetics, physical bodies (e.g., those which are in "excess" or out of control), and objects attribute value to social class distinctions, particularly dividing what is socially acceptable and what is not within the category of working class (Skeggs, 2004). Much of television perpetuates myths of a classless society by establishing the middle-class lifestyle as the norm (Henry, 2014; Kendall, 2011). Portrayals of working class individuals and their concerns are sparse. By one recent count, less than 10 percent of all domestic sitcoms feature working-class families (Butsch, 2016). Portrayals of working-class characters, particularly men, tend to be negative stereotypes that caricature them as buffoons, ignorant, and immature (Butsch, 2016; Kendall, 2011; Zweig, 2012). Furthermore, the few explicit treatments of social class in television serve to normalize neoliberal economic policies and associated ideologies of individualism, personal responsibility, and upward mobility (McMurria, 2008; Ouellette & Hay, 2008; Spangler, 2014; Wells, 2015). For example, to be poor and white is validated only when striving to improve one's condition and take care of one's body, voice, and manners (Rennels, 2015). One notable exception was *Roseanne*, a sitcom that famously dealt with various issues endemic to working-class families, such as job insecurity and lack of purchasing power.[1] Bettie (1995) argues *Roseanne* was about making class a visible marker of identity, particularly in terms of gender and labor, whether as employment or in the space of the home and family. Moreover, a show like *Roseanne* demonstrates how media represent, and thus define, social class as particularly gendered and racialized (Acker, 2006).

While a television program may feature working class people, the *practices* of class, such as types of and access to employment, relations to paid or unpaid labor, distribution of material goods, to name a few (Acker, 2006, pp. 50–60), are largely absent or merely present to move a plot. Kendall (2011) argues that narrative frames rarely address structural issues such as stagnant wages, access to education, affordable housing, cost of health care, and systematic racism and sexism. Instead, narrative frames across fiction and news programs tend to focus on the individual. The result is a reinterpretation of class conditions not as a facet of structural inequalities but instead "rooted in individual failures" (Rennels, 2015, p. 273). The ABC sitcom *The Middle* may offer an expanded representation of working class life marked by economic struggles, but ultimately each episode concludes with a moral lesson in locating happiness in one's family unit despite financial struggles and the "failure of the American dream's upward mobility" (Spangler, 2014, p. 485). While plots and dialogue in *Roseanne* pushed back against structural inequalities (e.g. access to employment opportunities) and advocated resistance, *The Middle* acquiesces and "invites resignation" (Grabowski, 2014, p. 136).

Baked into the sitcom form is the focus on individual relationships rather than how individuals relate to the multitude of structures that define their existence. Even though many television shows are often set in the workplace, their narratives rarely treat work in terms of labor. The political dimension of labor, as embodied by collective action, agitation, and unionization to improve working conditions, rarely makes its way into television comedies (Kendall, 2011; Zweig, 2012). The workplace sitcom, which applies family dynamics to an occupational setting, tends to reify individual moral responsibility and neoliberalism as the norm by taking attention away from the conditions of working in a service economy. For example, in one sitcom about a workplace family in a call center in India, this premise is a rich ground for narratives and stereotypes that rationalize global capitalism as individual freedom and mask systematic racism as an individual problem (Oh & Banjo, 2012).

Whereas past television tended towards stereotyping and erasing class differences, today's shows may "expose the injuries of class as the socio-psychological burden the current stage of capitalism puts on families and individuals" (Lemke & Schniedermann, 2017, p. 6). Narrative complexity itself does not guarantee critical commentary. The first season of *Superstore*, though, is a corrective to limited portrayals of work and working-class people as well as a text that does not ignore structural inequalities. These changes in representational and narrative strategies are not lost on the part of the actors in the show. America Ferrara, who is an executive producer and portrays a lead character, explained in the trade press: "We're representing working-class people in a setting that is the intersection of American consumerism and every race, religion and background. It's so ripe to have any conversation you want without it feeling forced" (Ryan, 2016). *Superstore* counters Kendall's (2011) observation that "the media portray those who produce goods and services as much less interesting than the people who excessively purchase them" (p. 215). The retail setting prompts stories about consumerism, but at its core, *Superstore* was designed to address the paucity of working-class representations and counter narrow stereotypes found across television portrayals.

Foregrounding Class in Narratives and Characters

Tracing plot lines, dialogues and aesthetic choices that paradigmatically belong in this particular workplace and the broader socioeconomic setting reveals our contemporary anxieties about class and labor. I argue that *Superstore*, at least in its first season, refracts to us the neoliberal condition through a prism that favors the perspectives of the working class given the sitcom's narrative form, setting, and intersectional characters.

However, such a representation of class alongside salient social issues is limited by what White (1992) calls the "ideological problematic," which is how a text reconciles seemingly progressive representations with the ways in which critical commentaries ultimately may be undercut by the overall text and commercial television context (p. 182). Examining the first season of this show is one means to engage with the contradictions in interpretative possibilities by evaluating narratives within individual episodes and across the whole arc of the season. The first season was a text constructed without knowing whether there would be a second season. Thus, a politically inflected season ending (and possibly series-ending) strike poses questions about the mainstreaming of class struggle. To leave the fate of characters amidst a strike meant an open-ended text with affinity for labor movements such as the Fight for $15.[2]

The cast of characters presents another ideological problematic. On the one hand, the ensemble cast of multicultural characters is progressive; characters are constructed with attention towards intersectional identities. Amy (America Ferrara), the floor manager, is Latina, and for the first three episodes we are led to presume she is a single mother (she is married). Glenn (Mark McKinney), the store manager, is a white Evangelical Christian with a large family of foster children. Dina (Lauren Ash), the assistant manager, is an unruly white woman, meaning that she is loud, blunt, sexual, physically larger than the rest of the characters, and often emasculates Glenn. Cheyenne (Nichole Bloom), an employee, is a pregnant teenager and appears to have an Asian background (never discussed, but visible). Garrett (Colton Dunn), an employee, is a Black man and in a wheel chair (although the actor is able bodied). Jonah (Ben Feldman), the new hire, is a white, heterosexual man, whose employment at Cloud 9 is treated with some ongoing suspicion given his attire and education, as will be explored in the analysis. Mateo (Nico Santos), also a new hire, is Filipino and gay. The show features an assortment of secondary and tertiary employee characters who are in no way a homogenous pool of background characters – they vary in age, race, and ethnicity, too.

On the other hand, the presence of such a diverse cast may indeed be a commercial strategy and, thus, problematic in erasing the specificity of experiences that are inextricably linked with race, gender, sexuality, and ability (Meyer, 2015). And there is little irony in pointing out that the fictional Cloud 9 workforce somewhat mirrors the reality of those who tend to work at Walmart and other retail jobs: women, people of color, and older individuals (Ehrenreich, 2016; Greenhouse, 2008; Lichtenstein, 2006). Between the workplace setting that foregrounds social class and the diverse cast, how do these intersectional identities function at the levels of both plot development and ideology?

Examining intersectional representations means attention to "the presence of identity politics manifested in the visual depiction of a character and/or story arc across multiple texts" (Meyer, 2015, p. 904). Cho, Crenshaw, and McCall (2013) call on intersectional analysis that "emphasizes political and structural inequalities" by critiquing the dynamics of identity *and* power structures (p. 797). By addressing constructions of identity as a "problem of sameness and difference," we critique how structural forces, be it our economic, educational, religious, and/or political institutions, define dominant or "common sense" values and pronounce the contours of our identities (p. 795). How are various configurations of identities along the axis of "working class" constructed and deployed to reify those in power?

Taking cues from ideological and intersectional analyses, I ask: What does this particular text convey about class and work as they relate to structural issues, at least those structural elements that are visible in the show as signified by the corporation? What are the portrayals of working-class people and how do they intersect with other markers of identity and experiences to create three dimensional and realistic characters? In foregrounding the sameness of socioeconomic class status – an identity that is sorely missed in much of our TV – are other markers of identity employed to develop a character's specificity? Overall, how does this text negotiate real-world discourses about low-wage labor and social class with the narrative and economic constraints of television? I begin with an examination of this particular workplace setting, followed by an analysis of how this text constructs working class consciousness and intersectional identities.

Cloud 9: the Bane of and the Reason for the Employee's Existence

The corporation is crucial in a number of ways, beginning with establishing the contours in which the characters develop and interact with one another (and with the corporation). I address the corporation in two ways: first, as a setting, meaning the connotations of the big box retail space, and second, as a character.

The setting itself is a departure from other workplace comedies in that it is the first in recent memory that takes place at a site of employment that is not a professional setting like that of the white-collar world in *The Office*. Cloud 9 is a retail giant modeled after Walmart, Target, and similar stores. Decisions about the overall set are designed with social class in mind. While the Cloud 9 color scheme closely resembles Walmart and the pilot episode was shot at a Kmart, the show creators included a note in the pilot script to create a set that felt more like Target than Walmart (Spitzer, 2015). Aesthetic choices regarding the set design (in addition to the single-camera style and cutaway shots of shoppers) carry ideological connotations (Gray & Lotz, 2012). Target is known as a higher-end big box retailer whose customers have a higher income and younger age than the average Walmart shopper (Peterson, 2016). The precision in identifying real-world models for Cloud 9 functions to appeal to the desired viewing audience. NBC's strategy is to aim for "quality" audiences (as in, higher income and higher education) instead of quantity. This show would be far different had it been set in a more upscale retail store, such as Macy's or Whole Foods, where the humor may still highlight the conditions of working in retail, but less foregrounded in socioeconomic status outside of middle-class norms. Instead, Cloud 9 is carefully staged to establish a sense of place and purpose, replicating the distinctive and yet mundane qualities of this work (and consumer) environment. From familiar store features such as stocked aisles and checkout stands to authentic signage such as the legally mandated Department of Labor federal minimum wage poster, Cloud 9 is a simulacrum of the consumer *and* worker experiences. The consumer side, though, is a backdrop to the characters' existence as workers. We do not see the characters at home in the ways we do in other sitcoms associated with working-class portrayals. All the characters, from the manager to the new employees, exist in relation to the corporation, as opposed to the fullness of their lives within work *and* home.

Cloud 9 is a character with a distinct voice that speaks through corporate representatives, store management, and the corporate printed material. Corporate representatives are seldom seen, let alone heard. The only corporate representatives are from the internal relations magazine and a union-busting expert. The corporation speaks to the employees primarily through Glenn, the manager. Glenn is an ideal middle-man. He is trusting and protective of his employees, whom he frequently refers to as his Cloud 9 family. He is timid and lacks assertiveness in dealing with both upper management and his employees. In other words, he is often unquestioning about the purpose of corporate policies while earnestly trying to sell those policies to an unenthusiastic workforce. The assistant manager, Dina, serves as a proxy for the corporation through her ruthless enforcement and surveillance.

While Glenn tries to see the good in everything – including the wisdom and actions of Cloud 9 – the rest of the characters intone about the corporation as uncaring and transparent in its attempts to *not* come off as a faceless multinational billion-dollar corporate entity. The corporation is the butt of jokes and one-liners that take aim at Cloud 9's true mission – to care more for profits than for people. For example, some employees treat the internal magazine as "corporate propaganda," and mock such stories as "Minimum wage is Maximum Fun" and "Walk it Off! A Guide to Workplace Injuries" (Hubbard & Jann, 2015). These jokes serve two functions. On one level, they create the conditions of antagonism between the Cloud 9 employees and the corporation. On a more ideological level, they serve as a persistent reminder about the power imbalance between the corporation and the workers, including middle management.

Kendall (2011) observed how all television forms with working-class representations rarely addressed structural problems. News and fictional programming tend to employ a frame about the individual without mentioning structural forces such as the circumstances of education or wage stagnation. Towards the end of the season, as the contours of Cloud 9's corporate ethos as well as the employees' personalities develop, a major episode plot addresses the sorts of structural issues that tend to be absent from sitcom plots in any sustained manner. The ninth episode, "All-Nighter," follows an arc that begins with a frivolous top-down directive that Glenn implements – to change all store signage from one indistinguishable shade of blue to another blue – and which results in all the employees locked in the store. Central to the plot is the not-so-subtle critique of retail monoliths such as Walmart, whose own labor practices and model of expansion have provided a template for other corporations in what is known as the "Walmart effect" (Greenhouse, 2008; Lichtenstein, 2006). "All-Nighter" draws on known actions taken by Walmart and similar corporations: centralized control over doors, locks, and lights (and music), and more alarmingly, employees locked in the store (Ehrenreich, 2016; Greenhouse, 2008).

The episode begins when Glenn is unable to reach anyone at Cloud 9's corporate offices, first to verify that the store signs need to be changed on a Friday night, and later, when the doors automatically lock. The lock-in is softened by the ensuing fun: using camping supplies for a sleepover, drinking alcohol, and creating a fashion show. But the writers crafted this episode to highlight the consequences of neoliberal capitalism as Glenn's backstory unfolds. We learn that Glenn's family used to own a hardware store, but it closed a month after Cloud 9 opened. Rather than merely a catalyst for typical sitcom antics, the premise of a lock-in drives a narrative that directly addresses Walmart's expansion and the industrial logic of the big box store. Glenn fails to see the irony of Cloud 9's destruction of his family's business until the others prod him to get angry. Garrett pushes Glenn to reflect about what he doesn't like about Cloud 9:

> Well, uh, I guess the aisles are a bit too close together. And sometimes the folks in charge don't treat me like I'm a human being with feelings.

> I mean, where do they get off? Keep us late. Locked in the dark. All in service of the bottom line. I hate this tie. I hate this shirt (tears off cloud-themed tie and shirt). And I hate regional manager Dicky Larson. But you know what I hate most of all? I hate Cloud 9! I hate Cloud 9!
>
> *(Ledgin & Gernon, 2016)*

Glenn's cheery positivity breaks, as he pushes a cart into a display and damages the labels on bottles of liquor so that they can all drink, which leads to the characters bonding over stories as they proceed to get drunk and play games in the store. The resolution of this episode focuses on Glenn's outrage and powerlessness as he leaves angry messages on the corporation's voicemail:

> This company is a sham. You lock us in. You control the music that we listen to ... And the color difference in your signage is marginal. Oh, and you can tell Dicky Larson that he can suck my big fat sweaty toe.
>
> *(Ledgin & Gernon, 2016)*

Garrett, who overhears this, appears to feel sorry for "breaking Glenn," who has lost his unflinching optimism. Although Garrett is alarmed by Glenn's angry messages, he sighs with relief when he hears Glenn erase and replace the messages with his usual sing-song positivity "Signs are great. Really popping!" The status quo is thus restored, literally contained within the confines of the store (after-hours) and Glenn's self-restraint.

Glenn's narrative arc in this episode provides a critique of consolidation and arbitrary corporate practices that hinge on his identity as an evangelical Christian. Glenn, always cheerful, frequently tries to bring the gospel into the workplace, although Dina, the secular enforcer, allows Glenn to bring religion into the workplace on only one occasion – when an elderly customer dies on a couch. More specifically, Glenn's identity demonstrates what Moreton (2007) calls the "soul of neoliberalism," or how Walmart's founder used religious practices, particularly the linguistic and cultural ethos of evangelical Christianity, to cultivate "servant leadership" and rationalize Walmart's domination as a provider of jobs, goods, and social services (p. 108). Glenn's temperament is such that he "doesn't waste time with anger," and his Christian identity dampens any indignation about Cloud 9. This character trait is also clear when Glenn trusts a stranger in the parking lot to retrieve the store key out of his car; the car is stolen, and everyone remains stuck inside (and figuratively remain stuck as a result of corporate and individual self-interest).

This episode, among others, provides a satirical account of working conditions under neoliberal capitalism. The form of the show is such that we do not have a conclusion that justifies how our economy and society works, particularly the sort of morality lessons that close out the conventional sitcom episode.

While there are ideological subtexts about the perseverance of one's own individual moral character (e.g., Glenn's Christian faith), the episode offers commentary about the corporate and broader political economic forces beyond the individual's control, such as consolidation and inadequate wages. In sum, the corporation and, by extension, the machinations of monopoly capitalism define the scope of the characters' existence, including the sameness of their powerlessness.

Constructions of Class

The portrayal of various working-class identities in a sitcom – and not just one version of a homogenous working class – feels like a radical act in a television landscape where sitcoms mostly feature affluent families and workplaces and, more broadly, narratives discursively construct the neoliberal subject as a consumer separated from socioeconomic structures. Cloud 9 as a setting and as a character engages with social class, both implicitly in the background connotations of this work and consumer space and explicitly through the main characters. The characters are well-rounded, three-dimensional people, as opposed to caricatures and stereotypes who have typically framed working class portrayals (Adams, 2016; Kendall, 2011). The socioeconomic label of "working class" includes those who work an hourly wage (typically close to the minimum wage) in jobs that do not require higher education (Kendall, 2011).

Contrary to media texts that reify American myths of a classless society or lampoon working-class characters, the characters regularly speak and act in ways defined by a sameness in economic positions. Each episode touches on the characters' economic hardships, such as working two jobs (e.g., Glenn's second job is as a driver-for-hire; Mateo, an immigrant, has a second job at a diner), struggling to secure childcare during work hours, and living paycheck-to-paycheck. The characters also rely on classed distinctions as a source of humor. The dialogue and antics, on the one hand, differentiate socioeconomic class status based on taste hierarchies; on the other hand, they exemplify class consciousness, meaning "the degree to which people at a similar location in the class system think of themselves as a distinctive group sharing political, economic, and social interests" (Kendall, 2011, p. 14).

Consider the following two examples, which rely on classed identities but demonstrate opposing functions. The pilot episode features a shopper complaining about false advertising to "get suckers in the door and push the expensive jewelry" when the $8 "cubic zirconium knock-off" engagement ring is sold out and his next best option is a few more dollars. Amy judges the shopper, from his choice in ring to his diction to his clothes. She is even more dismayed when he turns out to be Bo, Cheyenne's boyfriend and father of her unborn child (Spitzer & Fleischer, 2015a). Amy's interactions with him function to differentiate and fracture working-class identity as a means to denigrate and isolate undesirable features (Skeggs, 2004). In contrast, the midseason episode "Shoplifter" features an alleged shoplifter who insults Dina and Amy by stating: "Oh, I forgot. You work retail. Pitiful means sad." This person then continues to lodge classed insults at them, such as calling them "minimum-wage morons" and "backcountry idiots" (Clarke & Fleischer, 2016). This scene functions to activate solidarity against the sorts of stereotypes deployed to ridicule the working class.

The working-class representations in *Superstore* play off of a fish-out-of-water tale. Indeed, the premise of the show begins with perceptions of class status. Jonah is a new hire and quick to help Amy, who he thinks is a customer. Jonah is immediately self-conscious about his new employment as he tries to help Amy while flirting with her. "I don't seem like the kind of person that would work at a place like this," he tells her. Amy plays along, agreeing that he doesn't belong "because you have this very intelligent, educated, more cultured quality," then gestures to Cheyenne, an employee trying to pick up a box off the floor despite her very large, pregnant body. Jonah responds by sheepishly trying to point out that Amy's compliment may be condescending to the workers as Amy retorts with a tone that attacks Jonah's arrogance about the kinds of people that work in retail. He learns Amy is his supervisor and tries to remedy the awkwardness that resulted from him suggesting his superiority (Spitzer & Fleischer, 2015a). While the dynamic between Jonah and Amy suggests a romantic pairing, their interactions also emphasize class awareness as explored through antagonism about differences in status as well as solidarity.

Jonah's arrival is seemingly random since he is not from St. Louis and has no ties to the area. Mateo assumes that Jonah's appearance and education indicates that he must be a secret representative from Cloud 9 corporate offices, sent to the store to spy on employees: "I always wondered why an educated, privileged, pretty boy would decide to work here" (Zimmet & Hardcastle, 2016). His co-workers regularly tease him in ways that signify and skewer class distinctions such as croissants (pronounced with exaggerated accents), jazz, and documentaries. Jonah's coworkers shift towards scatological and carnivalesque humor that flattens class hierarchies (Bakhtin, 2007) such as placing the Jonah-esque mannequin on a toilet display, then on a leash eating dog food, and then as a bride to a gorilla. He attempts to prank them back, which ends up costing him $400, roughly the equivalent to what he makes in a week at minimum wage. His coworkers used the materials in the store; Jonah has the extra income to play pranks.

Other episodes further define Jonah's character in terms of social capital associated with privilege: endless tales about volunteering, didactic explanations about esoteric topics, and regrets that he did "Semester at Sea instead of absorbing one culture" in college (Ledgin & Gernon, 2016). In other words, a higher social class intersects with markers of what has been the televisual norm: whiteness. In the episode "Shots and Salsa," Jonah deploys a do-gooder ethic of care in helping the pharmacist dole out flu shots and allowing an elderly white woman to move to the front of the line, which leads to allegations of racism after the woman says "white people help our own," and Jonah is associated with white supremacy (Spitzer & Fleischer, 2015b). Jonah represents the politically progressive subject (and perhaps the viewer) who does not seem to belong at Cloud 9 because of his marked identity as white, educated, and male, or in other words, a contrast to the typical male working-class portrayals of past sitcoms (Bettie, 1995; Butsch, 2016; Kendall, 2011). This inversion destabilizes the representation of social class as characters defined by their sameness in working-class status are in a position to judge Jonah as an "other."

Nevertheless, the characters are all subject to the contingencies of the postrecession neoliberal economy. Despite Jonah's seemingly middle-class status, he is just as alienated as any of the employees at Cloud 9. In the sixth episode, we learn that Jonah flunked out of business school and just "took a long drive, then I wanted a snack, so I stopped at this random store in St. Louis, saw that they were hiring" (Zimmet & Hardcastle, 2016). Jonah's agency to control his time and space is a sign of privilege, in contrast to the other employees who have been stuck in this place. Glenn has worked at Cloud 9 for over 20 years, and his fate is to manage the very store that replaced his family's business. Cheyenne exhibits neither resentment about her economic status nor an imagination beyond her limited circumstances. She suggests that a better life for her daughter means that when she grows up, she can be an assistant store manager or maybe even manager (but is confused about what Glenn would do). She has few reservations about the timing of pregnancy except perhaps that she should have gotten pregnant later, or "sooner, like her friends" (Green, Miller, & Nelli, 2016; Ledgin & Gernon, 2016). And early on we learn that she did not choose to be a teenage mother but she could not get a ride to Planned Parenthood. Amy has worked for 10 years in a job that she thought was temporary; we learn that she has a 12-year-old daughter, is in an unhappy marriage, and was derailed from going to college. She may have little social power to change her immediate circumstances, but she is the only character who desires to leave and move on to something better, as evidenced by her attempts to finish her college degree via night classes.

The writers extend and then complicate the dichotomy between Amy and Jonah to further explore the ways in which all the Cloud 9 characters are bound by broader socioeconomic structures. In the pivotal "All-Nighter" episode, most of the employees are upset that they are missing out on family and social aspects of their lives while locked in the store. Jonah, though, is excited to have "the run of the store," which plays on his season-long fascination with taking a more whimsical approach to working in retail. Amy complains that she has to study for a midterm the next day, prompting the contrast between

Jonah's and Amy's degrees of access to pursue college and middle/upper class adulthood. As Jonah reminisces about his college days (e.g. late-night parties), Amy quips, "Did I ever tell you about the time I went to college as a grown-up and I had all these responsibilities?" She got into a good college, but she "got pregnant, got married … and someone had to pay the bills" (Ledgin & Gernon, 2016). In the second season, Amy challenges Jonah's claim that he is "just like everyone else" at Cloud 9 since he can leave at any time to return to business school. Wanting to prove he is no different, he calls the business school to cancel his deferment. He did not plan on actually cancelling – Amy called his bluff – but he learns his deferment has already expired. While this is a two-season narrative arc, it becomes clear that Jonah eventually does belong at Cloud 9 in the sense of foreclosed opportunities. As Amy tells him, "Welcome to the no options club. It's a cool club … most of America is in it" (Hubbard & Purple, 2017). Jonah, once cast as a fish-out-of-water due to his marked differences in socioeconomic status, is now defined by a degree of sameness.

Like past portrayals of the working class on most any sitcom, an essential component to these narratives is the idea of upward mobility as a means to leave or at least mitigate the conditions of the working class. Upward mobility will not happen given that the sitcom universe maintains a status quo, which in *Superstore* means staying in this workplace setting. As a narrative device, themes related to upward mobility focus less so on how structural inequalities shape class experiences and more so on limitations defined by individual and family interests, which are especially gendered. For example, Dina is upwardly mobile and cherishes her power over others, but she is quick to give that up to pursue a potential romantic relationship with an employee. Cheyenne, who cannot imagine a world beyond her hourly employment, also has no concept of the impending costs in raising a child. Amy, in contrast to the other characters who ignore or avoid Cheyenne's financial conditions, lectures Cheyenne about making rational, responsible choices (Ornelas & Nelli, 2016). And Amy's own struggle to regain the "right" path to middle-class adulthood best exemplifies the notion that education is the only way out (which is un-ironically negated by Jonah's story, who dropped out of business school). Glenn wants to promote Amy in the second-to-last episode of the season (Hubbard, Zimmet, & Mendoza, 2016). This path, though, is not a legitimate way to exit the working class – protecting her time to focus on evening college classes is a better choice for her, especially since the extra responsibility comes with no pay raise. She acquiesces, allowing her emotional labor – the work involved in caring for the well-being of her coworkers – to usurp her self-interest since she feels bad for Glenn's feeble attempts to do both jobs. She is rewarded with a benefit that Glenn failed to mention: Cloud 9 pays for half of college tuition. The episode ends with an optimistic promise of class mobility through a college education, but given that the next episode results in a strike, she no longer has access to this option and this corporate benefit is never mentioned again.

The ideological problematic of class within the cultural/commercial context of the sitcom formula has resulted in a steady stream of narratives that focus on neoliberal self-improvement and plots that take focus away from structural inequalities. Nevertheless, *Superstore* presents a slice of today's working class amidst television schedules with minimal working-class representation. The array of class-consciousness and backstories is a nod towards the collapsing distinction between the working class or middle class, with "middle class" serving more as political rhetoric than an actual descriptor of occupational or hierarchal position (Ehrenreich, 2016). Indeed, just as *Roseanne* re-presented economic restructuring of the American workforce and the "gendered and raced nature of class" (Bettie, 1995, p. 126), this text is re-presenting the contemporary version of the extenuating circumstances in low-wage, hourly retail.

Functions of Intersectional Characters

The context of the retail work environment assigns or implies a working-class identity for each main character but like any good story, the characters have their own distinct personalities. More importantly, characters develop as three-dimensional individuals whose identities are "always permeated by other categories" of identity (Cho et al., 2013, p. 795), thereby developing the specificity of working class identities. The writers use differences stemming from visible and experiential markers of identities to not only construct nuanced characters, but also create plots that connect identity to relations of power in the neoliberal environment. Three episodes in particular illustrate the deployment of intersectional representations as a means to critique the corporation and structural inequalities.

Superstore is self-aware regarding corporate strategies that fetishize and tokenize diversity, as evident in the second and third episodes. In "Magazine Profile," the plot highlights the construction of identity and plays with the visible markers of Garrett's identity (and also his personality) as a means to satirize corporate diversity. Glenn desperately tries to get the attention of the Cloud 9 photographer, who is more focused on capturing Garrett for the cover of the in-house corporate magazine. Garrett has no interest, as he explains to Jonah:

GARRETT: If you see the reporter show up today, please let me know so I can hide. I do not want them to put me on the cover.
JONAH: That's pretty cocky.
GARRETT: Oh, it's not ego. These corporate magazines *love* putting employees with disabilities on the cover.

JONAH: Yeah, I bet, and getting a black guy in a wheel chair on the cover is like their holy grail or something.
GARRETT: Whoa whoa, you trying to say that being black is a disability?

(Hubbard & Jann, 2015)

Garrett jokingly takes offense as Jonah tries to back pedal and claim knowledge about black culture. It is well within each character's personality to be cynical. As identities, though, this interaction reinforces Jonah's non-marked identity in comparison to Garrett's double-marked identity. The photographer is presumably not focused on Garrett's racial identity, but Jonah's cynical statement speaks to the hyper-awareness of neoliberal tokenization, both on the part of the corporation (Cloud 9) and the privileged subject (Jonah). The episode resolves with Garrett giving in to tokenization by posing with Glenn, who had failed to gain attention because he was too boring. Glenn is pleased with the final magazine cover, even though his face is obscured by a graphic with the text, "Cloud 9 supports our disabled heroes!" Glenn, a white male in a position of authority, is construed as invisible. Garrett's character development involves an identity that is not so much defined by his race or his body in a wheelchair as how his identity serves as ground for critical commentary. Throughout this and later seasons, his blackness and body are not the focus of any special plot points, yet his identity is not ignored. For instance, Garrett chastises Jonah when he tells Garrett he is lucky to be in a wheelchair and not on his feet all day.[3] He never discloses why he is in a wheelchair, which helps to normalize the representation of people with disabilities. However, the satirical jab at Cloud 9's practices may critique one part of neoliberal ideology – corporate inclusionist rhetoric that promotes people with disabilities as exceptional – but also reifies another part of that ideology that normalizes differently-abled bodies when they are productive for the economy (Mitchell & Snyder, 2015).

In the third episode, "Shots and Salsa," the main plot focuses on the presumptions and disputes about identity. In the opening scene, Glenn assumes Mateo is Mexican and, thus, qualified to distribute samples of Cloud 9's new salsa. Mateo identifies himself as Filipino and so Glenn turns to Amy because she has a "certain natural spiciness." She is offended and declines (and she is able to because Glenn's authority is easily undermined). Glenn then picks Carmen, another Latina employee (played by a guest star, who is not a regular secondary character), who has no problem with Glenn's identity requirements. Amy, irritated by Carmen's unproblematic agreement, confronts her about her exaggerated accent and pandering to Glenn's and the customers' stereotypes. A customer who overhears this exchange scolds Amy, telling her that she is wrong to judge Carmen's accent. Angered, Amy tries to tear away Carmen's sombrero and poncho, which causes Carmen to break her leg. Mateo takes over, and Amy chastises him for appropriating the identity of a Mexican villager. She explains, "It's not a role. It's a stereotype," and illustrates the offensive nature of his caricature by mimicking an Asian dialect and mannerisms. Meanwhile, a diverse group of customers interprets Jonah's attempt to help a customer as racist. Following both acts, Glenn forces the employees to watch an antiquated corporate video about racism with the tagline, "color blind is color kind." Corporate ideology states that calling attention to difference is a problem. However, this is contradicted by the commodification of difference as Amy agrees to the performance of "authentic" Mexican-ness because the salsa sales benefit a charity in Mexico. Amy wears a sombrero and Mexican poncho, speaks with a thick accent, and fabricates stories about her life in the village. She initially tries to educate customers – "It's important to remember that Latinos can be doctors and lawyers and architects" – but gives up when the customers and her coworkers look confused: "Never mind. You should see the look on your gringo faces. Ariba!" As Amy and Mateo resume singing to the customers, Carmen returns on crutches and calls out Amy's hypocrisy (Spitzer & Fleischer, 2015b).

The storyline demonstrates the stakes in who defines the contours of identities: Glenn insists on a required identity for a sales task, and Amy critiques his requirement and associated stereotypes. On one level, Glenn represents the corporate power structure and his authority to assign jobs, which enables him to require a Latina identity. On another level, Glenn represents social and cultural structures that re-presents identities in singular, essentialized stereotypes. He uncritically replicates difference when it is sanctioned by the corporation and society and dutifully takes action to reprimand difference when defined by corporate discrimination policies. He demonstrates no self-reflexivity about the imbalances in what is commentary on racism (as Amy called her impersonation) and what is interpreted as racism. A sitcom episode in the past might have used this subject matter as a morality lesson about respecting cultural diversity, but instead, this episode offers little resolution other than Amy's resignation to hypocrisy and Garrett's affirmation about the futility of getting involved with anyone in the store, whether fighting with a coworker over identity politics or helping customers.

In the final episode, the Cloud 9 employees are united against and by corporate decisions such as no health insurance; they are defined by their sameness in relation to the corporation. When the need for health insurance is more pronounced for one employee, though, the plot illustrates the construction of difference and how relations of power interact with intersectional identities. Cheyenne urgently needs health insurance and maternity leave. Having neither, her only choice is to work as long as possible and immediately return to work so as not to lose her position or wage. Cheyenne's pregnancy ultimately leads to talk of unionization and a strike, but this is not Cheyenne's choice because she believes she has no power to change her circumstances. Amy, who experienced her own teenage pregnancy and related hardships, has some agency and uses her limited power to orchestrate a plan for other employees to clandestinely cover Cheyenne's shifts. Nearly everyone expresses frustration at Cheyenne's situation but accepts the status quo and futility of their precarious working conditions.

Jonah, the most privileged of the workers, vocalizes dissent. The whole season narrative arc leads to this moment, where his identity as a white, straight, educated male and his didactic, righteous personality establishes his position of power to confront corporate actions. In the first part of the episode, he channels moral authority when he explains "in every other First World nation, paid maternity leave is just automatic!" and contrasts Cloud 9's corporate earnings to the lack of employee benefits. When Jonah finally convinces Amy to call employee services about maternity leave, they are reminded that is not an option. Amy is apologetic and ready to hang up, but Jonah resolutely notes how "other big companies" offer benefits. He mentions unions, which quickly triggers a corporate reaction (in contrast to Glenn's failed attempts to reach corporate in other episodes). Corporate sends a "labor relations consultant" (or as Mateo says, a "union buster") to lead a session to denigrate unions. Jonah spars with the consultant while his coworkers are more concerned with the availability of snacks. Despite complaints in the break room about wages, raises, work hours, and health care, the employees remain passive. Away from the store floor where the consultant continues his anti-union session, Jonah tries to persuade Amy to try to unionize and lead a wildcat strike. Amy, while sympathetic and conscious of structural inequalities, is cautious: "real people's jobs are at stake." Jonah's idealism versus Amy's pragmatism reflects their identities within an unjust status quo. Amy speaks from a position where the risks of collective action are far greater than from Jonah's position; she is a woman, Latina, mother, and head of household (her husband does not earn money) and would suffer greater repercussions than Jonah's more privileged identity and circumstances.

Meanwhile, Cheyenne gives birth in the store and tells Glenn she'll be late to work the next day. Absurd as it is, the in-store labor is the logical extension of the strains and impossible choices imposed by neoliberal conditions. Cheyenne suggests she will take care of herself and figure out care for her newborn when she returns. Glenn "punishes" Cheyenne for the disruption by suspending her for six weeks with pay, thereby mirroring maternity benefits. The consultant, who presumably carries corporate authority, then fires Glenn. Amy snaps into action and initiates a walkout. Dina, who values authority and structure over empathy and class solidarity, seizes a loud speaker and announces to the employees gathered in the parking lot: "Rest assured – Cloud 9 will be fine without you" (Ellickson, 2016).

The season ends on this cliffhanger. This is an important moment in a television landscape with few moments of collective action as a direct result of clearly laid out structural injustices. However, the representational strategies to mobilize class consciousness and critique corporate practices (e.g., no health care) are tempered by the powerful narrative frame of the workplace family. The differences between Jonah's and Amy's initial willingness to challenge the status quo reflects their intersectional identities and relations to power: corporate sent a union buster because of Jonah's power stemming from his privileged identity, while Amy could not even entertain the idea of asking corporate about maternity leave out of fear of losing her job. When Amy agrees that collective action is required, she is not so much persuaded by Jonah's arguments to enact a strike as she is confronted by an assault on her workplace family. Indeed, each episode features resolutions that hinge on themes of family and loyalty to one another rather than resolutions about solving structural problems. Nevertheless, these plots still *address* how the characters relate to the structure, even if they are powerless to rectify their status as workers or fail to stop others from reducing identities to a stereotypical and exploitative single axis of identity. The overarching value, though, continues to be in taking responsibility for one's self, which extends to taking care of those similarly affected by neoliberal inequities.

Conclusion: Critiques and Affirmations

Superstore emerged in the aftermath of Occupy Wallstreet and amidst the occasional news stories about ongoing class action lawsuits against Walmart, unionization campaigns for retail and fast food workers, and discussions about raising the minimum wage.[4] This show uses these issues to tell the kinds of stories that tend to be absent in most media texts. Here, the identity of the worker is central to the narratives, as opposed to "a steady, consistent representation of workers as consumers [that] undermines working class identity and weakens solidarity" (Zweig, 2012, p. 49). *Superstore* is a corrective text that broadens representations of working class individuals and draws on the conditions of working as source material.

Still, the mere inclusion of discourses about wages, health care, and worker subjectivity is not enough when we limit a television text to a season. The strike left the workers' fate in question, and I was hopeful that the second season's strike narrative would sustain a conversation about the fragility of a weakened labor force. The strike quickly diffuses, though, and the conditions of work as sources for plots are overshadowed by romantically driven narratives in Season 2. Cloud 9 as a character in this narrative is now a goofy overlord, embodied by a new district manager, rather than a faceless, controlling force that dictates conditions of work and the subsequent consequences to the employees' lives. Working class identities are mostly reframed in terms of culture wars, such as guns, religion, and partisanship. Granted, there are some narrative arcs that carry critical weight, such as further developing Mateo's identity as an undocumented immigrant, which limits both how he can function within the workplace and his romantic relationships. For the most part, however, the show's narrative resists structural changes while emphasizing the neoliberal mandate for individual responsibility (Miller, 2006).

At its best, *Superstore* gently corrals structural inequalities by fictionalizing real labor and work issues, thus accommodating oppositional storylines in a television environment that is biased towards affluence and shies away from class alienation. Gitlin (1979/1994) refers to this as television's hegemonic process, which serves in "domesticating divisive issues" (p. 531). As such, television contains divisive issues within narrative frames, such as the satirical sitcom, suited for our multi-platform and niche media environment. An audience exists for shows that wryly point out injustices and exploitative conditions of work and class subjectivities. This magnifies the ideological contradiction. Overall, the sitcom serves neoliberal corporate interests by deriding and challenging these same interests and practices. More optimistically, narrative complexity allows for stories to engage with structures of power and intersectional characters who experience the contingencies of labor in neoliberal capitalism.

Notes

1 The ABC sitcom, *Roseanne*, aired from 1988 to 1997. In 2018, the franchise was renewed and ran for two months before being cancelled by ABC in response to a racist tweet by the show's star, Roseanne Barr. Research about *Roseanne* mentioned in this chapter refers to the earlier series.
2 Fight for $15 is a political movement to campaign for and take collective action to raise the minimum wage to a living wage, where it is possible to work a minimum wage job and attain economic stability. See the political movement's website, https://fightfor15.org/about-us/.
3 It is important to note that Colton Dunn, who plays Garrett, is an able-bodied actor.
4 Occupy Wall Street represents a political and social movement that began as a protest against corporate power and wage inequality in 2011. For details about how the protest began and grew to be a political movement and rhetorical device as a catch-all for structural inequalities, see Gitlin (2012). For an example of news coverage of the status of workers, see Greenhouse (2008), and for unionization campaigns, see Caraway (2016).

References

Acker, J. (2006). *Class questions: Feminist answers*. Lanham, MD: Rowman & Littlefield.
Adams, E. (2016, September 21). "Mark McKinney on finding his *Superstore* voice and bringing back *Slings and Arrows*." *AV Club*. Retrieved from https://tv.avclub.com/mark-mckinney-on-finding-his-superstore-voice-and-bring-1798252146.
Bakhtin, M. M. (2007). *Rabelais and his world*. Bloomington, IN: Indiana University Press.
Bettie, J. (1995). Class dismissed? *Roseanne* and the changing face of working-class iconography. *Social Text*, *13*(4), 125–149.

Butsch, R. (2016). Six decades of social class in American sitcoms. In N. Cloarec, D. Haigron, & D. Letort (Eds.), *Social class on British and American screens: Essays on cinema and television* (pp. 18–33). Jefferson, NC: McFarland & Company, Inc.

Caraway, B. (2016). OUR Walmart: A case study of connective action. *Information, Communication & Society, 19*(7), 907–920.

Cho, S., Crenshaw, K. W., & McCall, L. (2013). Toward a field of intersectionality studies: Theory, applications, and praxis. *Signs: Journal of Women in Culture and Society, 38* (4), 785–810.

Clarke, J. (Writer), & Fleischer, R. (Director). (2016, January 11). Shoplifter [Television series episode]. In *Superstore*. Universal City, CA: NBC.

Ehrenreich, J. (2016). *Third wave capitalism: How money, power, and the pursuit of self-interest have imperiled the American dream*. Ithaca, NY: ILR Press.

Ellickson, O. (Writer), & McCarthy-Miller, B. (Director). (2016, February 22). Labor [Television series episode]. In *Superstore*. Universal City, CA: NBC.

Gitlin, T. (1979/1994). Prime time ideology: The hegemonic process. In H. Newcomb (Ed.), *Television: The critical view* (5th ed., pp. 516–536). New York, NY: Oxford University Press.

Gitlin, T. (2012). *Occupy nation: The roots, the spirit, and the promise of Occupy Wall Street*. New York, NY: It Books.

Grabowski, M. (2014). Resignation and positive thinking in the working-class family sitcom. *Atlantic Journal of Communication, 22*(2), 124–137.

Gray, J., & Lotz, A. D. (2012). *Television studies*. Cambridge, UK: Polity Press.

Green, J., & Miller, G. (Writers), & Nelli, V. Jr. (Director). (2016, January 4). Mannequin [Television series episode]. In *Superstore*. Universal City, CA: NBC.

Greenhouse, S. (2008). *The big squeeze: Tough times for the American worker*. New York, NY: Alfred A. Knopf.

Hall, S. (2011). The whites of their eyes: Racist ideologies and the media. In G. Dines & J. M. Humez (Eds.), *Gender, race, and class in media: A critical reader* (pp. 81–84). Thousand Oaks, CA: Sage Publications.

Henry, M. A. (2014). *The Simpsons, satire, and American culture*. New York, NY: Palgrave Macmillan.

Hubbard, M. (Writer), & Jann, M. P. (Director). (2015, November 30). Magazine Profile [Television series episode]. In *Superstore*. Universal City, CA: NBC.

Hubbard, M. (Writer), & Purple, B. (Director). (2017, January 12). Rebranding [Television series episode]. In *Superstore*. Universal City, CA: NBC.

Hubbard, M., & Zimmet, L. (Writers), & Mendoza, L. (Director), (2016, February 15). Demotion [Television series episode]. In *Superstore*. Universal City, CA: NBC.

Kendall, D. E. (2011). *Framing class: Media representations of wealth and poverty in America*. Lanham, MD: Rowman & Littlefield.

Ledgin, E. (Writer), & Gernon, C. (Director). (2016, January 4). All-Nighter [Television series episode]. In *Superstore*. Universal City, CA: NBC.

Lemke, S., & Schniedermann, W. (2017). *Class divisions in serial television*. Basingstoke, UK: Palgrave Macmillan.

Lichtenstein, N. (2006). *Wal-Mart: The face of twenty-first-century capitalism*. New York, NY: New Press.

McMurria, J. (2008). Desperate citizens and good samaritans: Neoliberalism and makeover reality TV. *Television and New Media, 9*(4), 305–332.

Meyer, M. D. E. (2015). The "other" woman in contemporary television drama: Analyzing intersectional representation on bones. *Sexuality and Culture, 19*(4), 900–915.

Miller, T. (2006). *Cultural citizenship: Cosmopolitanism, consumerism, and television in a neoliberal age*. Philadelphia, PA: Temple University Press.

Mitchell, D. T., & Snyder, S. L. (2015). *The biopolitics of disability: Neoliberalism, ablenationalism, and peripheral embodiment*. Ann Arbor, MI: University of Michigan Press.

Mittell, J. (2006). Narrative complexity in contemporary American television. *The Velvet Light Trap, 58*(1), 29–40.

Moreton, B. (2007). The soul of neoliberalism. *Social Text, 25*(3), 102–123.

Oh, D. C., & Banjo, O. O. (2012). Outsourcing postracialism: Voicing neoliberal multiculturalism in outsourced. *Communication Theory, 22*(4), 449–470.

Ornelas, S. T. (Writer), & Nelli, V. Jr. (Director). (2016, February 1). Wedding Day Sale [Television series episode]. In *Superstore*. Universal City, CA: NBC.

Ouellette, L., & Hay, J. (2008). *Better living through reality TV*. Malden, MA: Blackwell.

Peterson, H. (2016, October 7). This is what the average Walmart shopper looks like. *Business Insider*. Retrieved from www.businessinsider.com/walmart-shopper-demographics-2016-10.

Rennels, T.R. (2015). *Here Comes Honey Boo Boo*: A cautionary tale starting white working-class people. *Communication and Critical/Cultural Studies, 12*(3), 271–288.

Ryan, M. (2016, August 2). 'Superstore' takes on Olympics, unions, guns and other hot topics in season 2. *Variety*. Retrieved from http://variety.com/2016/tv/news/superstore-season-two-nbc-olympics-1201829090/.

Skeggs, B. (2004). *Class, self, culture*. London: Routledge.

Spangler, L. C. (2014). Class on television: Stuck in. *The Middle: Journal of Popular Culture, 47*(3), 470–488.

Spitzer, J. (2015, November 14). Pilot, network 3rd draft. *TV Calling Script Library*. Retrieved from http://scripts.tv-calling.com/script/nbc-superstore-1x01-pilot/.

Spitzer, J. (Writer), & Fleischer, R. (Director). (2015a, November 30). Pilot [Television series episode]. In *Superstore*. Universal City, CA: NBC.

Spitzer, J. (Writer), & Fleischer, R. (Director). (2015b, November 30). Shots and Salsa [Television series episode]. In *Superstore*. Universal City, CA: NBC.

Staff, G. (2015, December 6). Conference call: Ben Feldman and Justin Spitzer talk about NBC's new comedy Superstore. *Your Entertainment Corner*. Retrieved from www.yourentertainmentcorner.com/conference-call-ben-feldman-and-justin-spitzer-talk-about-nbcs-new-comedy-superstore/.

Thompson, E. (2007). Comedy Verité? The observational documentary meets the televisual sitcom. *The Velvet Light Trap, 60*(1), 63–72.

Wells, R. (2015). The labor of reality TV: The case of "The Deadliest Catch". *Labor Studies in Working-Class History of the Americas, 12*(4), 33–49.

White, M. (1992). Ideological analysis and television. In R. C. Allen (Ed.), *Channels of Discourse, Reassembled* (pp. 161–202). Chapel Hill, NC: University of North Carolina Press.

Zimmet, L. (Writer), & Hardcastle, A. (Director). (2016, January 18). Secret Shopper [Television Series Episode]. In *Superstore*. Universal City, CA: NBC.

Zweig, M. (2012). *The working class majority: America's best kept secret* (2nd ed.). Ithaca, NY: ILR Press.

INDEX

activism 39–40, 44–45, 49–55, 142, 166–167; feminist 64; *see also* philanthrocapitalism
Adams, J. 121
advertising 13, 24–32, 114–115, 131–143, 154, 181–189; *see also* cause marketing, *corporate social responsibility*
affect 110, 142; affective life 132–134
Affordable Care Act 113
Alexander, K. 176
Alger, H. 182
Allen, K. 133
Allison, S. T. 149
AllWorthIt 140–142
Almiron, N. 26
Althusser, L. 15
American Broadcasting Company (ABC) 169, 211
Americanism 108–109, 120, 124–125
Andrejevic, M. 32
Apple 12, 112, 143
The Apprentice 27, 29, 114
Arts & Entertainment Network (A&E) 96, 196
Avila-Saavedra, G. 169, 173
austerity 13, 26, 77, 81, 87, 112
authenticity 32, 35, 141, 179, 183, 187–188, 209; and cultural identity 156–158, 193, 197; gaze 156; and gender 32

Baldoni, J. 173
Banet-Weiser, S. 45, 141
Bannon, S. 9
Barclay, B. 195
Beggan, J. K. 149
Beijing Platform for Action 66
Bellah, R. 108–109, 124
Benjamin, W. 24, 33, 35, 153
Berlant, L. 79, 85–86
Berry, J. M. 30
Bessemer, H. 120
Bettie, J. 199–200, 202, 210
Big Brother 29
Bilge, S. 5, 67, 181
biopower 93–95, 97
Birdsall, W. F. 67
Black Lives Matter 69
Bloom, N. 212
Bockman, J. 193
Building Resources Across Communities (BRAC) 42–43, 52
Brands, H. W. 119
Breaking Bad 93
Breitbart News 4, 9
Bull, A. 133
Burke, K. 147, 150–151, 158
Byerly, C. 61, 66
Byers, T. 177

Cable News Network (CNN) 11, 13, 24, 27, 29–31, 33
Camil, J. 173

Carnegie, A. 114, 119–124
Case, S. 120
cause marketing 40, 42–43
CBS 23, 166
Center for Global Development 45
Center for Media Democracy 70
Center for Media Justice 68
Chambers, L. 158
Chan, A. 149
Chapman, R. 109
Chmielewski, J. F. 167, 169–171
Cho, S. 213
Christianity 77, 81–87, 109, 149, 212, 215–216
civil religion 108–110, 113, 124
class *see* gender; race
Clinton, B. 32, 166
Clinton Global Initiative 39, 50
Clinton, H. 31, 32–33, 35, 110
Cloud, D. 122
Colbert, S. 28
Collins, P. H. 5, 49, 67, 177–178, 181
colonialism 49, 157, 173, 185
Comcast 68
commodity capitalism 26
communication rights 62–64; in the Information Society (CRIS) 66–67
Cone, C. 43
conspicuous consumption 42, 149, 152, 155, 158
Convention for the Elimination of Discrimination against Women (CEDAW) 66
corporate social responsibility 45
Couldry, N. 61
Cramer, J. 116
Crank: Darkness on the Edge of Town 93
Crenshaw, K. 181, 213
Crichton, S. N. L. 66
criminality 97–98, 100, 179
Cruz, A. 149
Cuban, M. 115, 117, 118
CW network 165–166, 174

Daniels, L. 176, 184
Davidson, M. 141
Davis, D. A. 195
Davis, V. 178
De Fina, A. 166, 168, 174
Deery, J. 29, 32
Democratic party 21, 31, 67

deregulation 42, 61, 68–69, 79, 83, 110–111, 132
Deutsch, D. 114, 116
disease 92, 95, 97, 99–101
Disney 65, 169, 181
Dixon, S. 195
Dove 137–140, 143
Duck Dynasty 13, 192–193, 196, 198, 200–206
Duggan, L. 13, 166–167, 169–170, 172, 193–195
Dunn, C. 212

Empire 13, 176–179, 181–184, 186–189
empowerment 54–55, 79, 83, 86, 138, 159, 180; economic 46; girl empowerment 39; self-empowerment 11, 40, 44, 47, 135
entrepreneurialism 13, 27, 110, 114, 12, 177, 186; and subjectivities 42, 91, 133–136

Facebook 12, 39, 44, 49, 51–53, 67, 131
Faces of Meth (FOM) campaign 101
fake news 4, 9
Federal Communications Commission (FCC) 67–70
Fejes, F. 150
Feldman, B. 212
femininity 156, 198–199; Black 177, 184, 188; domestic 156, 200; middle-class 154, 206; normative 14, 134–135, 139, 141, 205
feminism 62–64, 66, 68, 137; scholars 5, 16, 17, 66–67; studies 61, 63, 135; *see also* postfeminism
Ferrara, A. 211
Financial Peace University 77, 79, 86
Fiske, J. 197
Fleras, A. 195
Food52 13, 148, 151–158
Ford, H. 114, 121, 125
Foster, J. B. 25
Foucault, M. 33, 91, 93–94, 181, 188, 193
Fox News 4, 11, 24; Network 176, 187
Frick, H. 123
Friedman, M. 41, 110

Gallagher, M. 62–63
Galvao, L. 160
Gealy, G. 177

gender 120, 122, 132, 134–135, 180–183, 194; bias 27, 32–33; blindness 23–24, 28, 167; and class 158, 193, 201, 206, 210, 221; and division of labor 44, 152, 200, 202, 205; and individualization 137, 140, 144; and intergenerational poverty 40, 44, 49, 51; makeover 135; patriarchal roles 179; and race 177, 181, 196, 198; and representation 13, 65, 82, 101–102, 213; and social divisions xii, xiii, 3, 5, 30, 44; structures and structural inequality 26, 35, 45, 52, 60, 62, 66–70, 220; violence 47; *see also* postfeminism
Gilens, M. 10
Gill, R. 194–195
Girls Count Report 40, 45, 47–48, 51, 56
The Girl Effect 13, 39–40, 43–54
Giroux, H. 12, 141
Global Media Monitoring Project (GMMP) 62–63
globalization 45–48, 79, 84, 142
Goldman, R. 137
Google 12, 112
Gould, J. 117
governmentality 93–94, 133, 180–181
Gray, B. Y. 177
Grey's Anatomy 176, 178
Grindstaff, L. 196, 203, 205
Guardino, M. 11
Guerrero, D. 173

Hall, S. 4, 14, 123, 133, 210
Hanson, L. 101–102
Harsin, J. 31, 33–34
Harvey, D. 4–6, 41, 61
Hay, J. 189
Hefner, H. 149
Henson, T. P. 177
Here Comes Honey Boo Boo 13, 192–193, 196–206
History Channel 108, 114
HIV 50–51
Hochschild, A. 134, 195
Holleman, H. 25
HBO 179
homophobia 177, 188
How to Get Away with Murder 178
How to Look Good Naked 138
Howard, T. 177
Howard University 69
Hubbs, N. 196
Hughes, S. N. 31
hypercommercialization 13, 25–28, 30–35

Ikard, D. 180
Illouz, E. 134
imperialism 185
individualization 11, 48, 79–84, 95, 109, 133–134, 183; and activism 44, 55; acts of 40, 55; and freedoms 5–7, 47, 210, 211; hyperindividualism 40; and individual choice 3, 50, 95, 136, 188; narrative of 137, 159, 171; sensibilities around 139, 148, 180, 186, 194–198
industrial capitalism 33, 116, 120–121, 123
inequality 26, 35, 45, 52, 60–62, 66–70, 220
Instagram 12, 149
InStyle 186
International Center for Research on Women 45
International Monetary Fund (IMF) 113
intersectionality 14; analysis of 132, 176, 213; approach i, 62, 67, 70; and identities 13, 103, 202, 213, 223, 225; and representation 14, 173, 193, 205–206, 211–213, 221, 226
Islamophobia 142

Jane the Virgin 13, 165–175
Jefferson, T. 121, 179
Jersey Shore 29
Jezebel 177–178, 186
Jones, V. 31
journalism 13, 21–28, 32, 60, 63; *see also* news
Judge Judy 11

Kafer, A. 137
Kanai, A. 134
Kendall, D. E. 211, 215
Kennedy, J. F. 121
Keyes, R. 28
Keys, A. 187–188
Kincaid, H. 167, 169–171
King, M. L., Jr. 121
Kmart 214
Koch, C. 7–10
Kranich, K. 64

labor 5, 8, 21, 29, 166, 192, 226; and class 155, 157–158, 192, 200–202, 204; erasure of 120, 123–124; fetishization of 157–158; and gender 124, 136, 152–155, 195–198, 205, 210; inequalities 4, 52, 124, 195, 213; markets 47, 48; and power 111–112, 211–212,

225; practices 45, 119–120, 215, 224; unions 112, 212
Lakoff, G. 77, 82
Landay, L. 149
Latinidad 165, 173–174
Latinx 14, 167; diaspora 168, 174; experience 165–166, 174; representation 165, 168–169, 171–175
Lemon, D. 31
Levine-Rasky, C. 196
Lewandowski, C. 30, 33
libertarian 12
Lincoln, A. 109, 114, 121, 125
Linnemann, T. 101–103
Littler, J. 42
Lord, J. 30–31
L'Oréal 13, 132, 137, 140–141, 143
Lowes, K. 176
Luhman, N. 28, 32

MacLean, N. 6–7, 10
Macron, E. 110
Mad Money 115
Magary, D. 159–160
Mahtani, M. 195
Mammy 177–178, 186
Manigault, O. 29
masculinity 27, 122, 179, 184, 196–198, 201; Black 177, 179, 184, 188; and class 195–198, 200–201, 204, 206; normative 14, 122, 195, 198, 201, 205; White 24, 27, 30
Mathisen, J. A. 109–110
Mayer, J. 7, 8
McCall, L. 213
McChesney, R. 12, 25, 41
McEnany, K. 30
McIver, W.J. 67
McKinney, M. 212
McNamee, S. J. 181
media ownership 13, 60–61, 64–66, 69–70, 181
The Men Who Built America 13, 108, 113–124
meritocracy 23, 176, 186; as a characteristic of neoliberalism 83, 95, 133, 182, 188, 195; and class 195; definition of 182; and erasure of identity 188, 195, 196
The Meth Project 13, 91–104
methamphetamine 91–104
MeToo Movement 60, 62
microlending 42–44, 52

The Middle 211
Miller, P. 93
Miller, R. K., Jr. 181
Mirren, H. 140, 141
misogyny 23, 28, 29, 31, 33
Mittell, J. 209
Moreton, B. 215
Morgan, J. P. 114, 121–122
Morton, J. 176
MSNBC 14, 33
Mukherjee, R. 45, 142
Multicultural Media Telecommunications Council 70
Muñoz, D. 176

National Abortion Rights Action League (NARAL) 68
National Broadcasting Company (NBC) 13, 29, 209, 214
National Organization for Women 63, 70
Navarro, A. 31
Navedo, A. 172
Negra, D. 186
neoliberal capitalism 4; characteristics of 6, 27, 104, 133, 215–216; as ideology 4, 83, 86; media's role in 12, 77, 87, 226
neoliberalism 13–16, 40, 95; challenging of 15–16, 125; characteristics of 25, 41–42, 48, 91, 136, 148; and class 193–194, 200, 205–206; definition of 3–6, 79, 109–111, 132, 166, 180, 193; and democracy 67, 113, 159; and gender 131, 134–136, 171, 180, 195; and globalization 45, 46; as hegemony 12, 113; as ideology 16, 54, 69, 77–78, 81–85, 122–123, 134; media's role in 4–5, 10–12, 24, 61, 77, 143; and pleasure 148; and policy 4, 6–7, 45, 47, 61, 67, 112, 194; post-neoliberalism 132; and power 34; psychic life of 131–132, 134, 137, 142, 144; and race 135–136, 172, 177, 180, 189, 195; representations of 171–172, 181, 193, 201, 209, 211, 216; as a sensibility 131, 137, 143, 147; and sexuality 170; *see also* meritocracy; *personal responsibility; post-race*
neoliberalized mediascape 23–24, 27–28, 33
net neutrality 61, 67–69
New York Times 14, 28, 60, 63, 147, 178
Newitz, A. 102
news media 4, 12, 15, 21–22, 28; coverage of U.S. elections 23; and gender 60–64;

and neoliberalism 4, 11, 23–24; production practices of 26, 29–32, 62, 64, 67, 215
The Newsroom 21
Nike 41, 45, 52, 54, 137
The Nike Foundation 39–40, 45–47, 50–51, 54
Nixon, R. 7

Obama, B. 8, 28, 68, 113, 180
Obama, M. xii
The Office 209, 214
Organization for Economic Cooperation and Development (OECD) 111
Ouellette, L. 27, 133, 189

Padovani, C. 66
Page, B. I. 10
patriarchy 77, 83, 86, 88, 135
Pepsi Co. 184, 186–188
personal responsibility 13; as a characteristic of neoliberalism. 3, 6, 83, 110, 166; and media representation 11, 139, 166, 171, 174–177, 183, 210
Pew Research Center 172
Phelan, S. 6
philanthrocapitalism 13, 39, 42–44, 52–56
Piketty, T. 111
Pinterest 149
Pitcher, K. C. 199
Playboy Magazine 149–150
The Population Council 40, 45
populism 4, 11, 88
pornography 147–150, 154, 160; and Burke 150–151; as kitchen porn 153, 159; and pornographic gaze 147, 149, 153, 158–160
post-colonialism 147, 159
postfeminism 167, 177, 180–181, 189; characteristics of 154, 186, 198, 202; definition of 135, 180; and neoliberalism 135–136, 143, 180, 183, 194–195; and subjectivity 135, 141, 186, 194
Postman, N. 22, 25–26, 31, 34
post-race 132, 136, 177, 189; characteristics of 185–186, 188; definition of 136, 142, 180; and neoliberalism 135–136, 143, 180–181, 183
post-truth 21, 24, 26–28, 32, 34
Powell Memo 7
The Prince's Trust 140, 141
Public Broadcasting Service (PBS) 13
public voice 61–62

Queer Eye 137

race 30, 62, 64, 67–68, 160, 222; and class 102, 181, 196–198, 206, 211, 221; erasure of 23, 28, 120, 122, 136–137, 158, 167, 213; and gender 7, 181; and inequality 183; and neoliberalism 5, 14, 27, 132–136, 194–195; and representation 13, 141–144, 177, 188, 205, 212; *see also* post-racism
racism 95, 133, 136, 142, 219; and Donald Trump 23, 28, 31; erasure of 177, 186, 188, 195, 223; and gender 181; and neoliberalism 3, 33, 177, 180, 195; normalization of 29; representation of 175, 183, 186, 211, 223
Rakow, L. F. 64
Ramamurthy, A. 142
Ramsey, D. 13, 77–88
Ramsey Solutions 77
Raphael, C. 29
Rasmussen, M. 67
Reagan, R. 41, 69, 166
reality TV 11, 24, 28–29, 31, 35; and class 192–193, 196–197; and Donald Trump 27, 30, 32, 35; and gender 178–179; and governmentality 181; and neoliberalism 14, 27–28, 33, 189; and race 178–79
The Real World 29
Republican party 8, 10, 21, 27, 67, 69, 113
respectability 100, 103
Rhimes, S. 176, 178
Ringrose, J. 135
Rios, D. 174
Roberts, D. J. 195
Robertson, K. 196, 200
Robertson, P. 196, 200, 203–204
Robertson, W. 196, 200–201, 203–206
Rockefeller, J. D. 114, 117–119, 121–125
Rodriguez, G. 166, 172
Rodriguez, N. S. 188
Romney, M. 28, 110
Room, R. 98
Roosevelt, F. D. 125
Rose, N. 93, 133, 195
Roseanne 199–200, 202, 210–211, 221
Ross, K. 66

Sanders, B. 27
Sapphire 177–178, 186
Scandal 13, 176–179, 181–186, 189
Scharff, C. 135, 194–195

Schwarzkopf, S. 159
Scott, T. 119
Second Life 149
self-discipline 13, 77, 81, 86; and gender 135, 199; and neoliberalism 198, 205
self-help 133, 135, 201; and finances 77–79, 84
self-regulation 93–94, 133, 180, 194
sexism 177, 181, 183, 186, 211
sexuality 142, 148, 213; and class 181; erasure of 120, 188; and gender 101–102, 168; hypersexuality 167, 177, 179; and neoliberalism 5, 137, 144, 167–170, 175, 188; and race 101–102, 168; representations of 101, 140, 144, 168, 174–177, 187
Shannon, J. (Mama June) 197, 199–203, 205
Siebel, T. 93
Smollett, J. 177
Sobieraj, S. 30
social capital 83, 218
social media 30, 39–40, 48, 52–53, 67
Sorkin, A. 21–23, 35
Spitzer, J. 209
Snyder, D. 11
Stanchfield, D. 176
Standard Oil 118, 121, 124
Stewart, M. 158
Stone, I. L. 25
Strong, D. 176
Superstore 13–14, 209–226
surveillance 94, 98, 132, 200, 214
Survivor 29

Taplin, J. T. 12
Target 214
Tasker, Y. 186
Tea Party 8, 11
Teasley, M. 18
telenovela 165,169, 173, 174
Tesla, N. 122
Thompson, A. 197, 202
Thompson, M. (Sugar Bear) 197, 201, 202–203
Time Warner 166, 181
thanatopolitics 91–95, 104
Toddlers & Tiaras 197
Tolman, D. 167, 169, 170–171
The Total Money Makeover 77–79, 81, 84–88

Trump, D. 7, 8, 10, 114, 118, 121; media coverage of 23–24, 27, 29–30, 32–33; and misogyny 23, 31; as neoliberal leader 15, 68; and racism 23, 30–31; and U.S. election 13, 21, 28, 31–35
Tuck, G. 148, 150, 158
Tumblr 134, 143
Twentieth Century Fox 181
Twitter 12, 49–50, 67

Ugly Betty 169
United Nations 41, 45, 66–67
United Nations Educational, Scientific and Cultural Organization (UNESCO) 67
United Nations Global Compact 39, 41
Universal Declaration of Human Rights 66
Urman, J. S. 174
U.S. Civil War 109, 114

Valentin, A. 66
Valluvan, S. 136
Vanderbilt, C. 114–118, 121–124
Verizon 65, 68
Vidal, G. 113
Vietnam war 110–111, 113

Walkerdine, V. 135
Wall Street Journal 187
Wall, T. 101, 103
Walmart 209, 213, 214, 215, 216, 225
Warner, K. 180, 185
Washington, G. 109, 125
Washington, K. 176, 186
Washington Post 15, 65
Weinstein, H. 60, 63, 64
Welch, J. 116, 119
Westinghouse Electric Company 122
Williams, L. 150
Williams, S. L. 101–102
Willoughby-Heard, T. 102
Wilson, C. 177
Wilson, K. 142
The Wire 179
Women, Action & the Media 68, 70
Women's Media Center 68–70
World Bank 39, 43, 45

World Economic Forum 39
World Social Forum 67
World Summit on the Information Society (WSIS) 67
World Trade Organization (WTO) 112
Wray, M. 102

xenophobia 34, 97

Yarrow, A. 197
Young, M. I. 100, 104
Young, M. 182
"Your Move" report 48, 49, 52
YouTube 12, 39, 49, 54, 137

Zimmerman, H. 156
Zucker, J. 29

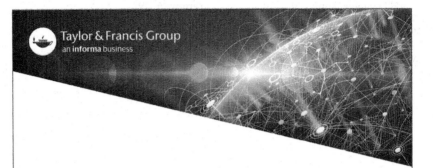